Understanding Prayer for the Dead

Understanding Prayer for the Dead

ITS FOUNDATION IN HISTORY AND LOGIC

JAMES B. GOULD

foreword by
Jerry L. Walls

CASCADE *Books* · Eugene, Oregon

UNDERSTANDING PRAYER FOR THE DEAD
Its Foundation in History and Logic

Copyright © 2016 James B. Gould. All rights reserved. Except for brief quotations in critical publications or reviews, no part of this book may be reproduced in any manner without prior written permission from the publisher. Write: Permissions, Wipf and Stock Publishers, 199 W. 8th Ave., Suite 3, Eugene, OR 97401.

Cascade Books
An Imprint of Wipf and Stock Publishers
199 W. 8th Ave., Suite 3
Eugene, OR 97401

www.wipfandstock.com

PAPERBACK ISBN: 978-1-62032-988-7
HARDCOVER ISBN: 978-1-4982-8610-7
EBOOK ISBN: 978-1-5326-0601-4

Cataloguing-in-Publication data:

Names: Gould, James B.

Title: Understanding prayer for the dead : its foundation in history and logic / James B. Gould, with a foreword by Jerry L. Walls.

Description: Eugene, OR: Cascade Books, 2016 | Includes bibliographical references and index.

Identifiers: ISBN 978-1-62032-988-7 (paperback) | ISBN 978-1-4982-8610-7 (hardcover) | ISBN 978-1-5326-0601-4 (ebook)

Subjects: LCSH: 1. Prayers for the dead. 2. Prayer—Philosophy. 3. Prayer—Christianity. 4. Philosophical theology. I. Walls, Jerry L. II. Title.

Classification: BV210.3 G69 2016 (print) | BV210.3 (ebook)

Manufactured in the U.S.A.   AUGUST 12, 2016

TABLE OF CONTENTS

Foreword by Jerry L. Walls vii

Introduction 1

1 Setting a Context: The Bible and Prayer for the Dead 11
2 Recounting the Past: Prayer for the Dead
  in the Historical Church 21
3 Surveying the Present: Prayer for the Dead
  in the Contemporary Church 40
4 Envisioning the Future: Prayer for the Dead
  in the Coming Church 60
  A Pause 80
5 God, Causality, and the Effectiveness of Praying for the Dead 83
6 Human Nature, Personal Identity, and Prayer for the Dead 97
7 Time, Eternity, and Prayer for the Dead 125
8 Creative Love Christianity: A Theological Framework
  for Prayer for the Dead 151
9 Hope, Expectation, and Prayer for the Dead 175

Afterword—Looking Ahead: A Preview of Volume Two 199
Appendix 203
Abbreviations 217
Bibliography 219
Name Index 235
Scripture Index 242

Foreword

ONE OF THE MOST moving stories in the New Testament is that of Jairus, a synagogue leader who had a little daughter on the point of death, who came to Jesus and "repeatedly begged" him to lay his hands on her, and heal her. As Jesus was on his way to Jairus's house, he was detained by a woman who had suffered from hemorrhages for many years, and she too was desperate for healing. She managed just to touch his clothes, and when she did so, Jesus realized someone had been healed and stopped to find out who it was. While he was talking with her, messengers arrived from Jairus's house with heartbreaking news: "Your daughter is dead. Why trouble the teacher any further" (Mark 5:35).

It is hard to imagine how devastating this must have been to this desperate father, whose hopes had been raised so high by the fact that Jesus was on the way to help. But then death intervened, and it seemed there was no reason to "trouble the teacher any further."

This story illustrates what many Christians believe about prayer. On the one hand, prayer is an incomparable source of hope because it puts us in touch with a God of love for whom nothing is impossible. Even when things are humanly or naturally impossible, God can act to redeem things. On the other hand, many Christians believe that death puts a sudden stop to our prayers.

The reasons for thinking this, however, are not due to any notion that God is powerless in the face of death, as the messengers from Jairus's house appeared to think. Rather, they come from another direction. In his final book, *Letters to Malcolm, Chiefly on Prayer*, C. S. Lewis strongly affirmed his own belief in prayer for the dead, noting that at his age, many of the people he most loved were already dead, and he wonders how the rest of his prayers would survive if prayers for the dead were forbidden. "The action," he writes, "is so spontaneous, so all but inevitable, that only the most compulsive case against it would deter me." And there is the rub. Many Christians do believe there is a "compulsive theological case" that strictly forbids at least certain kinds of prayers for the dead.

In this two-volume work—the present book, *Understanding Prayer for the Dead*, and its successor, *Practicing Prayer for the Dead*—James B. Gould argues powerfully not only that there is no good theological case against prayer for the dead, but also that there is a powerful theological case *in favor* of it. Gould's case is wide ranging in its argument, and he deals with the history of prayer for the dead in Christian theology as well as the philosophical and theological issues raised by the practice. His work will be recognized as a landmark on these vital issues for years to come.

The author distinguishes four kinds of prayers for the dead, and notes that the main Christian traditions have differed on the matter of which of these kinds of prayer are appropriate. The four kinds of prayer are for consummation, growth, purification, and salvation. While the first kind of prayer is most widely accepted and practiced, by many Protestants as well as Eastern Orthodox and Roman Catholics, the second and third types of prayer are accepted less commonly by Protestants, but are practiced by the Orthodox and Catholics. However, the fourth kind of prayer, for salvation, is generally rejected by all three traditions, on the ground that postmortem repentance and salvation are impossible.

Gould's ambitious project in these two volumes is to persuade Christians of all three traditions to embrace a more expansive theology of prayer for the dead than their official theology endorses. In short, he argues that there are good theological reasons to embrace all four kinds of prayer for the dead, and this requires Catholics to modify their views, as well as Protestants and Evangelicals.

As a Protestant who has written a book defending a doctrine of purgatory, including postmortem repentance, I am both intrigued by Gould's argument as well as attracted to it. Indeed, the early Christian practice of prayer for the dead, particularly prayer for purification, was one of the factors that led to the eventual development of the doctrine of purgatory. The traditional doctrine of purgatory however, pertains only to persons who die in a state of grace, so postmortem salvation is excluded.

Part of Gould's theological rationale for salvation prayer for the dead is his belief in universalism. His embrace of universalism is part of his transition from the views he held growing up as the son of missionaries in Nigeria, where he was taught that only those who heard the gospel in this life could be saved. While I reject universalism, it is worth noting that there are still good reasons to affirm postmortem conversion for persons who have not heard the gospel in this life, or who have not decisively rejected it. So the rationale for salvation prayers for the dead does not depend on the assumption of universalism—a point Gould himself acknowledges.

One of the most compelling aspects of these books is the case the author makes for the spiritually enriching power of a more expansive view of prayer, a case he develops in detail in the second volume. While theological truth is not determined by devotional practice, it is often shaped and informed by it.

These books are a challenge to rethink a fascinating and existentially engaging set of philosophical and theological issues, as well a warm invitation to enrich our relationship with God and the human community, whether living or dead. And as Jairus and his friends learned, death may not be the insurmountable barrier we think it is.

Jerry L. Walls
Professor of Philosophy
Houston Baptist University

INTRODUCTION

WE WERE STANDING IN the church's fellowship hall. "I'm puzzled," Larry said, "about this morning's Prayers of the People." "How so?" I asked, sipping coffee. "You see"—he stopped to remember, then continued—"we made this petition: 'we commend to your mercy all who have died, that your will for them may be fulfilled.'" "Yes . . . ."—I waited. "Well—why do we do that? Why do we pray for the dead *at all*? And why do we pray for *all* the dead?" C. S. Lewis, I reminded Larry, had the same question. He admits praying for the departed, but wonders why—since tradition teaches that at death a person's salvation or damnation is final.[1] That conversation led to this project.

In the fourth century, Cyril of Jerusalem reports having heard believers ask "what is a soul, leaving this world . . . , profited by being remembered in the prayer?"[2] In this work I answer his question, explaining and defending the practice of *petitionary* prayer for *all* the dead. I discuss one general prayer—*consummation prayer* concerns all the departed and asks for completion of God's plan, their resurrection in a new heaven and earth. And since the dead comprise three groups, I discuss three specific forms of prayer—*growth prayer* concerns the blessed in heaven and asks for their increasing participation in God's life, *purification prayer* concerns the imperfect in purgatory and asks for their moral transformation in love, and *salvation prayer* concerns the unsaved in hell and asks for their restored relationship with God. My thesis challenges Protestants, who seldom pray for the dead, to begin doing so—and Roman Catholics and Eastern Orthodox, who pray only for the Christian dead, to broaden their practice to include *all* departed persons. I argue that prayer for all the dead is part and parcel of an orthodox understanding of

---

1. Lewis, *Letters to Malcolm*, Letter 20, 107.
2. Cyril of Jerusalem, cited in Swete, "Prayer for Departed," 510.

salvation—one aspect of the web of doctrine including Trinity, creation, redemption, and eschatology. Petitions for consummation, growth, purification, and salvation are not inconsequential. Instead, they raise the most basic of all questions and go to the center of God's purpose in creating spiritual beings and redeeming sinful humankind. In this project I "read theology backwards"—to use Hugh Mackintosh's phrase—since in the last things, the conclusion of God's work begun in creation, "we find the truest index of the whole."[3] Prayer for the dead, because it illuminates and is illuminated by central themes of faith, is an excellent vantage point for seeing all of theology.

The Autobiography Behind This Project

The personal is philosophical—all reflective thinking is autobiographical, reflecting a person's dominant concerns and life narrative. This is certainly the case for me. The conservative Protestant subculture in which I grew up was framed by the afterlife: faith was about getting to heaven and the threat of hell was always present. My journey of thinking about the nature of salvation began much earlier than my conversation with Larry.

I experienced a fascinating childhood in Nigeria, where my parents served for many years as missionaries. A major motivation for their work was a belief in exclusive salvation—that in order to be saved a person must hear the gospel and believe in Christ. As a teenager I wondered how two ideas I was taught—that Jesus loves everyone and that those who do not believe in him go to hell—fit together. In college I became a Calvinist, partly to get answers.[4] Because salvation is not a deserved right but a free gift, God can in perfect fairness give grace to some but not others—saving and damning whomever God chooses. Eventually, however, my Calvinism collapsed. I kept finding Bible verses that indicate that God's love is indiscriminate (2 Pet 3:9; 1 Tim 2:4)—and I simply could not get

---

3. Mackintosh, cited in Robinson, *In the End, God*, 42.

4. There is great diversity in Calvinism (or, in Roman Catholic theology, Augustinianism). The particular version to which I was drawn is evangelical Calvinism that emphasizes predestination (see Calvin, *Institutes*, Book 4) and divine sovereignty—as expressed by historical theologians such as Charles Spurgeon, A. A. Hodge, Benjamin Warfield, and contemporary writers like J. I. Packer, John Piper, and R. C. Sproul. Calvinism of this type states that while God's *providential* love is universal, God's *saving* love is particular; it is restricted to the elect whom God purposed to save and for whom Christ died.

past the moral injustice of double predestination and exclusive salvation.⁵ The logic became obvious to me—since God truly loves everyone and wants them to be saved, exclusivism cannot be true—and I became an inclusivist.⁶ Believing the gospel is not possible for the unevangelized, and so salvation—while objectively based on Christ's death and resurrection—does not require subjective knowledge of and conscious faith in Christ.⁷ I am now a universalist. I accept the biblical depiction of a final triumph in which all things and people are reconciled to God (Col 1:16, 20)—and believe death is not a point-of-no-return beyond which all chance for reconciliation with God ends.

---

5. Arminianism (or, in Roman Catholic theology, Non-Augustinianism) affirms that, while God initiates salvation, human beings can and must cooperate with and respond to divine grace in order to be saved. Arminian exclusivism—the idea that God saves those who freely choose to believe in Christ and damns those who do not—fares no better morally than Calvinism. A decision for or against God must be informed—but the unevangelized are not informed and so cannot accept or reject faith in Christ. They are damned by luck of circumstance, through no fault of their own.

6. My experience during this time was spiritually and psychologically difficult. I felt too ashamed to share my conclusions with my parents because the beliefs that so troubled me were the very reason they went to Africa. To question, let alone reject, these beliefs was to betray them, to invalidate the core principle of their lives. I did not want to give them pain, and so I suffered in silence. To make a long story short, I eventually found a progressive church where the limitless love of God and amazing grace beyond measure were affirmed. When I did finally broach the topic with my parents, they were generous and open. We have discussed these issues many times since; my mother has told me that she and my father themselves wondered about exclusive salvation since—as Rob Bell (*Love Wins*, 8) puts it—what if they got a flat tire and people in the next village never heard about Jesus? A loving God would not make their eternal destiny rest on chance, on being in the right place at the right time.

7. Technically, exclusivism claims that salvation requires a person to 1. consciously believe in Christ 2. in this life—that is, before they die. This generates two forms of inclusivism. *Eschatalogical evangelism inclusivism* denies condition 2. If salvation is found only through hearing and believing the gospel, and if God truly offers salvation to all persons, and if some do not hear the gospel now—then they must hear later. Either at or after death all individuals are given knowledge of Christ that is adequate for saving belief. *Implicit faith inclusivism* denies condition 1. Explicit belief in the gospel is not necessary for salvation. It is subjective faith (a positive response to God in the heart as shown by sincere moral action and religious devotion) rather than objective knowledge (specific information believed about God in the head) that saves. The Second Vatican Council (*Lumen Gentium* Chapter 16) authoritatively rejects the traditional view that "outside the Church no salvation"; instead, those who Karl Rahner describes as "anonymous Christians"—the unevangelized who seek God with a sincere heart—may be saved. See my "Broad Inclusive Salvation" and Sanders, *No Other Name.*

While I was I morally troubled by hell as a child, in graduate school I became bothered by heaven—particularly the atheist accusation that Christianity is otherworldly. Religion, Karl Marx says, "is the opium of the people"—the promise of heaven is a drug that paralyzes political energy and diverts us from struggling for a just world here and now.[8] Having been raised as an evangelical, I thought in dualistic and otherworldly terms. Dualism divides reality into two categories—sacred and secular—and otherworldliness regards the spiritual realm (especially future heaven) as more important than this life. I knew, though, that the atheists were right, that this world matters—in Nigeria I had seen and lamented preventable poverty, illness, and hunger. I read Reformed scholars who draw on the doctrines of creation and the cultural mandate (Gen 1:28) to ground Christian involvement in public affairs and social action. Most important, I discovered Dietrich Bonhoeffer's "worldly Christianity"—his prophetic call for the church to embrace its earthly responsibilities as "salt" and "light" (Matt 5:13–16), to no longer "think in two spheres" because Jesus Christ, the God-human, unites the supernatural and the natural.[9] Jesus' life of compassion—his physical healings and table fellowship with outcasts—call a church that follows him to involvement in medical care and education, to work for justice in world trade, and to free vulnerable people from oppression and abuse. For many of their years in Africa my parents were involved in leprosy work.

This, in brief, is the autobiography behind my theology. Many readers, I suspect, have had similar journeys. The life of faith is just that—a journey—and faith that seeks understanding is likely to change in the process. "The habits of faith that served us well at earlier stages may not survive untouched," Rowan Williams says. "There is a necessary movement of faith beyond the images we have found comforting in the past. To cling to those pictures is to refuse growth."[10] In Lewis' *Prince Caspian*, Lucy, the child of faith, meets Aslan again for the first time since *The Lion, The Witch and the Wardrobe*.

> "Aslan," said Lucy, "you're bigger."
> "That is because you are older, little one," answered he.
> "Not because you are?"

---

8. Marx, *Early Writings*, 44.

9. Bonhoeffer, *Ethics*, chapter 1 and *Letters and Papers*. I discuss these themes in "Bonhoeffer and False Dilemma."

10. Williams, *Lion's World*, 122–23.

INTRODUCTION

"I am not. But every year you grow, you will find me bigger."[11]

Like Lucy, I have had to unlearn some false ideas and learn some true ideas concerning God—but I am convinced I now understand God better. Critical reflection has given my faith greater integrity and credibility; it has deepened, not destroyed, my relationship with God.[12]

The Method and Plan of This Project

The Second Vatican Council calls for "elements [of faith and practice] which have suffered injury through accidents of history ... to be restored to the vigor which they had in the days of the holy Fathers."[13] Prayer for the dead no longer has the prominence it once did, Robert Eno points out, even in Roman Catholic thought and piety—and now is the time to articulate the practice in a new way. "But theological reconstruction," he observes, "must begin with a knowledge of the foundations."[14] Knowing what we are doing when we pray for the departed requires developing—in some detail, at least—eschatological doctrines of the last things (from the Greek word *eschaton*, "that which comes last"): death, judgment, heaven, purgatory, and hell. Eschatology shapes all of theology. As Jürgen Moltmann says, eschatology "is not just one element of Christianity, but ... is the medium of Christian faith as such, the key in which everything else is set, the glow that suffuses everything here in the dawn of an expected new day."[15] Eschatology determines our understanding of prayer for the dead. In order to pray for the final consummation of history we must accept a two-stage afterlife in which the last things—resurrection, for example—do not occur immediately at death. In order to pray for the growth of those in heaven we must assume a dynamic experience of union with God. In order to pray for the purification of those in purgatory we must understand that heaven requires perfect holiness—and why

---

11. Lewis, *Prince Caspian*, 141.

12. This paraphrases Mordecai Kaplan, cited in Felten and Procter-Murphy, *Living the Questions*, xi.

13. Vatican II, cited in Witvliet, "Embodying Wisdom of Ancient Liturgical Practices," 196.

14. Eno, "Fathers and Cleansing Fire," 184.

15. Moltmann, *Theology of Hope*, 16. Polkinghorne (*God of Hope*, 140) agrees: "eschatology is ... the keystone of the edifice of theological thinking, holding the whole building together."

it is developed progressively rather than bestowed instantly at death. In order to pray for the salvation of those in hell we must believe that death is open and posthumous repentance possible. These necessary assumptions require analysis and defense. We are more likely to reach clear and justified conclusions about prayer for the dead if we start with a firm theoretical base.[16]

My account of prayer for the dead is *prescriptive* (it defines what we *ought* to mean), not descriptive (it does not aim to capture what people actually do think they are doing when they make such prayers). My argument is *orthodox*. My conclusions are revisionary in some ways, but my theological premises are conservative, drawing on basic doctrines—Trinity, creation, and salvation—that the historic churches and great theologians have held as fundamental to Christianity and that are common to all orthodox believers.[17] My position is *ecumenical*. I cite theologians of all persuasions to make a case for petitionary prayer for all of the departed that should be acceptable to all branches of the church. This project may appeal particularly to those in the emerging and ancient-future church who are attempting to move into the future through continuity with the past, to recover traditional wisdom of early church theology, spirituality and liturgy in a catholicity that crosses denominational lines.[18] I do draw, however, on the tradition of my own church—the Episcopal Church, part of the worldwide Anglican Communion. Finally, my analysis is *integrative*—it endeavors to discern the truth, as an Episcopal Church statement says, "through engaging the Bible, . . . the historic teachings and liturgy of the Church, and human reason."[19] Prayer for the dead involves complex and controversial issues—exegetical, theological, and philosophical. In addressing them I engage a range of academic disciplines and attempt to be biblically accurate, historically informed, and philosophically reasoned. Praying for the departed implies a wide range of theological topics and a large scope of practical concern—a vision of space and time, good and evil, creation, salvation, and final redemption. In addition, it engages

---

16. See the methodology outlined in Swinburne, *Christian God*, 3.

17. I draw this language from Kronen and Reitan, *God's Final Victory*, 2.

18. This trend of recovering ancient wisdom for the modern church was initiated by mid-twentieth-century Roman Catholic theologians. In post-Christian Europe these *ressourcement* theologians turned to the work of the great patristic and medieval theologians for revitalization. See Husbands, "Introduction," 10–12.

19. Episcopal Church, "Episcopal Faith."

almost all philosophical questions—mind-body, personal identity, free-will and determinism, time and eternity.

In this project I do not try to consider every issue or answer every possible objection; I sacrifice details for brevity and accessibility. While I have tried to balance logic and practice, some readers will want more philosophical analysis and others will want more practical application. I develop few new positions on prayer, heaven, purgatory, or hell; there is an enormous literature on each of the questions I discuss, and interested readers will find resources in the footnotes. My unique contribution is to summarize and synthesize what others have written, assembling from established positions an explanation of prayer for the dead—hence this project is packed with quotes. I do not defend belief in life after death. Instead, I take it for granted that if Christianity is true then life after death is also true. Frederick Buechner says it simply: "if I were God and loved the people I created . . . I couldn't imagine consigning them to oblivion when their time came."[20] William Hasker puts it more formally: "there is a close tie between theism and belief in an afterlife." We should "consider the two beliefs together as a package" so that "arguments for . . . theism [count] as arguments for . . . an afterlife." Life after death is a function and consequence of belief in God; others have done the work of defending the idea that we survive death.[21]

Finally, a caution about terminology. The words used for the three afterlife destinies—"heaven," "purgatory," and "hell"—are emotionally-charged terms that carry common meanings with all sorts of connotations. The popular conceptions are that *heaven* is an immaterial place where spirits float around on clouds, that *purgatory* is souls writhing in pain while demons screech around them, and that *hell* is an eternal and fiery torture chamber. I do not understand or use the words in these ways. It would be preferable, perhaps, to have new terms to mark the difference

---

20. Buechner, *Eyes of Heart*, 16. Robinson (*In the End, God*, 91) agrees: God "cannot, being eternal love, cease ever to hold [human persons] dear, nor consent to scrap them after three score years and ten." If God made human beings for relationship with God then it would be illogical to let them pass out of existence at death. If Christian theism is true, then human beings are made by a God who loves them and whose purpose for them includes life after death.

21. Hasker, "Afterlife," Section 5. For defenses of survival see Hasker's bibliography. Also see Davis, *After We Die*, as well as older works such as Badham, *Immortality or Extinction?*, Penelhum, *Immortality*, and Perrett, *Death and Immortality*. More skeptical volumes include Edwards, *Immortality* and Moore, *Philosophical Possibilities Beyond Death*.

between traditional and revised meanings—but it seems we are stuck with the usual words as convenient labels. Lexical definitions convey how a term is commonly used. Stipulated definitions, by contrast, give a specific—and sometimes different—meaning to a term for a particular purpose. I use the traditional words with the following stipulated meanings, meanings on which I elaborate later. *Heaven* is being in the presence of God. It includes both *present heaven* (the transitional place where we go when we die and where we await resurrection) and *future heaven* (the permanent place on a renewed earth where we will live forever with God and each other). *Purgatory* is the place, a lower part of heaven, where we mature into the love that prepares us for full union with God, the higher part of heaven. *Hell* is a place of separation from God. While hell is real, it is escapable—individuals can leave when they repent and turn to God; in the end, hell will exist but will be empty—like an abandoned warehouse. Readers should not dismiss what follows simply because I use traditional words like "hell." While they can miscommunicate—readers might immediately think of eternal torture, for example—inventing a novel vocabulary also carries risk. Nor should readers dismiss what follows because I use old words in new ways. Instead, I ask you to join me in the—at times hard—work of rethinking some key concepts and received ideas.

This project consists of two volumes, sequenced as follows. The first considers the history and logic of prayer for the dead. Chapter 1 addresses the biblical credentials of such prayers. Chapters 2 through 4 provide a historical and contemporary overview—and state my thesis. Chapters 5 through 7 identify the logical assumptions of prayer for the dead: the effectiveness of prayer—and the conscious, personal, and temporal nature of the life to come. These chapters are the most philosophically challenging. Chapter 8 outlines a theological framework—creative love theism—that grounds our prayers. Prayers for the departed are prayers of hope—and chapter 9 analyzes the nature of hope. The first volume makes a case for prayer for the dead in general.

The second volume concerns the practice and value of prayer for the dead. Chapter 1 briefly restates the philosophical and theological assumptions of volume one. Chapters 2 through 5 make a case for the four specific types of prayer for the dead. They discuss the substance of prayer for final consummation of all things, growth of the blessed in heaven, purification of the imperfect in purgatory, and salvation of the unsaved in hell—identifying the necessary conception of the afterlife required by

INTRODUCTION

each particular prayer. Chapters 6 and 7 reflect on the spiritual value of prayer for the departed—how it enhances faith, builds hope, and sharpens discipleship. Chapter 8 provides sample prayers that may be used both liturgically and devotionally. In each volume an Appendix includes detailed theoretical considerations.

Concluding Remarks

One morning at breakfast Larry and I were discussing a draft of chapter 6, which he had read. Suddenly I began laughing at my own presumption in thinking that my speculations truly represent eschatological reality. It reminded me of lines from Lewis' "Apologist's Evening Prayer": *"thoughts are but coins. / Let me not trust, instead of thee / their thin-worn image of thy head."*[22] My own amusement at supposing I understand the details of what happens after death, which we *do not* know, reminded Larry and me of what we *do* know—that we are made by a God whose overwhelming love surrounds us always, that we are called to friendship with that God, and that this destiny will be fulfilled eternally in a life beyond this life.

Ideas are created in community—and my thoughts in this book have been discussed, debated, refined, and corrected through conversation with trusted companions: my dear sister Beth Nolson (a kindred questioning spirit in whose home and heart I have always been welcomed and sheltered), my teaching colleagues Timothy Linehan (my philosophical sounding board, whose fine knowledge of metaphysics and epistemology helped me navigate some tricky waters), and James Campbell (who schooled me in the ways of Eastern Orthodoxy)—and my friend Larry Wild (who, as head librarian at Judson University in Elgin, Illinois, functioned as *de facto* research assistant tracking down numerous sources for me). Mary Jane Deja of McHenry County College was tireless in ordering and delivering inter-library loan material, even the most obscure. I am indebted to my editor, Robin Parry, for his consistent encouragement and insightful ideas. Above all, I am grateful to my wife Jenna Korenstra—living with her is a delightful foretaste of heaven and a school of virtue. She has been to me—in the words of our wedding prayer—"a strength in need, a counselor in perplexity, a comfort in sorrow, a companion in

---

22. Lewis, *Poems*, 129. Also see *Mere Christianity*, 135–36.

joy." She is an unmistakable sign to me, as to all who know her, of God's generous love which always offers second chances.[23]

Some of the material in this volume first appeared (in modified form) in previous publications of mine. Specifically, I have drawn material from the following articles:

"Broad Inclusive Salvation: The Logic of 'Anonymous Christianity.'"
    Philosophy and Theology 20 (2008) 175–98.
"God's Saving Purpose and Prayer for All the Departed." *Journal of*
    Anglican Studies 10 (2012) 1–29.
All materials are used with permission.

Unless otherwise indicated, Scripture is taken from the *New Revised Standard Version* of the Bible.[24] Scripture marked NIV is taken from the *Holy Bible, New International Version*.[25] Passages from the Apocrypha are taken from the *New Revised Standard Version with the Apocrypha*.[26] Scripture marked KJV is taken from the *King James Version* of the Bible.

When I quote authors who refer to God using masculine terms, I change these to the gender-neutral word "God." I leave masculine biblical quotations unchanged.

---

23. Episcopal Church, *Book of Common Prayer*, 429.
24. Division of Christian Education of the National Council of Churches of Christ in the United States of America, 1989.
25. International Bible Society, 1984.
26. Oxford: Oxford University Press, 2009.

chapter 1

SETTING A CONTEXT
The Bible and Prayer for the Dead

SITTING ON THE DECK on a warm summer day, swatting mosquitoes as we drink iced tea, the conversation drifts to my research and writing. My conservative Protestant friends quiz me on the biblical justification of praying for the dead—let alone all the dead. "Where do you get that from the Bible?" one asks. "Doesn't Scripture contradict the idea that people who reject God in this life get a second chance after death?" inquires another. In some respects the discussion is friendly and open, but in other ways their questions are skeptical, almost dismissive. Their concern is a legitimate one. The Bible, David Crump says, must take priority "in establishing the proper parameters of Christian theology."[1] As Christians we live under God's Word—and we become anxious and defensive when Scripture is interpreted in ways that are new to us. So how *does* praying for the dead fit with the Bible?

Scripture and Prayer for the Departed

There is no example, command, or prohibition of prayer for the dead in Scripture. The Bible does forbid attempts to communicate *with* the dead (Lev 19:31; 20:6)—but this is irrelevant to prayer *for* them. The few texts appealed to in support of the practice are difficult to interpret and cannot serve as simple proof texts.

---

1. Crump, *Knocking on Heaven's Door*, 281.

2 Maccabees 12:39–45. During the second-century-BCE war for Jewish independence from the imposition of Greek culture on Israel, Judas Maccabeus, while collecting the bodies of fallen comrades, found pagan emblems—forbidden by Jewish law—under their tunics. He immediately "turned to supplication, praying that the sin that had been committed might be wholly blotted out." The writer endorses Judas' behavior: "in doing this he acted very well and honorably, taking account of the resurrection. . . . . He made atonement for the dead, so that they might be delivered from their sin." This text clearly describes prayer for the departed, but there are two problems with it. First, while Roman Catholics and Eastern Orthodox accept this deuterocannonical book as revealed Scripture, Protestants do not. Second, interpretations of the story differ. Some scholars see it as evidence that prayer for the dead was a common practice in Palestinian Judaism (and thus part of Jesus' synagogue worship experience), while others see it as a single episode not repeated elsewhere. Given the difficulties with this text, we should be hesitant in using it to support prayer for the dead.

2 Timothy 1:16–18. In the opening greetings of the second letter to Timothy, St. Paul prays for God to bless an old friend: "may the Lord grant mercy to the household of Onesiphorus, . . . may the Lord grant that he will find mercy . . . on that day." Scholarly opinion is divided on whether Onesiphorus was dead or alive. The fact that other people—Prisca and Aquila—are greeted personally while only the "household" of Onesiphorus is mentioned suggests that he was dead.[2] Some, however, point out that since it is not directly stated, we cannot be certain that Onesiphorus was dead. Perhaps he had deserted the faith, which is why he is not addressed personally and why God is asked to show him mercy at judgment. This text most likely indicates prayer for a dead person, but may not.

1 Corinthians 15:29. In defending resurrection, St. Paul makes this enigmatic remark: if there is no resurrection "what will those people do who receive baptism on behalf of the dead? If the dead are not raised at all, why are people baptized on their behalf?" Baptism for the dead is illogical if there is no resurrection.[3] Most modern scholars see here a reference to substitutionary baptism of living people for the sake of some-

---

2. This interpretation is accepted by many scholars, including conservative Protestants such as Kelly, *Commentary on Pastoral Epistles*, 171 and Saarinen, *Pastoral Epistles*, 133–34.

3. See Reaume, "Another Look," 466.

one dead—an unbaptized catechumen or non-believer, for example. The natural reading of the text is that actions of the living can help the dead. There are, however, difficulties with this view. First, there is no historical parallel before or during St. Paul's time of baptism for the dead; this single reference might be due to the religious environment at Corinth, which had a unique preoccupation with the dead and the underworld.[4] Second, this practice contradicts St. Paul's teaching on the participatory nature of baptism; one person's baptism cannot substitute for someone else, and baptism alone without personal faith cannot save. Some scholars see the text as referring to unbelievers who decided to become believers and be baptized due to the influence of deceased Christians—in which case it does not concern the dead at all.[5] Because of the uncertain meaning of this text, it cannot bear much weight as biblical evidence for the idea that the actions of living people—including prayer—can affect the fate of the dead.

The Irrelevance of the Silence of Scripture

These few texts give no clear guidance for or against praying for the dead. Determining what the silence of Scripture means depends on a person's theological method. Some take this silence as definitive: since the Bible encourages prayer for the living but does not mention prayer for the dead—especially when it would be natural to expect it—it is not appropriate. The Thessalonian believers, for example, worried about the fate of those who had died before the second coming of Christ—but St. Paul does not comfort them by encouraging prayer for their dead (1 Thess 4:13–18).[6] The Reformation principle *sola Scriptura* declares that the Bible is the only true source of knowledge, the final authority which safeguards the church from false teaching. Thomas Boultbee claims that "the silence of Scripture is conclusive. It would be simply impossible for the writers of the Epistles to have omitted directions about prayers for the dead . . . if these had been any part of their system."[7] The Bible's lack of attention to prayer for the dead constitutes, some believe, a prohibition.

---

4. See DeMaris, "Corinthian Religion."
5. See White, "Recent Challenges" and "Baptized on Account of Dead."
6. Archbishops' Commission, *Prayer and Departed*, 39.
7. Boultbee, cited in Archbishops' Commission, *Prayer and Departed*, 86.

Other scholars see this silence as due to the early Christian setting. The ancient church expected Christ's imminent return and therefore did not develop its theology of the afterlife. St. Paul, for example, does not tell the Thessalonians to pray for their departed because there was simply no need for them to do so. What they needed was reassurance—which he gives—that the dead are not in danger of missing Christ's return but will be resurrected and share in his victory. Furthermore, Scripture is not an exclusive norm for faith and practice—reason and tradition also play a role. As Jerry Walls says, the fact that something is not mentioned in the Bible "hardly means that there is no way to argue the matter theologically or to arrive at a biblically-grounded view on the issue. For the question remains whether the doctrine coheres with things that are clearly taught in Scripture, or can even be inferred from them as a reasonable theological conclusion."[8] Certain beliefs, Crump suggests, are *biblically necessary*—basic truths directly taught in Scripture and drawn from exegesis. But since the Bible does not provide complete answers to many questions, we must go beyond what it says and develop positions that are *philosophically possible*—derived truths inferred from biblical teaching and systematized by rational reflection.[9] Many doctrines (such as the Trinity) and practices (like infant baptism) are not mentioned in Scripture, but are later theological developments. In praying for the dead, William Forbes says, the ancient church, far from ignoring the Bible, was "led . . . by the testimonies and examples of Scripture, from which it is evident that the prayers which just men offer for others are of great avail with God, and . . . that the righteous at their death do not cease to be."[10] Doctrines and practices that go beyond what the Bible says are legitimate, David Chapman concludes, "provided always that such development in no way contradicts Scripture and remains congruent with other doctrines."[11] For

---

8. Walls, *Purgatory*, 56.

9. Crump, *Knocking on Heaven's Door*, 18. MacDonald (*Evangelical Universalist*, 36) outlines several ways in which beliefs can be based on the Bible. First, a doctrine has positive biblical support if 1. it is explicitly taught (in a plain "proof text," for example), 2. it can be reasonably inferred from what is explicitly taught, or 3. it is consistent with the broader biblical meta-narrative. Second—and more controversially—a doctrine may be believed if it does not conflict with what is explicitly taught in Scripture.

10. Forbes, cited in Archbishops' Commission, *Prayer and Departed*, 77–78.

11. Chapman, "Rest and Light Perpetual," 43. It is not necessary for all matters of faith and practice to be contained in the Bible—but they must not contradict it. There are doctrines which are clearly taught in Scripture and those that are in harmony with (and thus allowed by) Scripture.

these reasons I believe that the silence of Scripture is irrelevant to the legitimacy of prayer for the dead.

Biblical Interpretation, Church Tradition, and Theological Method

I should say a bit more concerning the relationships between Scripture, tradition, and theology. Knowing what we are doing when we pray for the departed requires various assumptions about prayer, human nature, and time—as well as particular eschatological understandings of heaven, purgatory, and hell. Biblical material about these matters is imprecise and unsystematic. Its language is often symbolic and open (having multiple meanings) rather than literal and closed (having a single meaning). We cannot make dogmatic claims concerning the state of the departed. Intellectual humility requires awareness of the limits of our knowledge and insight, caution to not claim to know more than we actually know or with more certainty than is warranted—and sensitivity to bias in and weaknesses of our own viewpoints. Theological positions are always—in academic jargon—underdetermined by evidence. Biblical texts seldom conclusively support one interpretation and one interpretation only; there is always the possibility that another understanding is correct. But neither should we assume that we know nothing about the present condition or future expectation of the dead. As Tom Wright points out,

> all language about the future . . . is simply a set of signposts pointing into a fog. We see through a glass darkly, says St. Paul [1 Cor 13:12] as he peers toward what lies ahead. All our language about future states . . . consists of complex pictures that may or may not correspond very well to the ultimate reality. But that doesn't mean it's anybody's guess or that every opinion is as good as every other one.[12]

Socrates, facing execution for heresy and corrupting the minds of Athenian youths, says that "when a person is going to the other world, it seems highly proper for them to reason and speculate about the nature of our sojourn there." He continues: "it is impossible or at least very hard to attain any certainty about questions such as these . . . . And yet I should deem him a coward who did not prove what is said about them to the uttermost, not desisting until he had examined them on every side." We must test the available theories and consider them in every way, having

---

12. Wright, *Surprised by Hope*, xiii.

confidence that we can think coherently and logically and thus draw rational conclusions.[13] While Scripture does not give detailed information on the life to come, we can make reasonable inferences based on what it does say and our own theological commitments.

In this project I defend petitionary prayer for all the dead. This claim challenges each branch of the church—Protestants who do not pray for any of the dead and Roman Catholics and Eastern Orthodox who do not pray for the unsaved dead. Church traditions—whether Protestant, Catholic, or Orthodox—are often defended in the name of biblical authority, with the sense that Scripture plainly teaches a particular doctrine or practice. There are multiple problems with this view.

First, interpretations differ. "The text of Scripture, already in the second and third centuries," Brian Daley points out, was being "used to support a dazzling variety of positions"—not only on small matters, but on the greatest matters (such as the nature of Christ).[14] Equally sincere and reputable scholars find different meanings in Scripture, which suggests that the Bible is not as straightforward as we would like to think. "God has not provided enough guidance," John Suk states, "to prevent the church from disagreeing" on a good many topics.[15]

Second, interpretations may be just plain wrong. John Bowker points out that Christians have claimed biblical warrant for murdering Jews, burning women they regarded as witches, slavery and *apartheid*, aggressive unjust wars, and subordinating women to men—to name but a few misuses of Scripture.[16] Sharon Baker agrees: while tradition can be faithful to God's truth, it can also betray it—and so the church must always be open to rethinking its faith and practice. Theological ideas "become such a part of our belief system that we think they are scriptural. But often they don't come from the Bible at all. They come from our contexts, our communities of discourse, our friends and pastors and parents and Sunday school teachers. Upon closer examination . . . we find that the Bible teaches something quite different from what we have always believed."[17] This is why revising tradition—ordaining women, for example—need not necessarily undermine a high view of the Bible. "To affirm 'the authority of Scripture,'" Wright reminds us, "is precisely not

---

13. Plato, *Phaedo*, 61e, 411, and 85c, 441. Also see Paul, *Critical Thinking*, 553–54.
14. Daley, "Old Books," 62.
15. Suk, *Not Sure*, 128.
16. Bowker, cited in Ford, *Theology*, 126.
17. Baker, *Razing Hell*, 82–83.

to say, 'we know what Scripture means and don't need to raise any more questions.' It is always a way of saying that the Church in each generation must make fresh . . . efforts to understand Scripture more fully . . . , even if that means cutting across cherished traditions." Accepting biblical authority means letting it tell us things we have never heard before—and may not want to hear—rather than assuming that traditional understandings are correct.[18]

Third, interpretations are not neutral. It is epistemically naïve to think that we come to Scripture empty handed, without assumptions. "What we hear in the Bible," Douglas John Hall asserts, "is very often determined not by what is actually there, but by what we have come to expect to find there."[19] We never have Scripture in-itself as a pure thing, only Scripture as it appears to us. Biblical texts do not simply say what they say and we do not passively receive their truth just by reading words on the page. Instead, like a person wearing sunglasses that color the world, we actively impose our categories on Scripture. Interpretation is always mediated through subjective perspectives, the set of assumptions we bring to the Bible—which is why, Rudolf Bultmann observes, exegesis without presuppositions is not possible.[20] The fact that no interpretation is neutral, that we always stand somewhere, does not mean—of course—that we can never be reasonably certain of what Scripture says. Biblical interpretation is most accurate when we use the grammatical-historical method to discover what an author intended to say to the original readers. Competent scholars, after careful study of the Bible in dialogue with those who see things differently, may be confident in their conclusions (even if others disagree and epistemic humility is appropriate).

Finally, interpretation is too often undertaken as an individual activity. Protestants and Roman Catholics have long debated the importance of individual liberty *versus* church authority in matters of faith. Protestants hold that the Bible speaks for itself and can be interpreted by the individual according to the dictates of their own reason (not relying on the authority of church leaders). Liberty of conscience, individual freedom

18. Wright, *Last Word*, 84, 91 and 95.
19. Hall, *When You Pray*, 70.
20. Bultmann, "Is Exegesis Without Presuppositions Possible?" Rob Bell (*Velvet Elvis*, 54–55) puts it more strongly: "the assumption . . . that there is a way to read the Bible that is agenda- and perspective-free," that "everyone else approaches the Bible with baggage and agendas and lenses and I don't" is not only untrue but "the ultimate in arrogance." Everyone has their opinions and biases, and no one simply reads Scripture for what it says, unaffected by outside influences.

to make decisions about the Bible's meaning, however, can be dangerous. The principle of *sola Scriptura*—that Scripture alone is an unmediated guide to truth—can become, Christopher Hall says, *Scriptura nuda*: a plain, naked text to be interpreted by autonomous individuals under the personal illumination of the Holy Spirit.[21] The problem is that every heretic from the gnostic Christians and Arius of Alexandria to Charles Taze Russell (founder of the Jehovah's Witness sect) and Gwen Shamblin (founder of Remnant Fellowship Church) has relied on the Bible alone, claiming to understand it apart from a community of interpretation. Scripture is, of course, the key resource for knowing God and God's purposes in creation. The Bible's meaning, however, is not transparent; "while our own interpretations seem patently clear to us as the plain meaning of the text," Hall comments, "they are rarely so to those who disagree with us."[22] And so the meaning of Scripture as well as doctrinal development must be determined by the church. Biblical interpretation, Russell Ronald Reno says, "is a communal project . . . . Only a fool would imagine that he or she could work out solutions alone."[23] "No prophecy of Scripture is a matter of one's own interpretation" (2 Pet 1:20), St. Peter warns. Communal understanding provides the milieu for rightly understanding the Word of truth (2 Tim 2:15); it is a safeguard against any individual challenging any doctrine they dislike on the basis of an idiosyncratic reading of the text. "Scripture cannot be understood or interpreted authentically," Daley states, "apart from the community's 'rule of faith.'"[24]

Protestants in particular must beware the danger of reading Scripture in an autonomous way, without reference to communal authority. As

---

21. Hall, "Tradition, Authority, Magisterium," 31. This paragraph draws on Hall's essay. Currie (*Born Fundamentalist*, 56–57) points out that the principle that Scripture is the sole authority for faith and morals is self-refuting. Just as the statements "there are no absolute truths" and "the only truths are empirically verifiable" are self-destructive (since the former is itself an absolute truth claim and the latter cannot be validated by its own criterion of observation), so the statement "only doctrines taught in the Bible are to be trusted" is not taught in the Bible.

22. Ibid., 45.

23. Reno, cited in Hall, "Tradition, Authority, Magisterium," 38. Byassee ("Emerging from What?" 256) agrees: "Scripture is not to be read by solitary individuals trying to cook up their own belief systems from scratch . . . . Scripture is to be read with and through friends, both living friends . . . and dead friends." Daley ("Old Books, 54) points out that it was only with the Enlightenment's emphasis on the autonomy of the human intellect that biblical interpretation and theological argument based on tradition began to fade.

24. Daley, "Old Books," 66.

Daley contends, too many "attempt to encounter God's word in Scripture directly, apart from the creedal and doctrinal tradition in which it has been received and interpreted through the Christian centuries."[25] I emphasize, then, that the perspectives I offer in this project are not mine alone. My biblical interpretations and theological reflections are not peculiar to me; this is why I draw on and quote from a wide community of scholars across the Christian spectrum to support the positions I take. I do not stand alone; instead, my analyses and arguments stand within a communally determined understanding of Scripture's meaning and thus—I trust—represent good and faithful thinking. While I do call for revision at points—particularly concerning the doctrine of hell—this is not done simply on the basis of my own reading of the Bible. Instead, I am guided by and in the company of numerous theologians and philosophers; my claims are accountable to the wider church in that sense.

Concluding Remarks

The formation of knowledge and understanding is always holistic in nature, Julian Baggini observes; "any single thing we believe is connected, web-like, to any number of other beliefs."[26] Resolving difficult theological questions is not as simple as finding a verse to prove or disprove an answer; instead, it is about how a person assembles their entire web of theology. Once a particular understanding captures our imagination, Thomas Talbott says, it has a profound effect on how we put biblical ideas together and interpret specific texts of Scripture. There is, for example, biblical support for each of three inconsistent propositions:

1. God wants to save all persons (1 Tim 2:4; 2 Pet 3:9),
2. God can achieve God's purposes (Ps 115:3; Isa 46:10–11) and
3. some sinners will never be reconciled to God (Matt 25:46; 2 Thess 1:9).

The upshot, Talbott says, is that "every reflective Christian . . . must reject a proposition for which there is at least some . . . biblical support." Augustinians reject statement 1: while God's providential love is universal, God's saving love is restricted to the elect. Non-Augustinians

---

25. Daley, "Old Books," 54.
26. Baggini, *Pig That Wants to Be Eaten*, 182.

reject statement 2: while God's saving love is unlimited, God's redemptive power can be frustrated by free human choices. Universalists reject statement 3: God's love and power cannot be thwarted and so all persons will ultimately be saved. All three theological systems are in the *same* situation of having to reinterpret a proposition for which there is apparent biblical support—and all have defenders who take Scripture seriously.[27] Our understanding of God and God's work in the world, Terrance Tiessen says, "cannot be achieved through analysis of a few key passages of Scripture." Instead, the exegesis of particular verses (and an assessment of biblical silence) takes place within a wider theological context. We arrive at a theology "through a general impression drawn from the entire text of Scripture"—and "once one has become convinced of a particular overall framework in the biblical narrative . . . , it is very difficult to see texts in a way that would call for radical revision of the overall model."[28] The fact that different people give interpretive priority to different passages does not mean that they respect the Bible less. Traditionalists and revisionists on doctrinal and moral questions disagree about interpretation of Scripture, not its authority.

While prayer for the departed is not found in the Bible, it began early and quickly became a customary part of Christian practice. In later chapters I offer logical analysis and theological argument—not historical interpretation. A historical survey, however, will set my argument in context by identifying themes and issues to be examined. I turn to that next.

---

27. Talbott, *Inescapable Love of God*, 47–48. Origen (cited in Daley, "Old Books," 63–64) claims that only those who grasp the central drift and outline of Scripture's teaching are in a position to interpret particular texts correctly, to properly understand their place in the whole structure. "The most fundamental knowledge the scriptural interpreter needs, if he [or she] is to understand and proclaim the text correctly, is to grasp the message conveyed by the whole of . . . the biblical canon."

28. Tiessen, *Providence and Prayer*, 22. Also see Archbishops' Commission, *Prayer and Departed*, 40.

chapter 2

RECOUNTING THE PAST
Prayer for the Dead in the Historical Church

TURKU CATHEDRAL IS THE mother church of the Lutheran Church of Finland. In the sixteenth century the Cathedral, formerly Roman Catholic, became Protestant. Jenna and I are visiting it—along with Sarah, our daughter, who is in graduate school there. The funerary monuments are what grab my attention. Tombs in a church, the dead buried in the aisle floors. Why? Turku Cathedral was built in the thirteenth century, and in the fifteenth century side-chapels containing altars to various saints were added alongside the nave. These were subsequently converted into funeral vaults and graves were set into the floor as well. Among the figures buried in the Cathedral are several medieval and post-Reformation bishops and military commanders (those buried in cathedrals are uniformly of high social status—clergy, nobility, and gentry). But why is *anyone* buried there? What function of commemoration do cathedral tombs represent?

For centuries, Rob Moll points out, "church buildings were . . . graveyards." Christians were buried in a cemetery next to the church, under its floor, or inside its walls as an expression of the communion of saints that "integrated the community of the dead with that of the living." Such burials created a sense of the universal church across time—that "those who have died are still present with us as members of the body of Christ." Christians who sit in the pews each Sunday and entombed believers awaiting resurrection share one faith and one hope.[1] Burial of

---

1. Moll, *Art of Dying*, 40 and 166. Some churches today have memorial gardens with columbaria—where the cremated ashes of the dead are stored—on their property.

the faithful within cathedral precincts was also what historians call a "strategy of salvation." Nigel Saul explains that in the religious thought of the Middle Ages the dead were involved in a relationship of dependence on the living.

> The starting-point of medieval thinking on the afterlife was that, while the souls of the virtuous might well go straight to heaven and those of the damned straight to hell, the souls of most of us, neither wholly good or wholly bad, were likely to go to . . . purgatory—there to be tried and tested. And in the process of trying and testing, [God] would be swayed by the intercessory prayers of the living, most of all by the prayers of the clergy offered every day in the liturgy.

To be buried in a cathedral was to be close to where petitionary prayer is offered and to be in proximity to the saints; tombs also appeal to onlookers to pray for the dead person's soul. In short, funerary monuments and intercessory prayer go together—and burial in a cathedral helps in the salvation of the faithful departed.[2] To step into a medieval cathedral—Turku, the Domkerk in Utrecht, Hereford Cathedral in England—is to step back in history, and to encounter the tomb commemorations is to encounter prayer for the dead.

Christians have always prayed for the departed. The practice is not mentioned in Scripture, but in the ancient church remembrance of the dead began early and was widespread. Early Christians assumed the doctrine of the communion of saints—that there is one body of Christ in which *all* the faithful, both living and dead, are eternally united. This bond is not broken by death, and just as the living can be helped by our prayers, so can the dead. Prayer for the dead is rooted in the concept of spiritual interdependence. While Westerners are taught to value independence, in the church God gives us a family to help us in our pilgrimage to heaven; prayer for the dead is one of those helps.[3] The first prayers thanked God that believers are at rest in Christ and asked that they be brought safely to resurrection in God's eternal kingdom. Prayer for the dead gradually came to be associated with belief in a process of sancti-

---

These give a sense of the continuity of the church and a reminder of our own deaths (168).

    2. Saul, "Living and Dead," 3. Burial beside the shrines of the saints and martyrs, with candles always burning, provided protection at the last judgment (see Brown, *Ransom of Soul*, 20-21, 77-79, 122).

    3. I draw this language from Currie, *Born Fundamentalist*, 129-30.

fication after death—culminating in the medieval doctrine of purgatory. The idea that individuals suffering there can be helped by the works of the church on earth gave rise to abuses. The Reformers declared that believers are justified by faith alone and are made holy at death—so prayer cannot help the dead. Eastern Orthodox and Roman Catholics pray for the faithful departed in both private devotion and public worship. While most Protestants do not, some ecumenical churches have added ancient prayers as part of liturgical renewal.

The Ancient Church: Prayer for Peace and Pardon

There is no evidence of prayer for the dead in the first century, but second-century tomb inscriptions contain both declarations (such as *in pace*—"he rests in peace") and petitions (like *vivas in pace*—"may you rest in peace").[4] These prayers express confident assurance that the departed are with God—and believers would at times visit their tombs to pray for them.[5]

Early Christian literature often mentions prayer for the dead.[6] In the second-century apocryphal text *The Acts of Paul and Thecla*, the female apostle Thecla prays for the salvation of the unbaptized Falconilla, who was dead. In the early-third-century story *The Passion of Perpetua and*

---

4. Roman *tricliae* were walled enclosures with kitchens and eating spaces standing in the midst of ancient tombs so the living could celebrate loved ones with funeral meals close to their burial places. The meal was a symbol of the feast of refreshment and rest of the soul. Graffiti was written on the walls of these banqueting enclosures. See Brown, *Ransom of Soul*, 36–39.

5. This overview draws from Boggis, *Praying for Dead* and Lee, *Christian Doctrine of Prayer for Departed*. Also see Plumptre, *Spirits in Prison*, chapter 9; Swete, "Prayer for Departed" and Toner, "Prayers for Dead." Beyond these older histories, there is significant recent scholarship on prayer for the dead—tracing rituals and liturgies from the early Christian era (every pagan religion of the ancient Mediterranean assumed that the dead needed the living) through post-Reformation periods. An overview can be found in McLaughlin, *Consorting with Saints*, 1–23.

6. McLaughlin (*Consorting with Saints*, 181–82 and 28) cautions: "while there is a great deal of evidence from the second, third, and fourth centuries to show that Christians remembered their dead in various ways, that evidence is fragmentary and often obscure. There has been considerable debate over the interpretation of individual texts and the ways in which those texts fit together. Most scholars are now agreed . . . that rituals for the dead had more than one meaning for the earliest Christians. Some were apparently performed in accordance with beliefs which Christians shared with many of their Jewish and pagan neighbors, while others carried meanings which were more specific to the Christian message."

Felicitas, Perpetua prays for her dead, unbaptized brother Dinocrates—who is brought from suffering to joy. But as Henry Swete points out, "no importance can be attached" to these tales since "in both accounts we are dealing only with private speculations, which cannot be taken to reflect the general belief of the Church."[7] In the third century, Arnobius of Sicca writes that the church prays two things: "*peace* and *pardon* are asked . . . for those still in life, and those freed from the bondage of the flesh."[8]

The earliest prayers were for *peace*—commemorations (thankful remembrances of the dead) and commendations (entrusting them to God's care). In the second century, Tertullian of Carthage indicates that at burials and annual commemorative services "we make offerings for the dead . . . to celebrate their birthday" of eternal life. He declares it a duty for surviving spouses to "pray for [their dead partner's] soul, and request refreshment for them."[9] In the third century, Cyprian of Carthage exhorts clergy to remember the dead by name annually during the Eucharist: "take note of their days on which they depart, that we may celebrate their commemoration among the memorials of the martyrs."[10] In the fourth century, Cyril of Jerusalem reports that during Holy Communion "we commemorate . . . those who have fallen asleep before us . . . believing that it will be a very great benefit to the souls, for whom the supplication is put up."[11]

Prayers for *pardon* were soon added. In the Eastern Empire of the third century, Aerius of Pontus rejects intercession for the dead since it promotes moral laxity in this life: "if the prayer of the people here has benefited the people there, no one should practice piety or perform good works."[12] His objection is refuted by Epiphanius of Salamis: "as to naming the dead, what could be more helpful? . . . We pray for sinners, for God's mercy, and for the righteous."[13] John Chrysostom in the late third century states that the church "prays that God would be merciful to the sins of

---

7. Swete, "Prayer for Departed," 513.

8. Arnobius, "Against the Heathen," Book 4.36, 488; slightly modified and emphasis added.

9. Tertullian, "Chaplet," chapter 3, 237 and "On Monogamy," chapter 10, 67, slightly modified.

10. Cyprian, "Epistle 36," 315.

11. Cyril, "Catechetical Lecture 23," 154–55.

12. Aerius, summarized in Ephiphanius, *Panarion*, 506; cf. 411–12.

13. Epiphanius, *Panarion*, 113 and 509–10.

all, not only of the living, but also of the departed."[14] He exhorts believers to pray for the dead in order to improve their situation—encouraging what will eventually become prayer for the baptized but sinful dead in purgatory.

> Not . . . in vain [do we] make mention of the departed . . . and approach God in their behalf, beseeching the Lamb who . . . takes away the sin of the world . . . that some refreshment may thereby ensue to them. . . . For if the children of Job were purged by the sacrifice of their father, why do you doubt that when we too offer for the departed, some consolation arises to them? . . . Why therefore do you grieve . . . when it is in your power to gather so much pardon for the departed?[15]

In the fourth century, Cyril of Jerusalem reiterates that "we, when we offer to God our supplications for those who have fallen asleep, though they be sinners, . . . [are] propitiating our merciful God for them."[16] There are two categories of saved dead for whom prayer is made—the perfect who immediately enter heaven and the imperfect who require purification after death.

A common theme in the first three centuries concerns prayer for the unsaved who are rescued from hell.[17] The *Apocalypse of Peter*—an apocryphal document that some church fathers considered inspired scripture—refers to posthumous salvation brought about through prayer: "I

---

14. Chrysostom, "On the Priesthood," Book 6.4, 76.

15. Chrysostom, *Homily on First Corinthians*, Part 2, Homily 41.8, 592–93. Chrysostom is here giving an answer to a fictitious interlocutor concerned for a loved one who died in sin (a worry which assumes that if one dies in sin there is no remedy since salvation is impossible in the next life). Ramelli (*Christian Doctrine of Apokatastasis*, 554–61) argues that Chrysostom does not distinguish purgatory from hell; one either dies in grace or in sin. He thinks that prayer can purify those in hell who died in sin; God will grant them grace through the prayers of the church. Almsgiving on their behalf also extinguishes the furnace of hell and opens the gates of heaven, rescuing people from damnation in the world to come. The situation of the dead is improvable, thanks to the help of the church; it is not unchangeably fixed at death. "It is possible," Chrysostom says, "to put together forgiveness for the dead . . . with the prayers, with gifts offered on their behalf." It is unclear whether he limited posthumous salvation to baptized Christians or meant to extend it to all humanity.

16. Cyril, "Catechetical Lecture 23," 154–55.

17. This paragraph draws on Ramelli, *Christian Doctrine of Apokatastasis*, 67–87. Thanks to my editor Robin Parry for making me aware of this work. *Apocalypse of Peter*, cited at 69; *Apocalypse of Elijah*, cited at 72; *Epistula Apostolorum*, cited at 72; *Sibylline Oracles*, cited at 73; *Apocalypse of Paul*, cited at 76.

will grant to my . . . elect all those whom they ask me to remove from punishment. And I shall grant them a beautiful baptism in salvation . . . , a sharing of justification with my saints." The *Apocalypse of Elijah* states that dead sinners "will take part in grace. On that day the righteous will be granted that for which they will often have prayed"—that is, the salvation of sinners from hell, including those who betrayed and persecuted them. Successful intercession for the unsaved is also described in a conversation found in the *Epistula Apostolorum*. The disciples express concern for sinners being punished, and Jesus encourages them to "pray to God and implore" on their behalf. "I shall listen to the prayer of the just, which they utter for sinners," he assures them. The *Sibylline Oracles* reaffirm this idea: "when [the righteous] ask . . . , God will grant them to save the human beings from the fierce fire . . . , and will do so after pulling them out of the unquenchable flame and removing them, destining them . . . to the other life" of heaven. The *Apocalypse of Paul* also suggests postmortem repentance, deliverance from hell and entry to *paradise* caused by intercession. In one of his poems Prudentius of Tarraconensis states that every Easter (and perhaps every Sunday) souls in hell experience respite from suffering.[18] These apocryphal texts concerning prayer for the salvation of those in hell indicate that many in the early church did not believe the fate of the unsaved to be fixed forever at death.

In the Western church, the funeral orations of Ambrose of Milan in the fourth century contain prayers for the deceased—including the unbaptized emperor Valentinian II.[19] In the fifth century Augustine of Hippo reports—in *Confessions*—that after her death he prayed: "I now petition you for my mother's sins . . . . Please forgive her her debts if she contracted any . . . after she received the water of salvation."[20] In one of his sermons he declares, "it is not to be doubted . . . that the dead can be helped by the prayers of the holy Church, and the Eucharistic sacrifice . . . so that God may deal with them more mercifully than their sins have deserved."[21] In *Enchiridion* Augustine anticipates the doctrine of purgatory by limiting prayer to those in a middle state of character between perfect holiness and complete evil.

---

18. Brown, *Ransom of Soul*, 112.
19. Ambrose, "On Death of Valentinian," Sections 56 and 78, 280 and 297.
20. Augustine, *Confessions*, Book 9.35, 177–78.
21. Augustine, *Sermons*, Sermon 172.2–3, 252–53.

There is . . . a kind of life so good as not to require them; and . . . one so bad that when life is over they render no help. . . . When . . . sacrifices . . . of the altar . . . are offered on behalf of all the baptized dead, they are thank-offerings for the very good, they are propitiatory offerings for the not very bad, and in the case of the very bad, even though they do not assist the dead, they are a . . . consolation to the living. And where they are profitable, their benefit consists either in obtaining a full remission of sins, or at least in making the condemnation more tolerable.[22]

In *City of God* Augustine resists the idea that those who live wicked lives after baptism can be helped beyond death: "if any [person] keep their heart impenitent up to their dying day . . . are we to suppose that the Church still prays for them . . . when they have departed this life? Of course not!"[23]

In the sixth century, Gregory the Great also asserts that prayers help the dead only if they die in a state of grace and with "minor faults that remain to be purged away." He continues: "deceased persons . . . can be absolved from sins through the Mass. . . . But remember, the benefits of the holy sacrifice are only for those who by their good lives have merited the grace of receiving help from the good deeds others perform in their behalf." Gregory recounts numerous examples of dead believers who were helped by prayer. A member of his monastery who had stolen three pieces of gold, for example, was—after death—"freed from punishment by the sacrifice of the Mass." Gregory's emphasis on a "cleansing fire after death" and his practice of the Mass as a private service of specific intention for individuals, rather than a community commemoration, influenced medieval developments.[24]

Beyond the writings of the church fathers, prayer for the departed is found in all ancient liturgies, both Greek and Latin. Prayers for peace and pardon occurred at several places—in funeral rites, in anniversary commemorations and during ordinary services of the church. In the *Liturgy of St. James*, composed in the fourth century, the priest prays "that our offering may be acceptable . . . for the rest of the souls that have fallen asleep." Later the *memento* is recited: "remember . . . the spirits . . . who are of the true faith, from righteous Abel unto this day: unto them do you

---

22. Augustine, *Enchiridion*, Chapter 110, 272–73.

23. Augustine, *City of God*, Book 21.24, 1003.

24. Gregory, *Dialogues*, Book 4.52–59, 269–72 and Book 4.41, 248. See Atwell, "From Augustine to Gregory."

give rest there in the land of the living, in your Kingdom, in the joy of *paradise*, in the bosom of Abraham, and of Isaac, and of Jacob, our holy fathers; whence pain, and grief, and lamentation have fled: there the light of your countenance looks upon them, and enlightens them for ever." The prayers of the congregation ask for "the rest of our fathers and brethren who have fallen asleep."[25] The *Liturgy of St. Mark*, also from the fourth century, contains this petition: "give peace to the souls . . . who have fallen asleep in Jesus . . . . Especially remember those whose memory we this day celebrate." The deacon then reads a name-list of the departed and lays it on the altar, and the priest concludes "graciously bestow upon them in your Kingdom your promised blessing."[26] The *Liturgy of the Blessed Apostles*, which is among the oldest services, includes an element during the Eucharist called "At the Commemoration of Saints," where God is asked to "spare the offenses and sins of the dead."[27]

The *Liturgy of John Chrysostom* was developed in the fourth century and became the most common rite in the churches of the Byzantine Empire. It includes a litany in which the people "supplicate for the repose of the souls of the servants of God . . . who are fallen asleep, and that every offense . . . be forgiven them. That the Lord bestow their souls where the righteous are at rest." After reciting a list of the fathers and patriarchs, the priest continues, "remember all those who have fallen asleep in hope of the resurrection of life eternal." He then commemorates the departed by name, ending with "give them rest . . . where the light of your countenance watches over them." After the people have communed, he prays: "wash away . . . the sins of those who have here been commemorated."[28] The *Liturgy of St. Gregory of Nazianzus*, after naming the departed, asks God to grant them "a place of refreshment, light and peace."[29] The *Apostolic Constitutions*, a fourth-century manual on worship and doctrine, gives instructions regarding the "Bidding Prayer for Those Departed." Commemorations are limited to the faithful—"for our brethren that are at rest in Christ, that God . . . may forgive him every sin . . . ,

---

25. *Divine Liturgy of St. James*, 538, 540, 543, 546 and 542.
26. *Divine Liturgy of St. Mark*, 556.
27. *Divine Liturgy of the Blessed Apostles*, 564–65.
28. *Divine Liturgy of St. John Chrysostom*, 29, 46–47 and 59.
29. *Liturgy of St. Gregory*.

and give him his lot in the land of the pious;" prayers "do not at all profit the ungodly who are dead."[30]

In the early Christian era prayer for the dead was a well-established rite. Its subjects were the faithful; those who died outside the church were typically not remembered. Its purpose was intercessory and twofold—asking God for peace and refreshment and for pardon and forgiveness. In these centuries prayer for the dead did not presuppose purgatory.[31] But, as a Church of England report points out, "the spread of a belief that in the intermediate state the souls of the departed were subjected to a process of punishment and purification in purgatory, and, therefore, were in pain, altered the character of prayers for the dead, and made them to a large extent supplications for the delivery of the souls of the departed from suffering."[32]

The Medieval Roman Catholic Church: Prayer for Release from Purgatory

The fate of the dead in the afterlife, Peter Marshall says, "was the hub around which the theology of the [medieval] church revolved."[33] There was a change, first, in the *quality* of prayer for the dead. In the ancient church such prayer was consoling; there was no reference to a place of pain. While this remained true in the East, it gradually changed in the West.

---

30. *Constitutions of Holy Apostles*, Book 8.41–43, 497–98. Prayers for the dead are found in each of the early rites printed in Hatchett, *Seven Pre-Reformation Eucharistic Liturgies*.

31. In addition to prayer, almsgiving was an important afterlife ritual and a part of Christian funerals. Brown (*Ransom of Soul*) traces how fear of hell and last judgment motivated rich Christians to donate substantial wealth to the church as a form of *remedium*—healing and protection for the safety of the soul, to bring to heaven themselves and their loved ones (166). Money spent by the living could benefit the dead, purging sins not expiated in this life. These financial gifts stored up treasure in heaven (Luke 12:23; cf. Prov 19:17) and ransomed the soul by wealth (Prov 13:8; Dan 4:27); they provided funds for care of the poor and creation of magnificent works of art and architecture. Augustine taught that the rich could atone for sin (63, 91–96) and transfer earthly wealth to heaven through almsgiving. Acts of mercy by the rich to the poor reflected (and motivated) God's mercy to sinners (43). The links between fear of hell, atonement for sin, and almsgiving greatly increased the wealth of the church—by the eighth century, monasteries and convents serving as "powerhouses of prayer for the dead" had proliferated in Western Europe (20, 197, 205).

32. Church of England, *Report of Royal Commission*, 1.

33. Marshall, *Belief and Dead*, 7.

"The thought of the Church in regard to death passed," Richard Tollinton says, "from glad and confident serenity . . . into the somber theology of legalism and judgment."[34] Geoffrey Rowell agrees: "Easter joy and hope . . . characterized the funeral liturgies of the early church"—but by the Middle Ages had been replaced by "notes of fear and punishment."[35] The central hymn of the *Requiem* (Latin for "rest") Mass emphasized *dies irae* ("day of wrath and doom impending") and *lacrimosa* ("day of tears and mourning [which] man for judgment must prepare"). Joseph Ratzinger contrasts "the early Christian invocation *maranatha* [in which] there is a joyful hope for the Christ who will come soon" with the medieval *dies irae* where "we hear only of the fear of judgment."[36] This shift in the quality of prayer for the departed followed the establishment of Christianity as the official religion of the Roman Empire. In the period of persecution, the Fathers assumed "Christian universalism"—that salvation was guaranteed to all baptized church members no matter how sinful their lives. But, Megan McLaughlin explains,

> as the Church found a recognized place in society and attracted a growing number of converts, a new pessimism became evident in the writings of the Church leaders and in the prayers of the liturgy. Awareness of the sin to be found within a larger and . . . more worldly church grew, and as a result confidence in the salvation of the faithful slowly began to give way to anxiety about the fate of individual Christians after death.

By the Middle Ages "it was no longer assumed that those who died in the faith deserved to be welcomed into heaven. Only if their faults were forgiven or purged away could they . . . enter the company of the elect."[37] Prayers of hope for the dead became prayers of fear.

In addition to a change in quality, there was tremendous increase in the *quantity* of prayer for the dead. This was the result of two ideas, Marshall says: first, belief "that the majority of the faithful dead did not proceed immediately to the beatific vision of God in heaven, but underwent a painful purgation"—and second, the conviction that, in the

---

34. Tollinton, "Prayer for Departed," 630 and 637.

35. Rowell, *Liturgy of Christian Burial*, 102. Think of the ancient Easter refrain: "Christ is risen from the dead, trampling down Death by death, and upon those in the tomb bestowing life" (Episcopal Church, *Book of Common Prayer*, 500).

36. Ratzinger, *Eschatology*, 5.

37. McLaughlin, *Consorting with Saints*, 29 and 34; cf. 66 and 104.

communion of saints, "the living had the ability (and the duty) to ease the dead's suffering."[38]

In the thirteenth century, Thomas Aquinas explained the logic of medieval prayer for the dead. The doctrine of the communion of saints implies that "one man can be assisted by the merits of another"—and "hence the suffrages [Latin for 'supplication'] of the living profit the dead." Prayer cannot help unsaved adults in hell or unbaptized children in limbo—"we must not believe that the suffrages of the living . . . change their state from unhappiness to happiness." Nor can prayer benefit the blessed: "as the saints in heaven are free from all need, being inebriated with the plenty of God's house . . . , they are not competent to be assisted by suffrages." Prayer only assists those in purgatory, where "punishment . . . is intended to supplement the satisfaction which was not fully completed in the body. . . . The works of one person can avail for another's satisfaction . . . [and] the suffrages of the living . . . profit those who are in purgatory" by removing punishment and shortening time there.[39]

The first official pronouncement of these doctrines came at the Second Council of Lyons in 1274. The sinful baptized "are purged after their death, by purgatorial or purificatory penalties. . . . For the alleviation of these penalties, they are served by the suffrages of the living faithful." These teachings, elaborated in 1439 at the Council of Florence and reaffirmed in 1563 at the Council of Trent, became the defining doctrines of the late Middle Ages.[40]

Purgatory, McLaughlin says, was "an extension of the penitential system into the next world."[41] The idea was that while original sin is cleansed by baptism, post-baptismal sin is forgiven through absolution and penance. Penance has three parts: contrition (sorrow for sin), confession (to a priest who determines what punishment is owed), and satisfaction

---

38. Marshall, *Belief and Dead*, 7.

39. Aquinas, *Summa Theologica* Vol. 3, Supplement to the Third Part, Q 71, 2843–58. The Supplement was compiled after Aquinas' death by his close associate Fra Rainaldo da Piperno and draws from Aquinas' earlier writings, especially his commentary on Book 4 of Peter Lombard's *Sentences*, written some twenty years earlier.

40. Second Council of Lyons, cited in Le Goff, *Birth of Purgatory*, 285 and Roman Catholic Church, Council of Trent, Session 25, "Decree Concerning Purgatory."

41. McLaughlin, *Consorting with Saints*, 234 and 220. See Walls, *Purgatory*, 62–64. The Archbishops' Commission (*Prayer and Departed*, 35) points out that the shift in late antiquity from *public* confession and absolution *after* penance to *private* confession and absolution *before* penance led to the medieval idea of purgatory where incomplete penance was worked off.

(acts that pay that debt). The concept of satisfaction assumes a distinction between guilt (which is forgiven when we repent) and punishment, of which there are two kinds: eternal (which is entirely removed) and temporary (which we must endure in proportion to our sins). Purgatory was the theological solution to the problem of *deferred* penance. Robert Eno notes that in the Middle Ages "more and more people simply put off penance until their death beds.... The idea of purgatory as the 'locus' for satisfying temporal punishment due to sins emerged from this impasse."[42] Medieval prayer for the dead also assumed *tariffed* penance (that specific sins had set penalties and that every sin could be removed by a certain number of spiritual works) as well as *vicarious* penance (that satisfaction could be made as an act of charity by anyone on behalf of others).[43]

The idea that sins not atoned for in this life could be forgiven after death was accompanied by an instrumental view of the Mass as the most effective form of intercession, especially masses of special intention done with a particular purpose, such as assisting those in purgatory. Masses became what McLaughlin calls "intercessory 'units'" which were understood "in essentially mechanical terms. Each Mass . . . performed for the dead [was] seen as a unit of force which could push against the weight of sin until the soul was finally released from its sufferings." Since each Mass had a defined value, "the number of 'units' accumulated determined how quickly the soul would be freed from purgatorial torment."[44] Both clergy and laity were obsessed with securing as much prayer as possible. Single rituals became whole series of Masses for the dead—and where early Christians commemorated the departed collectively, medieval prayer was often performed in private services held apart from regular Sunday

---

42. Eno, "Fathers and Cleansing Fire," 200–201.

43. McLaughlin, *Consorting with Saints*, 11, 154, and 219. In the ancient church, Brown (*Ransom of Soul*, 125–26) says, "major sins that affected the community as a whole [were] subject to public penance. But there were so many other sins committed by so many other, small-time sinners.... [Once] Christianity became a majority religion and the Church was filled with average... sinners... the early Christian system of public penance became unworkable" and was replaced by private confession and penance. Sin came to be seen as a monetary debt which, like money, can be calibrated in precise amounts—and God came to be seen as a debt manager who could set harsh or lenient repayment schedules or remit debts entirely. Constant daily sin required regular confession and tariffed—precisely measured—penance for each offence (97, 191). Depending on their different mix of sins, souls moved through purgatory to heaven at different speeds, like runners spread out in a marathon, not like passengers grouped together in an airport waiting room (13).

44. Ibid., 234–35.

liturgy at side-altars in a church by hired clerics. Chantries—endowments which supported chapels and paid priests to say Mass for the souls of the founders—became common. Henry VII of England, for example, provided in his will for 10,000 Masses and built a chapel at Westminster Abbey to house monks who would pray for him.[45] Marshall explains that less affluent individuals established temporary chantries requiring prayer "for a specified period, most commonly a year" or "for a specific number of masses, usually the series of thirty known as a trental," made over thirty days. Gifts to a parish church meant inclusion in the "bede-roll"—a name-list "recited at least once a year in full, and in a shortened form during . . . weekly Sunday Mass."[46]

Funerals included the *placebo* (vespers on the evening before) and *dirge* (matins on the morning of Mass and burial) as well as processions from home to church to graveyard. These services were repeated four weeks later at "month's mind" and on the anniversary at "year's mind." From early times the church had celebrated the saints and martyrs on All Saints Day, November 1. All Souls Day, commemorated on November 2, was instituted in eleventh-century France as a day of prayer for those in purgatory. The practice spread across Europe, becoming an official feast in the fourteenth century.[47]

The Reformation Church: Prayer for the Dead Rejected

The medieval church, Marshall says, was a purgatorial institution—an "intercessory industry" focused on praying for the dead. Financial and clerical abuses created by Masses, invoking saints, and selling of indulgences were the precipitating cause of the Reformation. Lutherans, Calvinists, Anabaptists, and Anglicans all opposed purgatory and the "flood of intercessory prayer" that it generated—arguing that they are not found in Scripture but are part of a larger system of beliefs and practices that undermine justification by faith alone.[48] The Reformers also denied an intermediate state of imperfect bliss, since this encouraged prayer to improve the condition of the dead. They taught instead that the dead are either unconscious between death and resurrection (soul-sleep, sug-

---

45. Griffiths, "Purgatory," 442.
46. Marshall, *Belief and Dead*, 312.
47. Le Goff, *Birth of Purgatory*, 125.
48. Marshall, *Belief and Dead*, 81 and 25; cf. 312, 63, and 73.

gested by Martin Luther and some Anabaptists) or that they immediately enter heaven or hell (as John Calvin claimed). In either case praying for those in the next life is pointless since it has no effect on their state.

Lutheran Protestantism

Luther rejected any practice that undermines confidence in salvation; a person who thinks "I . . . must render satisfaction for my sins; therefore I shall make a will and shall bequeath a definite amount of money for building churches and for buying prayers and sacrifices for the dead by the monks and priests" dies with "a faith in works."[49] In *Confession Concerning the Lord's Supper* he accepts a kind of minimal, private prayer for the dead. "Since Scripture gives us no information on the subject, I regard it as no sin to pray . . . in this . . . fashion: 'Dear God, if this soul is in a condition accessible to mercy, be thou gracious to it.' And when this has been done once or twice, let it suffice. For vigils and *requiem* masses and yearly celebrations of *requiems* are useless."[50] In other writings Luther seems to reject the practice entirely: "funeral ceremonies . . . are to be retained . . . , not that there should be prayers for the dead."[51] The *Smalcald Articles* state that "when [Roman Catholics] have abolished the traffic in masses for purgatory . . . , we will then discuss with them . . . whether the dead should be remembered at the Eucharist."[52] In *Preface to the Burial Hymns* Luther writes, "we have . . . completely abolished . . . vigils, masses for the dead, processions, purgatory, and all other hocus-pocus on behalf of the dead."[53] In *Table Talk* he argues that early church practice "proves nothing;" instead, "it is necessary to stick to the clear Word of God."[54] He even objects to praying that "refreshment, light, and peace" be given to those "who have gone before us . . . and repose in the sleep of peace"—since they are already at rest "why should you pray for them?"[55]

Official Lutheran statements denounce purgatory but not prayer for the dead. *Defense of the Augsburg Confession* states that "no testimony

---

49. Luther, *Lectures on Genesis: Chapters 21-25*, 316.
50. Luther, *Word and Sacrament III*, 369.
51. Luther, *Lectures on Genesis: Chapters 31-37*, 273-74.
52. Luther, *Smalcald Articles*, Part II Article II: "Of the Mass," Sections 12-15.
53. Luther, *Liturgy and Hymns*, 326.
54. Luther, *Table Talk*, 259-60.
55. Luther, *Word and Sacrament II*, 322.

concerning the praying of the dead is extant in the Scriptures"—and yet does not condemn such prayers. "We know that the ancients speak of prayer for the dead, which we do not prohibit.... [Instead] we ... are contending with you who are defending a heresy..., namely, that the Mass justifies..., that it merits the remission of guilt and punishment."[56] Once separated from belief in purgatory, praying for the dead—while not encouraged—is permitted.

Reformed Protestantism

Calvin, in *Institutes of the Christian Religion*, condemns both purgatory and intercession for the dead. "When my adversaries... raise against me the objections that prayers for the dead have been a custom for thirteen hundred years, I ask them..., by what Word of God... is this done? ... Since the entire law and gospel do not furnish so much as a single syllable of leave to pray for the dead, it is to profane the invocation of God to attempt more than God has bidden us." Even if the early church was right to make such prayers, Calvin says, "there is a wide difference" between praying "in memory of the dead" and praying for deliverance of souls from purgatory. Finally, the saved dead already possess blessedness: "all godly men... immediately after death enjoy blessed repose. If such is their condition, what [benefit]... will our prayers confer upon them?"[57]

Ulrich Zwingli, in his sixty-seven theses on reform, rejects purgatory, but allows prayers for the dead: "that mankind earnestly calls to God to show mercy to the dead I do not condemn."[58] Reformed doctrinal standards deny both purgatory and prayer for the departed. The *Second Helvetic Confession* declares that "the faithful, after bodily death, go directly to Christ, and, therefore, do not need the... prayers of the living for the dead.... Likewise... unbelievers are immediately cast into hell from which no exit is opened... by any services of the living."[59]

The Reformers also rejected the Roman Catholic interpretation of the communion of saints as the whole family of God—living and dead. Instead of being the spiritual union of all Christians, it is a fellowship

---

56. *Defense of Augsburg Confession*, Article 21, "Of the Invocation of Saints" and Article 24, "Of the Mass: Of the Mass for the Dead."
57. Calvin, *Institutes*, Book 3.5.10, 681–84.
58. Zwingli, *Articles*, Articles 57 and 60.
59. *Second Helvetic Confession*, chapter 26.

between living believers, not with the departed. Luther restricts the communion of saints to "the whole Christian Church on earth," and the *Augsburg Confession* defines it as "the congregation of saints and true believers."[60] Calvin, too, identified the communion of saints with the visible and invisible church in this life. While acknowledging that "we are in fellowship with the holy patriarchs, who [are] dead," he denies that this includes prayer for them: while "believers . . . offer prayers before God for the brethren . . . this is inappropriately applied to the dead."[61] The *Heidelberg Catechism* states that the communion of the saints is the bond of fellowship between living "believers, all and everyone," but not between the living and the dead.[62]

The Church of England

The *Thirty-Nine Articles of Religion*—written under Thomas Cranmer's direction—declares that "the Romish doctrine concerning purgatory . . . is a fond thing, vainly invented, and grounded upon no warranty of Scripture." The preliminary draft of this article also condemned "prayer for the dead," but these words were removed.[63] The *Homily on Prayer* denies that prayer can help the departed: "Scripture teaches . . . that the soul of man passing out of the body, goes straightways either to heaven, or else to hell, whereof the one needs no prayer, and the other is without redemption. . . . Let us not therefore dream either of purgatory, or of prayer for the souls of them that be dead."[64] Parliament closed all chantries and monasteries founded to pray for the dead and banned indulgences—as well as practices like bede-rolls, intercessory Masses, and ringing of bells for the repose of the dead on All Souls Day.[65]

The 1549 *Book of Common Prayer* included petitions for the departed, both at Holy Communion and the burial service. These were eliminated in the 1552 revision—where prayer is for the living church

---

60. Luther, *Small Catechism*, Section II (The Creed) Article 3; *Augsburg Confession*, Article 8.

61. Calvin, *Institutes*, Book 3.25.6, 997 and Book 3.20.27, 887. Also see Book 4.1.3, 1015.

62. *Heidelberg Catechism*, Question 55.

63. Episcopal Church, *Book of Common Prayer*, "Thirty Nine Articles," Article 22. Also see Hardy, "Blessed Dead," 172.

64. Church of England, *Homily on Prayer*, chapter 19.3.

65. See Kreider, *English Chantries*.

on earth, not for the whole of Christ's church (which includes the dead); the funeral Eucharist was also removed.[66] The 1545 *Primer*—a book of private devotions for laypeople—declared that the intercessions of the living "avail . . . to purge away sin and make [the departed] partakers of thy redemption." The 1559 revision replaces prayers for forgiveness with petitions for "peace and rest."[67] Books of prayer by Lancelot Andrewes and John Cosin, however, contain petitions for the departed.[68] The *Westminster Confession of Faith*—an official standard of Presbyterian churches—rejects purgatory and declares that "prayer is to be made . . . for all sorts of men living . . . , but not for the dead."[69]

The mainline Reformers were not alone in denying the doctrine of purgatory and dismantling the structures of prayer for the dead. Anabaptists, too, rejected such rituals. These sixteenth-century Radical Reformers opposed both Roman Catholicism and mainstream Protestantism—from which the practice of praying for the dead had already been jettisoned. The *Schleitheim Confession* simply condemns "all Catholic and Protestant works and church services."[70]

Concluding Remarks

Eastern Orthodox and Roman Catholics continue to pray for the departed—Protestants remain opposed to the practice. Only in Anglicanism has it been cautiously accepted.[71] While the seventeenth- and eighteenth-century divines condemned intercession to release souls from purgatory,

66. Marshall, *Belief and Dead*, 110 and Rowell, *Liturgy of Christian Burial*, 87.

67. Rowell, *Liturgy of Christian Burial*, 89–90.

68. See Archbishops' Commission, *Prayer and Departed*, 74; Boggis, *Praying for Dead*, 219; Hardy, "Blessed Dead," 163.

69. *Westminster Confession*, chapter 32, 81–82 and chapter 21.4, 58.

70. *Schleitheim Confession*, Article 4. Currie (*Born Fundamentalist*, 22) points out that "at the time of the Reformation there were two very different groups of Protestants. The Lutherans, Calvinists and others rejected only those doctrines of the Catholic Church they believed directly contradicted Scripture. Everything else remained. Anabaptists, on the other hand, rejected all doctrines . . . that they could not directly support from Scripture. This was much more radical. The changes were far more extensive."

71. This section draws on Bennett, "Prayer for Departed"; Cocksworth, *Prayer and Departed*, chapter 2; Plumptre, *Spirits in Prison*, chapter 9; and Welsby, "Prayers for Dead." For a collection of writings in Anglicanism since the sixteenth century, see Archbishops' Commission, *Prayer and Departed*, Appendix 2.

some—such as James Ussher and Jeremy Taylor—accepted remembrance of the Christian dead as practiced by the early church. In the 1662 Prayer Book, commemoration was added to the Eucharistic prayer.

John Wesley, who founded the Methodist movement but remained within the Anglican Church, prayed for the dead. His *Collection of Forms of Prayer* includes this ancient petition: "grant them to rest in the region of the living . . . and . . . give them . . . a happy resurrection."[72] In defending the practice against dissenters, Wesley asserts that "in this kind of general prayer . . . for the faithful departed, I conceive myself to be clearly justified, both by the earliest antiquity, by the Church of England and by the Lord's Prayer. . . . Praying thus for the dead, 'that God would shortly accomplish the number of God's elect and hasten God's Kingdom,'" he concludes, "you will not easily prove to be any corruption at all."[73]

The nineteenth-century Anglo-Catholic movement sought to recover the Roman Catholic roots of the Church of England. John Henry Newman argued that, rightly understood, various practices—including prayer for the dead and funeral Eucharists—are compatible with the *Thirty-Nine Articles*. Many churchmen, while rejecting a punishing purgatory, accepted a sanctifying process after death and prayer for the increased bliss of the Christian dead. The evangelical Church Association, on the other hand, opposed such practices. They repeated the arguments of earlier formularies, condemning all prayer for the departed as unscriptural, incompatible with salvation by grace, inseparable from belief in purgatory, and rejected in Anglican tradition. In 1873 a guild was founded to promote celebration of All Souls Day with Masses of intercession for those in purgatory, practices that a 1906 commission declared inconsistent with Anglican teaching.[74]

During World War I, with its massive deaths, praying for the dead as acts of pastoral care became common. Randall Davidson, Archbishop of Canterbury at the time, observed that "the abuses of [past practice] need not now, four centuries onward, . . . hinder . . . the absolutely trustful prayer . . . for him whom we shall not greet on earth again, but who, in his Father's loving keeping, still lives, and . . . still grows from strength to

---

72. Wesley, cited in Chapman, "Rest and Light Perpetual," 40.

73. Wesley, cited in Holden, *Wesley in Company*, chapters 10 ("Of the Communion of Saints," 82–83) and 11 ("Of Prayers for the Dead," 84–87).

74. See Russell, "Intermediate State and Prayer for Departed" and Church of England, *Report of Royal Commission*.

strength . . . in deepened reverence and love."[75] The 1938 Archbishops' Commission on Christian Doctrine studied the matter and concluded: "if there is any such fellowship of living and departed as Christians have always believed, and if the thought of growth and of purification after death is not to be dogmatically excluded, there is no theological objection in principle to prayer for the departed."[76]

There is no obvious mention of prayer for the dead in Scripture—but by the third century commemoration at the Eucharist was well-established. The nature of prayer for the dead changed over time; where the ancient church prayed with hope (for peace and pardon of those in God's presence), the medieval Western church prayed with anxiety (for release of souls from suffering in purgatory)—and Protestants abandoned the practice almost entirely. The next chapter examines the current practice of prayer for the dead in the three main branches of the Church—Roman Catholic, Eastern Orthodox, and Protestant.

---

75. Davidson, cited in Bell, *Randall Davidson*, 823.
76. Archbishops' Commission, *Doctrine in Church of England*, 216.

chapter 3

SURVEYING THE PRESENT
Prayer for the Dead in the Contemporary Church

IT IS ALL SAINTS' Day—and I am in church taking Holy Communion. Kneeling at the rail, I look at the altar. Draped over its surface and around its sides, on sheets of paper, are the names of those from the congregation—and others whom we knew and loved—now departed. My father's name is among them—and I am deeply conscious of being in the presence of "angels and archangels and all the company of heaven" gathered before the throne of God.[1] The earlier reading from *Wisdom of Solomon* (3:1–9) reminded me that "the souls of the righteous are in the hand of God. . . . In the eyes of the foolish . . . their departure was thought to be a disaster, and their going from us to be their destruction. But they are at peace." This celebration of the communion of saints and the dead—especially the inclusive prayer "may all the departed, through the mercy of God, rest in peace"—would have been unthinkable in the evangelical church of my youth.

Roman Catholics and Eastern Orthodox have always prayed for the dead. While the Reformers abolished it, Anglicans and ecumenical Protestants include some commemorations and petitions in their liturgies; conservative Protestants do not. This chapter summarizes the current practice of prayer for the dead in the three main branches of the

---

1. Episcopal Church, *Book of Common Prayer*, 362. Many symbols can be used: some churches provide prayer flags for those whom members would like to remember on All Saints Day.

church—Roman Catholic, Eastern Orthodox, and Protestant (both progressive mainline Protestants and conservative evangelical Protestants).

The Roman Catholic Church

Prayer for the dead is part of Roman Catholic practice and remains linked with belief in purgatory. Prayer cannot change a person's spiritual destiny of heaven or hell, which is settled at death; it is limited to the saved and excludes the unsaved. The Second Vatican Council affirms the efficacy of interceding for the dead: in the communion of saints the church, "because it is a holy ... thought to pray for the dead that they may be loosed from their sins, ... offers suffrages for them." While Vatican II does not use the word "purgatory," it claims that some "having died, are still being purified; and it proposes again the decrees of ... the Council of Florence and the Council of Trent."[2]

The *Catechism of the Catholic Church* declares that "from the beginning the Church has honored the memory of the dead and offered prayers in suffrage for them, above all the Eucharistic sacrifice, so that, thus purified, they may attain the beatific vision of God."[3] When celebrating funerals the church "asks [God] to purify God's child of his sins ... and to admit him to the *paschal* fullness of the table of the Kingdom."[4] Prayer for the blessed in heaven already enjoying union with God is pointless and prayer for the unsaved in hell, who are beyond hope, is of no use, so prayer only benefits the dead in purgatory.

The 2001 Vatican *Directory on Popular Piety and the Liturgy* declares that "suffrage for the souls of the faithful departed ... is an urgent supplication of God to have mercy on the souls of the dead, to purify them by the fire of God's charity and to bring them to God's Kingdom of light and life." It notes that the liturgy contains varied forms of prayer for the dead—funeral rites, All Souls Day intercessions, and the daily celebration of the Mass—and warns that memorial of the dead in popular devotional practices must not contradict the gospel. Finally, the *Directory* states that "the Church's prayer ... for the souls of the faithful departed implores eternal life not only for the disciples of Christ who have died in his peace,

---

2. Second Vatican Council, *Lumen Gentium*, Chapter 7.49–51.

3. Roman Catholic Church, *Catechism of Catholic Church*, Sections 1030–32, 268–69.

4. Ibid., Section 1689, 20.

but for the dead whose faith is known to God"—thus acknowledging that the company of the saved extends beyond baptized Christians.[5]

Commemoration of and intercession for the dead is part of every celebration of Holy Communion. The current canon of the *Roman Missal* has four approved Eucharistic prayers, all of which mention the departed. Prayer 1 asks, "remember . . . your servants N. and N., who have gone before us with the sign of faith and rest in the sleep of peace. Grant them . . . and all who sleep in Christ, a place of refreshment, light, and peace." Prayer 2 says, "remember also our brothers and sisters who have fallen asleep in the hope of the resurrection, and all who have died in your mercy: welcome them into the light of your face." Prayer 3 asks, "to our departed brothers and sisters and to all who were pleasing to you at their passing from this life, give kind admittance to your Kingdom." And prayer 4 says, "remember also those who have died in the peace of your Christ and all the dead, whose faith you alone have known. To all of us, your children, grant . . . that we may enter into a heavenly inheritance." The departed are always commemorated in the Eucharist—which "is celebrated in communion with the entire Church . . . , living and dead."[6]

The dead are also prayed for in the funeral Mass. Unlike medieval practice, a Roman Catholic ecumenical statement says, the *dies irae* is no longer found in funeral liturgy—which "focuses on the promise of resurrection rather than on the threat of divine judgment."[7] The service includes prayers for rest ("grant that he/she may be led to our true homeland to delight in its everlasting joys") and pardon ("should any stain of sin have clung to him/her [may it] be forgiven and wiped away"). Prayers for unbaptized children ask God to reassure parents that their child "has been entrusted to your divine compassion"—and other prayers reference church officials, young people, friends, and family. Prayers are offered on the anniversary of the death, and daily Mass may be celebrated for the

---

5. Congregation for Divine Worship, *Directory on Popular Piety*, Sections 251, 255 and 250. Two other magisterial sources reaffirm traditional Roman Catholic teaching on the afterlife and prayer for the dead—the Sacred Congregation for the Doctrine of the Faith's 1979 *Letter on Certain Questions Concerning Eschatology* (131–33) and the International Theological Commission's 1992 statement *On Certain Current Issues in Eschatology* (209–43.) Also see Roman Catholic Church, *Catechism of Catholic Church*, Sections 988–1065.

6. U.S. Conference of Catholic Bishops, *Roman Missal*, 494, 501, 506, 513 and *General Instruction*, 41.

7. U.S. Lutheran-Catholic Dialogue, *Hope of Eternal Life*, 67.

dead. Roman Catholic practice allows private prayers and Masses for the unbaptized who are denied a church funeral.[8]

On All Souls Day—"Commemoration of All the Faithful Departed" (November 2)—the church gathers in solemn prayer for those in purgatory. Every priest may celebrate three Masses, remembering and praying for all Christians who have died—and may visit the cemetery to bless graves with incense, lights, and flowers. "Look mercifully on your departed servants that . . . they may . . . receive the joys of eternal happiness," the prayers ask—"wash away . . . the sins of your departed servants."[9] The entire month of November emphasizes "the need to pray for the dead as an act of faith, hope and charity within the body of Christ."[10]

Public rituals, as well as specific devotional resources, are used by Roman Catholics praying alone. There are prayers at the time of death and for parents and siblings, children and spouses, for those who die in old age or after long illness, who die suddenly, accidentally, violently, or by suicide, even for the forgotten dead. Novenas and rosaries can be made for the dead, each including the ancient versicle "eternal rest grant unto them, and let perpetual light shine upon them. May they, and the souls of all the faithful departed, through the mercy of God, rest in peace."[11]

Prayers for the dead continue to be an important part of Roman Catholic practice—a Catholic ecumenical declaration reads—"as expressions of [the] confident entrusting of the departed to the care and mercy of God."[12]

The Eastern Orthodox Churches

The churches that make up Eastern Orthodoxy all pray for the dead. "Christians here on earth have a duty to pray for the departed," Timothy

---

8. U.S. Conference of Catholic Bishops, *Roman Missal*, 1217–27. Also see *General Instruction*, 126–27.

9. Ibid., 842. Also see Elliot, *Ceremonies of Liturgical Year*, 187–91.

10. Elliot, *Ceremonies of Liturgical Year*, 188.

11. Numerous websites provide sample prayers: see "Prayers for Faithful Departed," "Prayer for Dead," and "Prayers for Deceased." A novena is nine days of prayer; it is derived from the time the apostles prayed in Jerusalem between Christ's ascension and Pentecost (Acts 1:12–14). The rosary is a circlet containing five rows of beads and involves saying four prayers in a certain combination.

12. U.S. Lutheran-Catholic Dialogue, *Hope of Eternal Life*, 68.

Ware says.[13] Doing so has seldom "been a subject of controversy within the Christian East, and so there has been little occasion to make formal definitions about them. In this realm there exists ... a profound inner consensus, expressed not through doctrinal formulae but through the worshipping practice of the Church."[14] Nikolaos Vassiliadis summarizes Orthodox teaching: "because our love remains, our Mother Church has, from the very beginning, established the practice of saying special prayers for those who have fallen asleep.... Petitions for the dead ... are addressed to God because we hope and believe in God's ... mercy and loving kindness."[15]

Eastern Orthodoxy rejects the idea of a punishing purgatory—a third place between heaven and hell where individuals make satisfaction for their sins by suffering in fire.[16] Paul Fedwick notes, however, that "the soul has to undergo purification" in preparation for eternal happiness— and "because the dead person cannot by [their] own resources achieve this, a great emphasis is placed upon the offering of prayers and sacrifices on behalf of the dead."[17] Prayer is made, Vassiliadis adds, "both for those who have departed 'in repentance' and those who have departed 'in sin.' The Church prays for all"—including "for sinners"—but "does not teach or promise that those who departed unrepentant will receive forgiveness of sins ... or [be removed] from the place of punishment to *paradise*."[18] These doctrines are not authoritatively defined in councils and canons having ecumenical authority—as in the teaching magisterium of the Roman Catholic Church—but are consensus beliefs and practices of the Eastern Orthodox Church.

Every Divine Liturgy includes commemoration of the dead. The forms are ancient; the *Liturgy of John Chyrsostom* is still used on most Sundays. When beginning the Eucharist, the priest breaks particles,

---

13. Ware, *Orthodox Church*, 259. Professor James Campbell of McHenry County College provided me with information on prayer for the dead in Eastern Orthodox traditions.

14. Ware, "One Body in Christ," 179.

15. Vassiliadis, *Mystery of Death*, 27.

16. This issue divided Eastern Orthodox and Roman Catholics at the fifteenth-century Council of Florence, when the Western Church attempted to impose acceptance of purgatory on the Eastern Church as part of reunification (in exchange for military support against the advancing Muslim Turks). See Louth, *Introducing Eastern Orthodox Theology*, 154–55.

17. Fedwick, "Death and Dying," 161. Also see Vassiliadis, *Mystery of Death*, 444f.

18. Vassiliadis, *Mystery of Death*, 434.

representing the living and the dead, from the communion bread and places them on the *paten* (or small plate). This ritual action, Vassiliadis explains, symbolizes the communion of saints.

> At the center . . . the Lamb is placed; to its right is the portion of the *Theotokos*; to its left are the portions for . . . all the saints; at the bottom are the portions for the living and the dead. Thus, there on the *paten* . . . the whole catholic Church both the heavenly and the earthly is symbolically present. . . . Because of this bond which exists between us the living and those who have fallen asleep . . . we have an obligation to offer memorials for their souls.[19]

Alexander Schmemann adds: "all of us—both living and fallen asleep—[are] gathered on the *diskos*. . . . In taking out particles and pronouncing names . . . we offer and return them to God . . . in order to make them participants in the 'inexhaustible life' of the Kingdom of God."[20] In the liturgy, the departed are remembered three times: prior to worship, as the bread and wine are prepared, at the litany, following the Gospel reading, and after the consecration of the holy gifts.[21] The celebrant prays for individuals by name, asking for rest and forgiveness: "for the repose of . . . the servants of God departed this life, N. . . . , that you will pardon all their sins, both voluntary and involuntary" and "establish their souls where the just repose." Again the priest asks God to "give rest" to the departed "in a place of brightness, a place of verdure, a place of repose, whence all sickness, sorrow and sighing have fled away. Pardon every transgression which they have committed."[22] After the people have communed, these commemorative particles are brushed into the chalice with a prayer that Christ will "wash away . . . the sins of all who are here remembered."[23]

During the Coptic liturgy the prayers ask that God "remember all the saints who have pleased you since the beginning" and a list of prophets, apostles, and patriarchs is recited. After this commemoration, names of the departed are read with the words: "graciously . . . repose all their souls in the bosom of our holy fathers Abraham, Isaac and Jacob. Sustain them in the green pasture, by the water of rest in the *paradise* of joy, the

---

19. Vassiliadis, *Mystery of Death*, 421–22.
20. Schmemann, *Eucharist*, 111–12.
21. Russian Orthodox Convent, "Church's Prayer for Dead."
22. Orthodox Church, *Service Book of Orthodox Church*, 91.
23. Ibid., 118.

place out of which grief sorrow and groaning have fled away in the light of your saints."[24] In the Byzantine tradition the prayers ask for a good trial at final judgment: "from every punishment deliver . . . all who have died in faith."[25] And—in a practice unique to Orthodox churches since the fourth century—on Pentecost evening prayer is made for the unsaved: "O Christ our God . . . , who didst shatter . . . the bolts of hell, . . . who didst descend into hell, and break the everlasting bars, and show a way up unto those who abode in the lower world, . . . accept propitiatory prayers for those who are imprisoned in hell, promising unto us who are held in bondage great hope of release from the vileness that doth hinders us and did hinder them; and that thou wilt send down thy consolation."[26] Vassiliadis comments: "on this day we do not pray only for Christians. . . . We pray for all those who have died . . . and who worshipped God with a pure life; we pray for every person who has served his life well."[27] While the church may only intend to pray for believers, private individuals may pray for anyone who has died.

Particular days of commemoration are also set aside. Saturday, the day of death before Sunday, the day of resurrection, is for remembrance of the dead. Special prayers take place on the Sunday before Lent asking for God's mercy at judgment; several Saturdays in Lent are also days of intercession for the dead. The second Tuesday after Easter is a day of rejoicing when survivors visit the graves of loved ones and pray for them in the joy of Christ's resurrection. The Saturday before Pentecost is another day of special commemoration when God is asked to wash away all sins from the departed.[28] The daily offices of the church also include numerous petitions for the dead—all asking rest "in the land of the living, where flow the streams of joy and the fountains of eternal life" and forgiveness "from all their sins."[29]

The funeral practices of the Eastern Orthodox churches include prayers which begin at the moment of death and continue through the official period of mourning—with memorial *requiem* services held on

---

24. Pope Shenouda III, *Divine Liturgy*.
25. Cited in Ware, "One Body in Christ," 187–88.
26. Orthodox Church, *Service Book of Orthodox Church*, 255.
27. Vassiliadis, *Mystery of Death*, 425.
28. A Monk of St. Tikhon Monastery, *These Truths We Hold*.
29. Orthodox Church, *Lenten Triodion Supplemental Texts*, 337 and 109. Also see *Lenten Triodion*. A quick perusal of these service books reveals the ubiquity of petitions for the departed.

the third, ninth and fortieth days. These prayers for rest "in the mansions of the saints, where fair is the voice of those who keep high festival" and pardon "from every transgression which they have committed" are repeated over and over and mirror those in the regular liturgy.³⁰ According to one traditional teaching, during the first six days after death the soul is judged for its virtues and vices. As it passes through tollhouses where its deeds on earth are examined by demons and guardian angels struggling for its fate, the person is assisted by the prayers of the church.³¹ On the anniversary of the death a special service is conducted using boiled wheat and honey cakes symbolizing the grain that must fall into the ground and decay before experiencing the sweetness and joy of resurrection life (John 12:24).

Prayer for those who have died in hope of eternal life is an important part of Eastern Orthodox practice. It is also long and widely held that prayer can assist the unsaved dead, but how it does so is not settled. Vassiliadis claims that prayers ease their suffering so that those in hell "receive . . . a certain consolation [and] their punishment becomes somewhat lighter."³² Jean-Claude Larchet suggests that prayers can free the unsaved from hell, but only in the period before Christ's second coming; even "grave sinners [can be] delivered from hell through the prayers of the faithful."³³ Hilarion Alfeyev speculates that salvation is possible even after final judgment: "as long as the Church lives . . . the prayer of Christians for those outside the Kingdom of heaven [both living and departed] will not cease . . . . Even when time is transformed into eternity . . . , the Church will pray to the Lord for the salvation of all people who were created by God."³⁴ The Eastern Orthodox churches—alone among Christians—pray for all the dead, including the unsaved, convinced that God's

---

30. Orthodox Church, *Service Book of Orthodox Church*, 444 and 565.

31. See Daley, *Hope of Early Church*, 27, 70, 121, and 185; Louth, "Eastern Orthodox Eschatology," 240; and Vassiliadis, *Mystery of Death*, 385–92. Brown (*Ransom of Soul*, 120, 162, 199) points out that in Egyptian monastic literature demons were said to wait for the soul as it left the body. Like tax officials, they demanded payment for every sin; as they passed through these checkpoints, they were protected by ranks of angels.

32. Vassiliadis, *Mystery of Death*, 343.

33. Larchet, *Life After Death*, 215. Cavarnos (*Future Life*, 35) agrees: "in regard to the possibility of a change in a soul's condition during the interval between the particular and general judgments, the Orthodox Church teaches that it is possible for it to change for the better."

34. Alfeyev, "Eschatology," 119–20.

grace can in some way alter their fates. And yet this aim of assisting those presently in hell could be made more explicit in the official prayers and liturgies where—apart from the Pentecost prayers—it is only implicit.

The Protestant Churches

Protestants are generally uninterested in prayer for the departed. While few denominations have actually banned such prayers, few have approved them either. It has seldom been raised for formal discussion and so there are few official statements on the topic. Ecumenical liturgical renewal has restored some prayers regarding the dead in the liturgy of mainline Protestant denominations.

Reformed Churches

The Calvinist churches are most opposed to prayer for the departed.[35] John Calvin denounced them as mistaken and useless, and Reformed and Presbyterian standards condemn them. Prayer for the unsaved dead is pointless (since eternal destiny is fixed at death) and prayer for the saved dead is equally useless (since purgatory is a fiction and they are already safe in God's presence). There are no prayers for the dead in liturgies of the *Christian Reformed Church* or the *Reformed Church in America*—apart from traditional funeral commendations and committals.[36]

The *Presbyterian Church USA* liturgy has a "Commemoration of Those Who Have Died in the Faith"; these are not petitions for the dead, but reminders that the church on earth is part of a larger company of saints with the church in heaven. Several "Prayers of the People" combine thanksgivings for the dead with petitions for the living—such as Form F: "for all who have died in the communion of your Church . . . [that we may] join them in life eternal, we pray to you." The Eucharistic prayer asks: "in union with your Church in heaven and on earth, we pray, O God, that you will fulfill your eternal purpose in us and in all the world." If these prayers constitute petitions, they ask that God complete God's

---

35. Professors John Witvliet and Lyle Bierma of Calvin Theological Seminary provided me with information on prayer for the dead in Reformed traditions. My search for prayer for the dead on the "Reformed Worship" website yielded no results.

36. To commend—to entrust something into another's care—is at least implicitly to ask and petition them to actively care for that thing. There is, then, no sharp division between commendation and intercession.

plans by bringing history to its end. The funeral liturgy contains explicit intercessions taken from the Episcopal Prayer Book: "for our brother/sister N., let us pray to our Lord Jesus Christ.... You raised the dead to life; give to our brother/sister eternal life.... You promised *paradise* to the repentant thief; bring N. to the joys of heaven.... He/she was nourished at your table on earth; welcome him/her at your table in the heavenly Kingdom." Traditional prayers for rest are recited at the commendation and committal.[37]

Anabaptist Churches

Anabaptist churches, which come from the sixteenth-century Radical Reformation (which took issue with both Roman Catholicism and mainstream Protestantism), do not pray for the departed. Neither historic documents nor contemporary statements of faith address the issue. The *Mennonite Church* has no such prayers for public worship, but does include funeral prayers that commit and commend the dead to God's loving mercy. The *Church of the Brethren* does not have a set form for prayers of the people, and while the communion service can incorporate the idea of all the saints, it does not mention any departed individual. Funeral prayers are primarily to comfort the family, but should "express appropriate thanksgiving for the deceased" and entrust them to God.[38]

Evangelical Churches

Evangelicals—including free, non-denominational, *Baptist* and *Pentecostal* churches—reject prayer for the dead entirely. It is a Roman Catholic practice that needs no discussion; the condemnation of the Reformers is sufficient. At death believers go directly to heaven and unbelievers to hell, and since there is no purgatory, nothing can be gained by praying for the departed. However, Donald Bloesch, a progressive evangelical, does accept the practice: we "can pray for the faithful departed, but . . . should

---

37. Presbyterian Church USA, *Book of Common Worship*, 116, 72, 121–22 and 922f. See Episcopal Church, *Book of Common Prayer*, 497.

38. Church of the Brethren, *For All Who Minister*, 407. Professor Jamie Pitts of Anabaptist-Mennonite Seminary provided me with information on prayer for the dead in Anabaptist traditions. Professor Denise Kettering-Lane of Bethany Theological Seminary provided me with information on prayer for the dead in the Church of the Brethren.

not pray for their justification and redemption. . . . We may, however, pray for their progress toward final glory, since we can surmise that there is spiritual growth beyond the grave." Bloesch goes even further. "What about prayers for the lost? We may hope for the final reunion of all souls and even pray for this." While he does not affirm universal posthumous salvation, "it is not wrong to pray 'may God have mercy on their souls' if we fear that the deceased have separated themselves from the love of God."[39] Bloesch, however, is a lone voice, and prayers for the departed are completely absent from evangelical worship.

Lutheran Churches

Lutheran churches allow prayer for the dead, at least in principle. Martin Luther did not encourage or forbid them, and neither do the Lutheran confessions. A formal study by the *Lutheran Church-Missouri Synod* states that there is no biblical support for the practice, condemns Roman Catholic prayer for souls in purgatory, and cites the synodical catechism: "we should pray for ourselves and for all people . . . , but not for the souls of the dead." The document declares that there is no reason to pray for the departed; those in heaven have no need of our prayers and those in hell cannot be helped by prayer. "Though we do not approve of intercessions for the benefit of the souls of the dead, we nevertheless declare that the Church may not object to such prayers offered . . . as: a) supplications for the rest of the body in the grave; b) thanksgivings . . . for the deliverance of deceased believers from all temptations and tribulations [of this life, and] for all the glorious blessings which God promised to those who . . . persevered in faith." The service books of the Lutheran Church-Missouri Synod do not contain any prayers for or commendations of the dead.[40]

---

39. Bloesch, *Last Things*, 149 and 167–68.

40. Joint Theological Faculties, "Study on Intercessory Prayers." The Lutheran Church-Missouri Synod (LCMS) does not allow petitions or commendations of the dead in the Litany, the Prayers and Intercessions, or the Eucharistic prayer. The inclusion of such prayers was one of the grounds for the LCMS not accepting the 1978 *Lutheran Book of Worship*. The committal prayer in the funeral liturgy in the LCMS *Lutheran Service Book* (281) replaces the traditional commendation ("into your hands . . . we commend your servant. . . . Acknowledge . . . a lamb of your own flock. . . . Receive him into the arms of your mercy") with a factual statement ("you gather the lambs of your flock into the care of your mercy and bring them home"). The concluding collect asks only that God "keep these remains to the day of the resurrection of all flesh." See U.S. Lutheran-Catholic Dialogue, *Hope of Eternal Life*, 69 and 72.

The *Evangelical Lutheran Church in America* remembers the faithful departed in the Prayers of the People every Sunday, including those who have recently died and those commemorated on the church calendar of saints. The evening prayer service gives "thanks for all who have gone before us and are at rest, rejoicing in the communion of saints"—and All Saints Sunday is part of the liturgical year. The deceased are prayed for in the funeral rites with commendations: "keep our sister/brother . . . in the company of all your saints. And at the last . . . raise her/him up to share with all the faithful the endless joy and peace won through the glorious resurrection of Christ our Lord." After this the ancient prayer of committal—"rest eternal grant him/her, O Lord; and let light perpetual shine upon him/her"—is recited.[41]

Wesleyan Churches

The Wesleyan tradition nowhere condemns prayer for the dead. John Wesley rejected purgatory, but encouraged intercessions for rest and resurrection. The *English Methodist Church* "has prayers for the dead, the use of which is optional, and those . . . who pray for the dead thereby commend them to the continuing mercy of God."[42]

The *United Methodist Church* explicitly encourages prayer for the dead. "Protestant aversion to the Roman doctrine of purgatory and reaction against abuses of the Mass for the dead have too often become unthinking overreaction and should no longer blind us to the fact that prayer for the dead has been a widespread practice throughout Christian history," a denominational publication says. "If one doubts the truth of intercessory prayer for the dead, it would be well to rethink one's understanding of God, one's Christology and one's doctrine of the Church." Such prayer "is a profound act of love addressed to a God of love. . . . And if love as prayer has been offered for people until the moment of death," then it is also appropriate to offer "love as prayer after death."[43]

---

41. Evanglical Lutheran Church in America, *Evangelical Lutheran Worship*, 106, 317, 279 and 283–84. Professors Kurt Hendel and Ben Stewart of Lutheran School of Theology at Chicago provided me with information on prayer for the dead in Lutheran traditions.

42. English Roman Catholic–Methodist Committee, "Justification," 90. Professor Byron Anderson of Garrett-Evangelical Theological Seminary provided me with information on prayer for the dead in Methodist traditions. See Tucker, *American Methodist Worship*, chapter 8: "Methodist Funerals."

43. United Methodist Church, *Service of Death and Resurrection*, 28–29.

Prayers of thanksgiving for the deceased are made at the Eucharist: "we bless thy name for all thy servants departed this life in thy faith and fear" or "we remember with thanksgiving those who have loved and served thee . . . , who now rest from their labors (especially those most dear to us, whom we name in our hearts before thee)." The "Litany for the Church and for the World" includes a petition from the Episcopal Prayer Book: "we commend to your mercy all who have died, that your will for them may be fulfilled"—and the hymnal includes a "Canticle of Remembrance" of the righteous.[44] Thanksgivings are made on the anniversary of a death, in the liturgy for All Saints Day and on other occasions when the church celebrates "the communion of saints as we remember the dead, both of the Church universal and of our local congregation" by reading the names of those who have died recently.[45]

Specific prayers, including commendations ("we entrust him/her to your boundless love and eternal care"), are part of ministry following death. The funeral "Service of Death and Resurrection" includes remembrance of the deceased in the Eucharistic prayer—ending with the words "to all these, grant your peace. Let perpetual light shine upon them."[46] The commendation asks God to "receive N. into the arms of your mercy. Raise N. up with all your people." The committal requests that God "grant N. entrance into your light and joy" or to "receive . . . your servant N., and grant that [he/she] increase in knowledge and love of you."[47] One prayer suggests a gradual process of purification and growth after death—"fulfill in N. your purpose that reaches beyond time and death. Lead N. from strength to strength, and fit N. for love and service in your Kingdom." There are prayers for a child—and, in words that hint at post-mortem conversion, for persons who did not profess Christian faith: we "commit those who are dear to us to your never-failing love, for this life and the life to come."[48] This service for the non-Christian asks God to "look favorably . . . upon those . . . who scarcely knew your grace. . . . Grant mercy also

---

44. United Methodist Church, *United Methodist Book of Worship*, 43–44, 495 ,571 and *United Methodist Hymnal*, 652 and 877.

45. United Methodist Church, *United Methodist Book of Worship*, 74–75, 413–14, and 739.

46. Ibid., 167 and 143. Also see *United Methodist Hymnal*, 872.

47. United Methodist Church, *United Methodist Hymnal*, 875; *United Methodist Book of Worship*, 150 and 156; and *Service of Death and Resurrection*, 76 and 90, slightly modified.

48. United Methodist Church, *United Methodist Book Of Worship*, 163, 162, and 165.

to those who have departed this life in ignorance or defiance of you. We plead for them in the spirit of him who prayed, 'Father, forgive them, for they know not what they do.'"[49] The 1975 *Methodist Service Book* also contains a funeral petition which is not restricted to the saved but includes all we love who have died: "Father of all, we pray to you for those we love, but see no longer: grant them your peace; let light perpetual shine upon them; and . . . work in them the good purpose of your perfect will."[50]

The Anglican Communion

Anglican churches include prayer for the dead both in regular Sunday worship and the funeral liturgy. While acknowledging that prayer for the dead is a divisive issue, the 1970 *Archbishops' Commission on Christian Doctrine* recommended three general prayers that it believed would be acceptable to all Anglicans. The first is a general intercession for the church, including the Christian dead: "may God in God's infinite love and mercy bring the whole Church, living and departed, . . . to a joyful resurrection and the fulfillment of God's eternal Kingdom." The second remembers specific individuals: "we commend to God almighty this our brother N. here departed," and "we thank thee, O God, for the life and witness of thy servant N." The third is a general prayer for all the departed—including the non-Christian dead—which acknowledges both that we do not know how God deals with those who have died outside of faith in Christ and that God desires the salvation of all people: "O God of infinite mercy and justice, who has made man in thine own image, and hatest nothing that thou hast made, we rejoice in thy love for all creation and commend all men to thee, that in them thy will be done."[51]

The *Episcopal Church* catechism teaches that we pray for the dead because "we still hold them in our love, and because we trust that in God's presence those who have chosen to serve God will grow in God's love, until they see God as God is."[52] The prayers of Good Friday ask God to give "pardon and rest to the dead."[53] Eucharistic Rite II has six forms of Prayers of the People, all of which include a petition for the dead. Form

49. United Methodist Church, *Service of Death and Resurrection*, 83.
50. 1975 *Methodist Service Book*, cited in Chapman, "Rest and Light Perpetual," 41.
51. Archbishops' Commission, *Prayer and Departed*, 51, 52, and 55.
52. Episcopal Church, *Book of Common Prayer*, 862.
53. Ibid., 282.

I includes those who died in hope of resurrection and all the departed; Form II mentions the departed, those who have died; Form III refers to the departed and the saints; Form IV prays for all who have died; Form V includes those who have died in the communion of God's church and those whose faith is known only to God; Form VI is for all who have died. There are two appointed collects for the departed; one says "we remember . . . your faithful servant N.; and we pray that, having opened to him the gates of larger life, you will receive him more and more into your joyful service." One of the Eucharistic prayers includes this petition: "remember all who have died in the peace of Christ, and those whose faith is know to you alone; bring them into the place of eternal joy and light."[54] Non-American worship books contain similar prayers. The Church of England's *Common Worship* contains these general prayers: "we commend all those who have died to your unfailing love, that in them your will may be fulfilled; and we pray that we may share with them in your eternal Kingdom" and "Conqueror of death, remember for good those whom we love but see no longer"—as well as "give rest to the departed and bring them, with your saints, to glory everlasting." There is also this more inclusive petition: "we remember those who have died in the peace of Christ, both those who have confessed the faith and those whose faith is known to you alone, and grant us with them a share in your eternal Kingdom."[55] The Scottish Liturgy, Intercession Form 1, has a petition for all the dead ("for those who are separated from us by death; that theirs may be the Kingdom which is unshakeable, we pray to you, O Lord")—as does the New Zealand Prayer Book ("we remember those who have died. Father, into your hands we commend them").[56]

The Episcopal burial service expresses Easter joy and hope; it begins by asking God to give the deceased "entrance into the land of light and joy." In the Prayers of the People the priest recites a petition for all the dead:

---

54. Ibid., 383–93, 253, and 375.

55. Church of England *Common Worship*, Funeral Prayer 67; Prayers 10 and 16; Forms of Intercession 4. Some prayers concerning the dead are *thanksgivings* ("receive our thanks and praise that . . . your child N. . . . shares with your saints in the joy of heaven"); others are *declarative statements of fact* ("you protect the soul of N. . . . and . . . will show mercy to all the faithful departed") or commendations ("we commend N into the arms of your mercy"). Only a few are *imperative statements of request* ("we pray for those who have fallen asleep in the hope of rising again, that they may see God face to face").

56. Episcopal Church of Scotland, *Scottish Liturgy* and Anglican Church in New Zealand, *New Zealand Prayer Book*, 483.

"we pray to you for N., and for all those whom we love but see no longer. Grant to them eternal rest. Let light perpetual shine upon them." Prayers for the repose of the departed continue through the commendation and as the body is taken from the church: "into *paradise* may the angels lead you. At your coming may the martyrs receive you, and bring you into the holy city Jerusalem." These intercessions are repeated at the committal of the body to the ground. Rite I includes older prayers: "into thy hands, O Lord, we commend thy servant N. . . . beseeching thee that he may be precious in thy sight. Wash him . . . in the blood of that immaculate Lamb that was slain to take away the sins of the world; that, whatsoever defilements he may have contracted . . . being purged and done away, he may be presented pure and without spot before thee"—and "grant that, increasing in knowledge and love of thee, he may go from strength to strength in the life of perfect service in thy heavenly Kingdom."[57] Similar prayers occur in other Anglican prayer books.

Even conservative Anglicans like Tom Wright allow prayer for the dead. True prayer is "an outflowing of love," which does not end at death. Since "God chooses to work through our prayers for other people's benefit," prayer for the departed is appropriate—"not to get them out of purgatory, nor because [we] are unsure about their final salvation, but because [we want] to talk to God about them." The most theologically correct prayer, Wright suggests, is "may the faithful departed, through the mercy of God, rest in peace and rise in glory." He concludes: "once we rule out purgatory, I see no reason why we should not pray for . . . the dead and every reason why we should, . . . that they will be refreshed and filled with God's joy and presence" as they await resurrection.[58]

Mormon Churches

The *Church of Jesus Christ of Latter Day Saints* has a unique practice—baptism for the dead. "Baptism is essential to the salvation of all who have lived on earth," a church publication says. "Many people, however, have died without being baptized. . . . Because God is merciful, God has prepared a way for all people to receive the blessings of baptism. By performing proxy baptisms in behalf of those who have died, church members offer these blessings to deceased ancestors." This does not mean "that

---

57. Episcopal Church, *Book of Common Prayer*, 491–505 and 488.

58. Wright, *For All Saints*, 73–76 and *Surprised by Hope*, 172. Also see DeSilva, *Sacramental Life*, 130–33.

when baptisms for the dead are performed, deceased persons are baptized into the church against their will. . . . The validity of a baptism . . . depends on the deceased person accepting it and choosing to accept and follow the Savior while residing in the spirit world." Baptism for the dead is not prayer for them, but an opportunity for them to hear the gospel and choose to accept or reject it. Still, it shares with such prayers the assumption that the living can do things to help the dead. And it assumes that God is loving and wants all to be saved—including people who, through no fault of their own, never had the opportunity for baptism—and that post-mortem conversion is possible.[59]

Judaism

In addition to Christians, Jews—since the Middle Ages—pray for the dead. "Through *kaddish*," Lisa Miller writes, "family members on earth can help expedite a soul's eventual ascension . . . to God. . . . The eleven months of *kaddish* . . . is . . . the time when the soul is cleansed of the stains of the world."[60] Prayer helps the dead move up to heaven.

Ecumenical Convergence on Prayer for the Dead

Geoffrey Wainwright points out the obvious: issues concerning the dead—their fate and whether the living can affect it—have been church-dividing.[61] Robert Boggis notes that Protestants "have generally regarded praying for the dead as one of the inherent differences that distinguish them from Catholic [and Orthodox] Christendom."[62] Confessional controversy and ecclesiastical separation—broken fellowship with those with whom we disagree because we are sure we possess the truth—contradict Jesus' desire that his followers "all be one" (John 17:21). As Leo Piguet observes, "we have not followed that command. Those of us who believe in Christ have separated ourselves from each other and cemented our differences into walls." The ecumenical movement of the last century has attempted to heal denominational division and strengthen the bonds of love among all followers of Jesus.[63] The foundation of agreement,

---

59. Church of Jesus Christ of Latter Day Saints, "Baptism for the Dead."
60. Miller, *Heaven*, 16–17; cf. 146.
61. Wainwright, "Saints and Departed."
62. Boggis, *Praying for Dead*, 245.
63. Piguet, *100 Prayers*, 103 and 107, slightly modified.

Robert Webber says, must be the classical Christian faith of the first five centuries—the one catholic church must be an apostolic church. "The unity that exists among ... Catholic, Orthodox and Protestant Christians [goes] back to the common era, and to those convictions that precede a time when the Church became Eastern Orthodox, Roman Catholic or Protestant."[64] In recent years some ecumenical convergence on prayer for the dead, both doctrinally and liturgically, has occurred.

Example 1 Anglican and Orthodox churches both believe that prayer helps the departed—although the ways in which it does so is not specified. The 1984 *Dublin Agreed Statement* declares that "the communion of saints finds its fullest expression in the ... Eucharistic prayers ... which commemorate the saints and intercede for the departed as well as for the living." The declaration concludes:

> for the righteous ... further progress and growth in the love of God will continue forever. After death, this progress is to be thought of in terms of healing rather than satisfaction or retribution. ... The traditional practice of the Church in praying for the faithful departed is to be understood as an expression of the unity between the Church militant and the Church triumphant, and of the love which one bears to the other.[65]

Anglican and Orthodox churches are in substantial agreement on praying for the dead.

Example 2 The Lutheran and Roman Catholic churches of Germany, in their report *Communio Sanctorum*, agree that "it corresponds to the communion in which we are bound together in Christ ... with those who have already died to pray for them and to commend them ... to the mercy of God." There is some consensus on a process of sanctification after death: purification "becomes complete as ... persons come with their love to give the perfect response to the love of God. That this may take place, the communion of the faithful on earth may constantly pray."[66] These denominations have much in common.

Example 3 The United States Evangelical Lutheran and Roman Catholic churches, too, have reached some agreement on praying for the departed—expressed in the statement *The Hope of Eternal Life*. Prayer

---

64. Webber, *Ancient-Future Faith*, 29.

65. Anglican-Orthodox Dialogue, *Dublin Agreed Statement* Section III: "Worship and Tradition: The Communion of Saints and the Departed."

66. Bilateral Working Group, *Communio Sanctorum*, Sections 201, 240, 223, and 228.

for the dead "arises primarily out of the bonds of grace that unite us in God and continue to unite us with our loved ones who have died. We confidently trust that God will continue to embrace our loved ones. Such prayer does not express anxiety, uncertainty or the fear that our love for the deceased is greater than God's love for them." Prayers for the departed "ask for the forgiveness of . . . sin, acceptance by God and eternal life." The report observes that "Catholic and many Lutheran funeral liturgies contain a prayerful commendation of the dead into the hands of a merciful and gracious God. While this convergence . . . does not extend to a common practice of prayer for the dead beyond funerals, it does indicate a growing unity in [their] practices in relation to those who have died in Christ." Lutherans and Catholics agree, then, that "there is communion among the living and the dead across the divide of death. . . . Prayerful commendation of the dead to God is salutary within a funeral liturgy. . . . Insofar as the resurrection of the dead and the general final judgment are future events, it is appropriate to pray for God's mercy for each person, entrusting that one to God's mercy." Thus "prayer for the dead, considered within the framework of the communion of saints, need not be a Church-dividing . . . issue."[67]

Example 4 The Roman Catholic and English Methodist churches both pray for the dead. Their consensus statement confirms that "over the centuries in the Catholic tradition praying for the dead has developed into a variety of practices, especially through the Mass. . . . The Methodist church . . . [also] has prayers for the dead, the use of which is optional, and those Methodists who pray for the dead thereby commend them to the continuing mercy of God." Given agreement on basic theological principles, a variety of practices of praying for the dead can be allowed within a united church.[68]

On the question of prayer for the departed there is growing ecumenical convergence as the churches dialogue across ecclesiastical boundaries and remove the barriers that divide them.

---

67. U.S. Lutheran–Catholic Dialogue, *Hope of Eternal Life*, 67, 61, 69, 70, 72, and 76.

68. English Roman Catholic–Methodist Committee, "Justification," 90-91.

Concluding Remarks

Several conclusions can be drawn from the historical and contemporary survey of the last two chapters.

1. Prayer for the dead is an ancient practice of the church that began in its earliest days.
2. Roman Catholics and Eastern Orthodox have always prayed for the dead. Protestants—with the exception of some Anglicans—generally have not.
3. Much of the church offers *consummation prayers*: prayers for final culmination of God's plan—*parousia*, resurrection, judgment, and new creation.
4. Some of the church offers *growth prayers*: prayers for the rest and continual increase of joy for those in God's presence. Consummation and growth prayers are the narrowest, most restricted form of prayer for the dead.
5. Some of the church offers *purification prayers*: prayers for the moral transformation of those who die in a state of grace yet unready for heaven (in the case of Roman Catholicism—those in purgatory).
6. Few in the church offer *salvation prayers*: prayers for the repentance and escape of the unsaved from hell. These are the broadest, most inclusive, form of prayer for the dead.

In the next chapter I outline the position I defend in the remainder of this work.

chapter 4

ENVISIONING THE FUTURE
Prayer for the Dead in the Coming Church

GROWING UP IN CONSERVATIVE Protestant circles I never heard of praying for the dead until, in college, I encountered banks of burning votive candles at side-altars or placed before statues of saints in Montreal's Notre Dame Basilica. The practice of lighting candles for the dead struck me as odd at best, pagan at worst. Little did I know that in the Roman Catholic tradition candles symbolize the light of Christ (John 1:4, 9; 8:12; 12:46) and are a form of prayer—particularly a remembrance of deceased loved ones. As the candle keeps burning, so our prayers continue when we leave and go about our daily business. I was well into adulthood before I began to seriously doubt that the theology I had been taught as a child was the absolute truth—and started to take seriously the notion that there were other, perhaps more faithful, ways of being Christian.

My experience, of course, is not unique since all of us—Protestants, Roman Catholics, and Eastern Orthodox alike—are raised with particular understandings. Too often committed Christians develop a narrow mindset—what John Suk calls a "self-righteousness that looks down its nose at everyone who doesn't heed" its doctrines and practices.[1] We believe that we possess the truth and that it is our job to guard it. But by refusing to join conversation "with those who do not share our specific interpretation of the faith," Merold Westphal points out, "we pretty much terminate the possibility of critical reflection on the truth [and] significance of the various components of our theology, rendering our

---

1. Suk, *Not Sure*, 187.

current understanding of the faith final for all intents and purposes."[2] It is not easy, of course, to become humble about our own grasp of truth and to listen to the ideas of others—to develop what Brian McLaren calls a "generous orthodoxy," an ecumenical and progressive faith that is open to revision.[3]

This work concerns praying for the departed, and I invite all readers—those not used to such prayers and those who are—to rethink their traditions. My argument will challenge, even disturb, some people and may require intellectual courage—which Richard Paul defines as the willingness to face and assess fairly viewpoints to which we have not given serious hearing, regardless of our strong negative reaction to them. We all experience disorientation and distress, cognitive dissonance, when our cherished convictions—which often confer identity and self-understanding—are cross-examined, dismantled, and revised. Courage arises from the recognition that ideas considered dangerous are sometimes rationally justified and that beliefs espoused by those around us and which we uncritically accept are sometimes false.[4] Struggling with confusion and unsettled questions, having faith stretched, Anne Lamott contends, is a good thing.

> If we stay where we are, where we're stuck, where we're comfortable and safe, we die there. We become like mushrooms, living in the dark, with poop up to our chins. If you want to know only what you already know, you're dying. You're saying: Leave me alone; I don't mind this little rathole. It's warm and dry. Really, it's fine. When nothing new can get in, that's death. When oxygen can't find a way in, you die. But new is scary, and new can be . . . confusing—we had this all figured out, and now we don't.[5]

Critical reflection will benefit the reader, whether my conclusions are accepted or not.

Clarifying My Position

Descriptive statements assert the way things are—and the previous two chapters describe how the church has and does pray for the dead, without

---

2. Westphal, "Faith Seeking Understanding," 217, slightly modified.

3. McLaren, *Generous Orthodoxy*.

4. Paul, *Critical Thinking*, 553. The psychological and relational penalties for nonconformity to our social group, for being true to our own thinking, can be severe.

5. Lamott, *Help, Thanks, Wow*, 86.

UNDERSTANDING PRAYER FOR THE DEAD

taking a position on whether the practice is right or wrong. Prescriptive statements assert how things ought to be, and in what follows I say what prayer ought to be (rather than what it actually is). I defend the position that Christians should offer

1. petitionary prayer
2. for
3. all the dead.

First, I defend *petitionary prayer* for all the dead. There are many genres of prayer—praise, lament, confession, petition—and prayers for the departed may be thanksgivings or intercessions. Intercessions may be funerary (commendations that entrust the deceased person to God's care) or non-funerary (occurring in regular rounds of public worship or private devotion). The prayers for the departed that concern me are not commendations and thanksgivings (which all Christians should agree are legitimate), but non-funerary petitions that ask God to do something (which raise a whole set of questions and are thus more controversial).[6]

Second, I defend petitionary prayer *for* all the dead. Three types of prayer mention the dead. Prayer *about* the dead—such as "we praise . . . your holy name for all your servants who have finished their course in your faith and fear"—thanks God for their lives and for the hope of resurrection.[7] Prayer *to* the dead—invocation of the saints, as in "Holy Mary . . . , pray for us sinners"—directs them to assist us or to make requests of God for us.[8] Prayers *for* the dead—like "receive him more and more

---

6. While some scholars make a technical distinction between *petition* for oneself and *intercession* for others, I use the terms interchangeably. See Archbishops' Commission, *Prayer and Departed*, 16–17.

7. Episcopal Church, *Book of Common Prayer*, 504.

8. Prayer *to* the saints began when, in the late Roman Empire, they came to be seen as *patroni*—patrons standing between the living and God as noblemen representing clients at the court of the emperor (Brown, *Ransom of Soul*, 43). Wright (*For All Saints*, 40 and *Surprised by Hope*, 172–74) objects to invocation of the saints because it "seems to . . . undermine, or actually deny by implication, something which is promised again and again in the New Testament: immediacy of access to God through Jesus Christ. . . . Every single Christian is welcome at any time to come before the Father." Wright's argument assumes a false dilemma, as Ford ("Prayer and Departed Saints," 14) points out. "Just because we pray, on our own, directly to God, does not mean that we never ask other people for their prayers. Indeed, we are commanded many times in the Scriptures to pray for one another. . . . So, just as we feel comforted and strengthened when we ask friends, family and church members here on earth to intercede for us in a time of need, how much more can we feel comforted and strengthened when

into your joyful service"—bring their needs before God and petition God to do something for them.⁹ In such prayers requests are made on behalf of—in the interest and for the benefit of—the dead. It follows from these distinctions that Roman Catholics and Eastern Orthodox pray *for* the dead—while most Protestant references count only as prayer *about* them.

Third, I defend petitionary prayer for *all the dead*. In a classification that goes back to the church fathers, the dead comprise three groups—the blessed in heaven, the imperfect in purgatory, and the unsaved in hell.¹⁰ Each form of prayer corresponds to a different group of the dead.

1. *Consummation* prayers concern all people, both living and dead: they ask for completion of God's plan—Christ's return, joyous resurrection and new creation. These events, which end history, remain future for all the dead.

2. *Growth prayers* concern the blessed in present heaven; they ask for rest and increasing participation in God's life.¹¹

3. *Purification* prayers concern the imperfect in purgatory; they ask for moral transformation into characters of holy love.¹²

4. *Salvation* prayers concern the unsaved in hell; they ask for repentance, forgiveness, and restored relationship with God.¹³

---

we also ask the Church in heaven for her prayers." Also see Currie, *Born Fundamentalist*, 161–62.

9. Episcopal Church, *Book of Common Prayer*, 253.

10. This division is found in 1 Corinthians 3:1–3 (*KJV*)—the natural (unsaved), the carnal (imperfect), and the spiritual (blessed). The Archbishops' Commission (*Prayer and Departed*, 46) is divided on whether to itemize specific petitions for the dead or to simply pray for their well-being whatever their particular situation. I take the former stance.

11. In volume two, chapter 3, I distinguish *present heaven* (the transitional place where we go when we die; the intermediate state where we await resurrection) from *future heaven* (the culmination of salvation history—the permanent place where we will live forever with God and each other after resurrection). I also distinguish *static* heaven (where spiritual growth plateaus and reaches finality) from *dynamic* heaven (where spiritual growth in love and knowledge of God continues).

12. In volume two, chapter 4, I distinguish *sanctification purgatory* (where what gets purged is the disposition to sin) from *satisfaction purgatory* (where what gets purged is the penalty of sin). While the term "purgatory" carries all sorts of connotations, I use it for ease of reference.

13. In volume two, chapter 5, I distinguish *closed hell* (where posthumous salvation is impossible and damnation is permanent) from *open hell* (where posthumous salvation and escape from hell are possible).

If Christians pray for the dead at all, they restrict it to consummation, growth, or purification prayers for those who died in faith. My position departs from historic practice by including salvation prayers for those who lived apart from the church—those whose faith is known only to God, who were adherents of other religions, or who had no faith. "We commend to your mercy *all* who have died," the Episcopal Church Prayers of the People say, "that your will for them may be fulfilled."[14] For none of the departed has God's will been completed: none have been resurrected in God's new creation—meanwhile the blessed continue to grow in love of God, the imperfect lack mature love and are not fully united with God, and the unsaved are separated from God.

Balancing Tradition and Revision

Certain theological understandings and religious practices are "entrenched"—they are established traditions that are shared by large sections of the historical and contemporary church (or by particular branches of the church). Even highly entrenched positions that are taken for granted, however, may not be true or justified—and may need revision.[15] "If you are conservative," David Ford says, "you want to preserve some version of the past and are resistant to change." If you are liberal, by contrast, "you sit more lightly to the authority of the past and are more open to change."[16] Revision, of course, should never be undertaken lightly; we need good reasons for rejecting entrenched views. Traditionalists claim that their particular church practice concerning prayer for the dead (and the theological understandings that frame those practices) is correct and should be maintained. Protestant traditionalists pray for none of the dead while Roman Catholic and Eastern Orthodox traditionalists pray for some of the dead—the saved. Revisionists think that the traditions of their churches should be changed. Protestant revisionists will begin praying for the dead, while Roman Catholic and Eastern Orthodox revisionists will broaden their prayer to include the unsaved.

---

14. Episcopal Church, *Book of Common Prayer*, Prayers of the People Form VI, 393. Form IV, 389, is similar: "we pray for all who have died, that they may have a place in your eternal Kingdom."

15. The term "entrenched" comes from Carter, *Elements of Metaphysics*, 12–13.

16. Ford, *Theology*, 21.

There are two arguments for conserving past practice. The first, the *argument from tradition*, claims that, unless there are compelling reasons, churches should err on the side of history—Protestants being reluctant to start praying for the dead, and Roman Catholics and Eastern Orthodox being hesitant to stop.

Since the Reformation—chapter 1 points out—the question of who is entitled to determine the true meaning of the Bible has divided Protestants (who think that individuals should read and decide for themselves) and Roman Catholics (who confer authority for biblical interpretation on church leaders). Martin Luther's notion that individual conscience supersedes the judgment of the church has never been accepted by Roman Catholics.

Robert C. Roberts and Jay Wood identify two different intellectual practices: autonomy (regulation by self, thinking for oneself) and heteronomy (regulation by others, following the thoughts of other people). Total auto-regulation is not possible since there are no self-made thinkers. Much of what we know is mediated to us by others, inherited through reading and education; other people serve as knowledge-imparters, knowledge-critics, and knowledge-models. We are all limited in what we can learn or think on our own, and so we consult others and receive help from them. Accepting their authority, Hans Gadamer says, "is based not on the subjection and abdication of reason but on . . . the knowledge . . . that the other is superior to oneself in judgment and insight and that for this reason their judgment takes precedence . . . over one's own."[17] No one is immune from hetero-regulation, from being influenced noetically by others.

This is especially true for Christians: traditional truths of faith and morals are external sources that carry weight in contemporary thought and practice. Owen Thomas defines tradition—creeds, conciliar decisions, confessions of faith, liturgies, and theological writings—as "the Church's continuing attempt under the guidance of the Holy Spirit" to understand the central message of the Bible.[18] In ancient Israel the teachings of Judaism were passed down in oral instruction from generation to generation. Jesus commands his followers to obey the traditions

---

17. Gadamer, cited in Roberts and Wood, *Intellectual Virtues*, 277, slightly modified. Epistemic individualism is the idea that we must depend on only ourselves as isolated knowers for intellectual justification. Social epistemology—by contrast—recognizes that many, if not most, of our beliefs come from other people.

18. Thomas, *Introduction to Theology*, 40.

of the Pharisees (Matt 23:2–3), but also warns them not to replace the commandments of God with human tradition (Mark 7:8). St. Paul indicates that oral tradition—teachings transmitted by word of mouth—has equal authority with written teachings (2 Thess 2:15; 2 Tim 2:2), but also warns about being taken captive by human tradition (Col 2:8). Roman Catholics believe that God's leaders in the church are the determiners and guardians of truth, the deposit of faith, across the centuries. "The Protestant assumption that Scripture existed first and that tradition was slowly . . . added to it," David Currie says, is false. Instead, the church created Scripture and dogma through the decisions of bishops, ecumenical councils, and papal pronouncements. The Council of Trent declared in 1564 that truth is "contained in written books [of the Bible] and the unwritten traditions [of the church]."[19] The Bible and church are authoritative because they are divinely inspired and appointed—traditional positions, then, should be *prima facie* (Latin for "at first inspection," "on first appearance") accepted. Protestants agree that doctrinal development—in Thomas' words—"is never made *de novo*," but "is always guided provisionally by tradition."[20] Beginning with tradition protects us from ourselves—from our own biased assumptions, unconscious presuppositions, and culturally-shaped interpretations, from over-reliance on popular but transient philosophies and novelties.

But what happens when traditions conflict? There is an obvious inconsistency between these two propositions:

1. praying for the dead is appropriate and
2. praying for the dead is not appropriate.

So both cannot be correct. Because they are mutually exclusive claims, if one is true then the other must be false.

---

19. Currie, *Born Fundamentalist*, 62 and the Council of Trent, cited in Thomas, *Introduction to Theology*, 41. Origen (cited in Daley, "Old Books," 62) argued this in the second century: "only that position is to be believed as truth that in no way varies from the tradition of the Church." The basic apostolic message was summarized in the "rule of faith," a list of basic Christian tenets. Vatican II's decree on revelation, *Dei Verbum* (cited in Daley, "Old Books," 58–59), states that "the Church has kept and keeps the Scriptures, together with tradition, as the supreme rule of its faith." These do not constitute two sources of truth but "a single sacred deposit of the word of God," a single *traditio apostolica*.

20. Thomas, *Introduction to Theology*, 36. Also see Aben, *African Christian Theology*, 182.

In addition, simply claiming that a practice is long-standing is insufficient to establish its truth. While we depend on the resources of tradition, tradition is not an infallible authority to which we must slavishly adhere, to which we owe unconditional obedience. The Church of England's "Articles of Religion" state that councils "may err, and sometimes have erred."[21] Tradition, Thomas says, "must always be kept under the judgment of . . . the Bible"—and so we should not simply accept received teaching and stop thinking for ourselves. Total hetero-regulation by tradition is unwise.[22] We should listen to how the church has understood Scripture in the past, but these understandings are not absolute and unreformable. As our knowledge and understanding of God's truth grows, official doctrines and practices must be re-examined. Since tradition does not constitute a final understanding of Scripture or a perfect system of theology, it should be affirmed only *pro tanto*—only to the extent that it is correct. Christian scholars can criticize and revise old positions in light of new insights. Appeals to tradition cannot take the place of evidence, T. Edward Damer says: "when there are good reasons for changing a way of . . . thinking or for not continuing a particular practice, then reverence for the past is an irrelevant consideration in the process of determining the future."[23] Tradition should be accepted as correct until proven otherwise—but an initial affirmation can be rebutted by new evidence, by strong reasons which overturn it.

The second argument for maintaining past practice, the *argument from consensus*, claims that, unless there are compelling reasons, we should err on the side of doctrines or practices on which all branches of the church agree. Vincent of Lerins famously insists that "care must be taken that we hold that faith which has been believed everywhere, always, and by all." In determining what to believe we must "follow universality, antiquity, and consent (of priests and doctors)." We should depart from tradition cautiously—since it represents the consensus of many individuals across time.[24] Protestant, Catholic, and Orthodox churches generally agree that prayer for *all* the dead is not appropriate.

The problem with this argument is twofold. First, on some matters there is no consensus; the church remains divided on many issues,

---

21. Episcopal Church, *Book of Common Prayer*, 872, Article XXI.
22. Thomas, *Introduction to Theology*, 36.
23. Damer, *Attacking Faulty Reasoning*, 93.
24. Vincent, cited in Thomas, *Introduction to Theology*, 34; also see 42.

questions on which the Bible is not decisive. The existence of eternal punishment in hell, I argue in the next volume, is one such matter. Second, even if there was universal consensus, widespread opinions can be mistaken—so the fact that the churches uniformly teach something does not make it true. The principle that correct doctrine is what has been held universally in the history of the church, Thomas says, "turns a descriptive judgment into a normative judgment.... The hidden assumption is that the universal consensus will in fact always be true doctrine." This presumes an infallible church—and "yet it is certainly possible that a majority of the Church may be in [error] at any one time. This was clearly the view of the Reformers."[25] Numerous examples of false but cherished beliefs, later revised, can be given. For eighteen hundred years the church lived, for the most part, at peace with slavery; then in the nineteenth century some people began to find it objectionable—and now all Christians do. In that same century, the growing academic consensus about the Bible's literary composition (such as that the Pentateuch is the work of several authors and that St. Paul did not write the pastoral letters) challenged traditional convictions regarding authorship—and scientific evidence supporting human evolution upset literal interpretations of the opening chapters of Genesis. The ethics of divorce and remarriage and questions of gender equality are today being rethought by many in the church. Popular opinion is not a reliable indicator of truth—for truth, Damer says, "is in no way dependent upon the number of people who support it."[26]

Traditional and consensus positions, while valuable, are not infallible and may be changed in light of further reflection. The Reformers believed that *ecclesia semper reformanda est* (Latin for "the church is always to be reformed"). God, says Pope Francis, "is not afraid of new things. That is why God is continually surprising us, opening our hearts and guiding us in unexpected ways."[27] Static theology, intent on preserving tradition, assumes that it has reached a full understanding of truth; progressive theology, by contrast, acknowledges that Christian understanding evolves as human knowledge and experience grow and as the Spirit speaks new words. This is why, Sharon Baker quips, "the tradition is to reinterpret the tradition." Doctrinal change may take three forms:

---

25. Thomas, *Introduction to Theology*, 34.
26. Damer, *Attacking Faulty Reasoning*, 95.
27. Pope Francis, "Homily at the Beatification Mass of Paul VI."

refinement (which develops and clarifies existing truth), reversal (which creates new, perhaps contradictory, understanding), and recovery (which returns to older ideas and practices).[28]

Authentic developments in theological understanding are what Jason Byassee calls "faithful innovations."[29] There is a balance between regulation by church teaching and having a mind of one's own. Both hyper-obedience and hyper-individualism are flawed intellectual practices. Intellectual autonomy, having rational control of our beliefs, Paul says, means conforming when it is reasonable to conform and questioning when it is reasonable to question. Theological reflection, Roberts and Wood conclude, is a "dependent independence."[30] There are, then, two truths concerning tradition. *Tradition is necessary*—if faith and practice are not communally-determined then any individual can overturn any precedent in light of their own idiosyncratic ideas. But, while reliable, *tradition is not infallible*—it can both accurately represent and badly misrepresent God's truth. Christopher Hall gives an analogy: "the Church's tradition in its best moments represents the music the Holy Spirit is singing"—while "in its worst moments, the tradition may fail to interpret the divine composer's musical score well."[31]

As a *Protestant* I deny an infallible tradition and official teaching magisterium, since the church can err in understanding Scripture. Tradition contains mutations and distortions. But as a *traditionalizing Protestant* I am wary of going to the other extreme and making each person their own individual authority. Individuals can err as well, using their own personal beliefs to pick and choose, cafeteria-style, which traditions to accept and which to reject. This is the circular dilemma of tradition: tradition must be accountable to Scripture which guides it, but interpretations of Scripture must be accountable to tradition, which creates it. If tradition automatically overrides fresh insight into the Bible, then the church can go wrong in understanding the gospel—and if private interpretations of the Bible automatically trump tradition, then individuals can err. "Our reading needs to be corrected by tradition," Hall concludes, "and tradition needs to be corrected by our reading."[32]

28. Baker, *Razing Hell*, 153. See Currie, *Born Fundamentalist*, 83–84.
29. Byassee, "Emerging from What?" 261.
30. Paul, *Critical Thinking*, 553 and Roberts and Wood, *Intellectual Virtues*, 284.
31. Hall, "Tradition, Authority, Magisterium," 39. This paragraph draws on Hall's essay; the term "traditionalizing Protestant" in the next sentence comes from page 43.
32. Ibid., 45.

Rob Bell suggests that we find a biblical model for revision in the practice of the Jewish rabbis—who understood that revelation is open-ended and that their role was to interpret how to live *torah*. They "had technical terms for this . . . process of forbidding and permitting and making interpretations. They called it 'binding' and 'loosing.' To 'bind' something was to forbid it. To 'loose' something was to allow it. So a rabbi would bind certain practices and loose other practices. And when he gave his disciples the authority to bind and loose, it was called 'giving the keys of the Kingdom.'" When Jesus uses these words (Matt 16:19; 18:18)—Bell says—"he is giving his followers the authority to make *new* interpretations of the Bible. He is giving them permission to say, 'hey, we think we missed it before on that verse, and we've . . . come to the conclusion that this is what it actually means.'" Doctrine and practice are like springs of a trampoline that stretch and flex, not like a brick that is fixed in size and has no room to move.[33] Walter Brueggemann suggests that we find a biblical model for "newness . . . . that runs beyond the tradition" in St. Peter's encounter with Cornelius (Acts 10). The apostle was commanded to adopt the "odd, shocking and dangerous" behavior of eating with a man who was excluded from table fellowship with Jewish Christians. "The crisis Peter faced was that he learned in that moment of trance, in which God spoke to him afresh, that he had to move beyond his faith tradition." Like early Jewish believers, today's church must be open to fresh understanding prompted by the Spirit. "In many ways," Brueggemann warns, "we want to keep things the way they used to be, the way the tradition . . . taught us it should be. But comes the voice . . . , 'Take and embrace' what you thought was scary and forbidden."[34] St. Peter came to see that Gentile inclusion was not a break with Jewish tradition, but an extension of it—the fulfillment of the promise to Abraham that through him all nations would be blessed (Gen 12:2–3) and of the prophetic utterance that God's love is not limited to Israel, whose purpose was to be "a light to the nations, that . . . salvation may reach to the end of the earth" (Isa 49:6).

My point should now be clear. In its ongoing attempt to understand its faith, the church, John Kronen and Eric Reitan say, must "not only receive the teachings of the past—in the sense of listening respectfully—but

---

33. Bell, *Velvet Elvis*, 47–50; cf. 11 and 22–27.
34. Brueggemann, *Collected Sermons*, 174–77.

also question, challenge, supplement and refine these teachings."[35] Theologians should balance firmness (holding to core commitments) with openness (adjusting beliefs and practices in light of new understandings). "The Christian community"—Thomas Oden agrees—"is constantly seeking an equilibrium of tradition and renewal." Without the anchor of tradition the church drifts into accommodation with prevailing trends— and without the winds of renewal the church stands still and becomes archaic.[36] Tradition should be respected (where appropriate) and revised (when necessary).

Christians should not modify long-held positions without good reason. There are, however, good reasons for Christians to reform their views of prayer for the departed. Protestants will change their modern tradition by recovering ancient church practice, returning to older, pre-Reformation prayers. Catholics and Orthodox will change their traditions by revising existing church practice, expanding prayer in new directions. Neither adopting prayer for the dead for the first time nor broadening such prayers to include the unsaved are a departure from biblical truth; instead—as I argue at length in volume two—they constitute an enlargement of theological understanding.

Recovering Tradition: The Challenge to Protestants

I challenge Protestants to *begin* praying for the dead. A century ago Robert Boggis made several observations concerning Protestant attitudes that remain relevant today.[37] First, "speaking generally, Protestants are averse to the practice of praying for the departed." Second, with the exception of churches whose doctrinal standards condemn praying for the dead, "Protestants are . . . constitutionally free in the matter. . . . While . . . such prayers have not been sanctioned, neither have they been con-

---

35. Kronen and Reitan, *God's Final Victory*, 66. Robinson (*In the End, God*, 38) agrees: "every statement of doctrine"—including those which have stood the test of generations—"is open to revision in the light of a fresh understanding of the evidence." Theories of atonement, for example, have undergone "constant readjustment." Tradition, Moltmann (*Sun of Righteousness*, 2–3) says, "is the starting point, not the boundary . . . . Theology must always be reformed, not always be the same."

36. Oden, *After Modernity*, 52–54. Paul Ricoeur sees a tension between the "hermeneutics of suspicion" (which rejects traditions as distorting and oppressive) and the "hermeneutics of retrieval" (which is suspicious of widespread opposition to tradition)—see Ford, *Theology*, 138.

37. Boggis, *Praying for Dead*, 258–59.

demned," and so—third—Protestants can reconsider them. "The progress of the study of theology, and the fuller appreciation of biblical and doctrinal and historical truths," Boggis reasons, can "diminish prejudice and error" and "dispose people more favorably to [the] topic." Randall Davidson agrees: while protest was necessary at the time of the Reformation, "the abuses of [past practice] need not now, [many] centuries onward," hinder Protestants from praying for the dead.[38]

McLaren urges the Protestant church to "move forward by looking back," to "look to its ancient practices to help it reset its future course."[39] Robert Webber, too, insists that "the road to the future runs through the past," that ancient truth—the framework of faith and practice developed in early Christianity—will revitalize the future church.[40] One of the most important movements in recent Roman Catholic thought, Brian Daley explains, is *ressourcement* (French for "return to the sources") theology, "the recovery of an awareness of the importance of pre-Reformation Christian literature—especially the writings of the first several centuries of Christianity—... as sources for a deeper understanding of the gospel ... and for the renewal of our liturgy and the sustaining of our spiritual life."[41] Tradition, I have said, is not superfluous; it provides a milieu, a safeguard, for properly understanding Christian faith and practice—we ignore tradition to our detriment. That is why I began this book with a study of patristic theology and historic Christian liturgy.

Many mainline and evangelical Protestants are beginning to question their long-standing suspicion that post-apostolic Christianity became distorted and betrayed the gospel, until the Reformers purged it. From the emergent church movement to the new monasticism, *ressourcement* Protestants are adopting ancient forms of liturgy and time-honored spiritual practices. This is due, Phyllis Tickle suggests, to a "hunger born of five hundred years of living and worshipping ... without liturgical connection to the prior fifteen hundred years of the pre-Protestant Church."[42]

---

38. Davidson, cited in Bell, *Randall Davidson*, 823.

39. McLaren, *Finding Our Way Again*, 146; slightly modified.

40. Webber, *Ancient-Future Evangelism*, 9–10.

41. Daley, "Old Books," 54. *Ressourcement* theology turns to patristic and medieval texts as primary sources of doctrine, exegesis, and liturgy. Williams ("*Similis et Dissimilis*," 70–72) examines the "high ideological and historiographical walls that have separated evangelical forms of faith from the faith of the early church"—ahistoricalism, anti-Catholicism, and anti-creedalism.

42. Tickle, "Liturgy and Cultural Engagement," 103.

Protestantism will be renewed, Webber says, by "drawing wisdom from the past and translating these insights into the present and future life of the Church."[43]

The first Christians prayed for the dead in public worship—I challenge Protestants to recover this ancient practice. When a tradition is consistent with Scripture it should be honored and upheld by the church (1 Cor 11:1–2; 2 Thess 3:6). Protestants, then, should adopt the pre-Reformation tradition of praying for the dead found in the early and medieval church (over their own historically-recent Reformation traditions that reject it).

Many Protestants see prayer for the dead and purgatory as inseparable—and finding the latter problematic, reject the former. Two responses are in order. First, as David Chapman points out, the ancient church prayed for the dead without purgatory. "It is not the case that belief in purgatory gave rise to prayer for the Christian dead. On the contrary, the medieval doctrine of purgatory arose as a consequence of scholastic reflection upon the practice of prayer for the departed." Therefore, he concludes, "we should not let difficulties over . . . purgatory weigh against prayer for the Christian dead."[44] Consummation and growth prayer, in particular, have nothing to do with purgatory. Besides, the medieval abuse of a long traditional practice does not invalidate its proper use.

Second, even if prayer for the dead does entail purgatory, there is more than one way to construe that concept. The notion that Protestants have in mind is a satisfaction purgatory where individuals pay the temporary punishment for sins not repented of before death. We must distinguish, however, a punishing purgatory aimed at pardon from a purifying process aimed at moral transformation. As Timothy Ware says, "someone who dies in a state of genuine repentance, but who is in other respects ill-prepared to come face to face with God, may well require to undergo *purification* after . . . death, and this purification may cause . . .

---

43. Webber, *Ancient-Future Evangelism*, 10. In returning to the post-apostolic period, we must admit, Williams ("*Similis et Dissimilis*," 77, slightly modified) warns, "that not everything the patristic Fathers taught is true or even valuable." We must not romanticize and idealize the early church as a "golden age," blindly assuming "that most everything it said and did provides good guidance for today's church." Anti-Judaism, acceptance of slavery, and an elevation of asceticism and celibacy—for example—are found in many ancient Christian writers. Modern utilization of the fathers must be critical and selective (without treating them simply as a theological grab-bag for our own agendas).

44. Chapman, "Rest and Light Perpetual," 47.

some suffering; but it makes no sense to say that he is undergoing *punishment* for sins that God in God's mercy has already forgiven."[45]

The Roman Catholic Church is now rethinking its traditional formulation. Joseph Ratzinger, for example, says that "purgatory is not . . . some kind of supra-worldly concentration camp where one is forced to undergo punishment. . . . Rather it is the inwardly necessary process of transformation in which a person becomes . . . capable of [a loving relationship with] God."[46] Some Protestants are open to the idea of a sanctifying process after death. Baptist theologian Clark Pinnock, for instance, suggests that "evangelicals would not think of purgatory as a place of punishment or atonement because of our view of the work of Christ, but . . . can think of it as an opportunity for maturation and growth."[47] Even if prayer for the dead does entail purgatory, the sanctifying purgatory it implies is fully compatible with the doctrine of justification by grace through faith—and should not be automatically rejected by Protestants as mistaken.

The survey of early church practice in chapter 2 can be taken as a historical argument, an argument from tradition: since prayer for the dead began early and was widespread, it should continue today. Protestants ought to respect "the authority of long-standing practice in the greater part of the Church," the Church of England Archbishops Commission says. Unless clearly unbiblical, "the Church's habits in early times [constitute] a rule of practice for later ages."[48] In the seventeenth century, William Forbes begged Protestants—"let not the ancient practice of praying . . . for the dead, received throughout the universal Church of Christ, almost from the time of the apostles, be any more rejected. . . . Let them reverence the judgment of the primitive church, and admit a practice strengthened by the uninterrupted profession of so many ages."[49] What the early Christians thought and how they prayed must be taken seriously. Embracing ancient church tradition has a place, and Protestants should begin praying for the dead. Some contemporary Protestants are appropriating this heritage of early Christianity to enrich both corporate

---

45. Ware, "One Body in Christ," 185; emphasis added.
46. Ratzinger, *Eschatology*, 230. Also see Ombres, *Theology of Purgatory*, 186 and Rahner, *Theological Investigations* Vol. 19, 181–93.
47. Pinnock, "Response to Zachary Hayes," 130.
48. Archbishops' Commission, *Prayer and Departed*, 48–49.
49. Forbes, cited in Lee, *Christian Doctrine of Prayer for Departed*, 164–65.

worship and individual discipleship. This renewed use of ancient practices is a hopeful sign.

Revising Tradition: The Challenge to Roman Catholics and Eastern Orthodox

The challenge to Protestants to retrieve ancient truth suggests that in matters of faith and practice novelty (believing something simply because it is new) can be a fallacy. Newer is not necessarily better.[50] But sometimes it is—tradition (believing something simply because it is old) can also be a fallacy. The pursuit of truth, including theological truth, is endless (since few beliefs have the finality of certitude) and progressive (as knowledge is enlarged and disagreements resolved). At times tradition should be revised—in light of this, I challenge Roman Catholics and Eastern Orthodox to *broaden* the scope of their prayers for the dead to include salvation prayers.

The simplest reason to pray for *all* the departed is the fact that we do not know who is saved and who is not.[51] A Lutheran-Roman Catholic declaration argues that since "it is not for us to judge those who . . . do not believe or refuse to repent," we should include all the dead in our prayers. This argument from ignorance is complemented by an argument from knowledge. The declaration encourages us to entrust all the dead "to the mercy of God, whose love for the world is so great that God 'gave his only Son' [John 3:16] to save . . . all humanity."[52] The Archbishop's Commission agrees: "it seems inconceivable that a God . . . who hates nothing that God has made, and who wills that all [persons] should be saved, would not welcome the sort of concern expressed" in prayer for the non-Christian dead.[53] Nikolaos Vassiliadis emphasizes that in praying for the unsaved dead "we only ask from God what is pleasing to God, since God as the source of love and mercy 'desires all men to be saved' (1 Tim 2:4)."[54] Thomas Howard argues that "the Church prays for all the

---

50. Lewis rejects chronological snobbery—the idea that the thinking of the past is inferior to that of the present, simply by virtue of its being earlier in time. See "On the Reading of Old Books" in *God in Dock*.

51. Daley (*Hope of Early Church*, 140) says "it is . . . because she is ignorant of any particular person's true standing before God that the church prays for all the dead."

52. Bilateral Working Group, *Communio Sanctorum*, Section 215.

53. Archbishops' Commission, *Prayer and Departed*, 53.

54. Vassiliadis, *Mystery of Death*, 427.

dead since the unbelieving are still part of the huge fabric of creation, and nothing in that fabric is beyond the scope of mercy."[55] We *do not know* who is saved and not saved—but we *do know* that God wants and works for the salvation of all, and so we should pray for all the dead.

The main obstacle to praying for the unsaved dead is the idea that death is an absolute limit ending all chances for salvation. This notion—that divine grace and human freedom end at death—is now being reconsidered by theologians of all persuasions. Roman Catholics such as Hans Urs von Balthasar believe that God's love reaches even into hell, and Karl Rahner claims there might be "opportunities . . . for a post-mortal history of freedom [to accept grace for] someone who had been denied such a history in their earthly life."[56] Many Protestant theologians—including some conservatives—are open to posthumous salvation. Methodist bishop William Willimon takes the parable of the lost sheep (Matt 18:10-14) to imply that "Jesus seeks us . . . as long as it takes, . . . not only in life but also in death."[57] "Hell is not outside the compass of God's mercy," progressive evangelical Donald Bloesch asserts. "The gates of the holy city are depicted as being open day and night (Isa 60:11; Rev 21:25), which means that access to the throne of grace is a continuing possibility. . . . Even when one is in hell, one can be forgiven."[58]

If post-mortem conversion is even possible, then the church should make salvation prayers. While uncommon, such prayers are not without precedent. Pseudo-Dionysus—an unknown Syrian from the sixth century—mentions intercessory prayer for the unsaved dead, that they might be forgiven their sins and be received into heaven.[59] The eighth-century Roman Catholic *Sacramentary of Gellone* has a Mass for one "whose soul is in doubt": "we humbly pray . . . that while we despair for the quality of his life, we may be consoled from the abundance of your kindness. And if we cannot obtain full forgiveness for his soul, let him at least . . . feel some refreshment from the abundance of your mercy."[60] In the thirteenth century, Hadewijch of Antwerp argued that the church should intercede for

---

55. Howard, *Evangelical is Not Enough*, 124-25.

56. Balthasar, *Dare We Hope* and Rahner, *Theological Investigations* Vol. 19, 191, slightly modified. Also see Ludlow, *Universal Salvation*.

57. Willimon, *Who Will Be Saved?* 84.

58. Bloesch, *Essentials*, 226-28.

59. Pseudo-Dionysus, cited in Ramelli, *Christian Doctrine of Apokatastasis*, 705.

60. *Sacramentary of Gellone*, cited in McLaughlin, *Consorting with Saints*, 203-4 and 257.

the salvation of the unsaved dead—and Hildegard of Bingen refers to the final unity, not only of the saints, but of all sinners. A pre-Reformation English devotional manual contains this prayer:

> be merciful, O Lord, ... to those souls ... for whom there is no consolation or hope in their torment, save that they were made in thine image. Spare them, O Lord, spare them, and defend thy work in them, and give not the honor of thy name ... to another. Despise not the work of thy hands in them, but ... free them from the intolerable pains and anguish of hell, and lead them to the fellowship of the citizens on high.[61]

In the nineteenth century, Sophornius Sacharov refers to "praying for those in hell"—the intercessor "prays for the remission of sins for all," asking "repentance for the whole world, for all humankind." In the twentieth century Nikolai Berdyaev discusses the role that the prayers of the church play in the restoration of all persons to Christ.[62]

Roman Catholic Eucharistic petitions now include the non-Christian dead. Prayer 2 says, "remember ... our brothers and sisters who have fallen asleep in the hope of the resurrection *and* all who have died in your mercy: welcome them into the light of your face"; prayer 3 says, "to our departed brothers and sisters *and* to all who were pleasing to you at their passing from this life, give kind admittance to your Kingdom"; and prayer 4 says, "remember ... those who have died in the peace of your Christ *and* all the dead, whose faith you alone have known. To all of us, your children, grant ... that we may enter into a heavenly inheritance."[63] Technically, none of these are prayers for the unsaved; they are prayers for the saved, a category of persons which is more inclusive than practicing Christians. But the point stands—the church's prayers extend beyond baptized believers.

---

61. Plumptre, *Spirits in Prison*, 274–75.

62. Hadewijch, Hildegard, Sacharov, and Berdyaev, cited in Ramelli, *Christian Doctrine of Apokatastasis*, 75, 626, 509 and 75 respectively.

63. U.S. Conference of Catholic Bishops, *Roman Missal*, 501, 506, 513, emphasis added. In each prayer the phrase preceding the conjunction "and" refers to Christians while the clause following refers to non-Christians. Also see Congregation for Divine Worship, *Directory on Popular Piety*, Section 250. Vatican II, while more open to inclusive salvation of the unevangelized continues to reject posthumous salvation, insisting that individuals can only be saved in this life. But if the Roman Catholic Church can officially revise its centuries-old stance on exclusive salvation in favor of inclusivism, it should also be open to rethinking its long-held belief that death closes opportunities for repentance and be open to the possibility of posthumous salvation.

An Anglican-Orthodox statement recommends prayer for the unsaved: "even those in hell are not deprived of the love of God. . . . The Orthodox Church in the prayers of Pentecost, believing that Christ has the keys of death and hell (Rev 1:18), and hoping that the love of God will find a response in the souls even of some who are in hell, prays for their salvation."[64] The Episcopal Church includes petitions for the unsaved dead; Form IV in the Prayers of the People asks "for all who have died, that they may have a place in your eternal Kingdom"—and in Form VI "we commend to your mercy all who have died, that your will for them may be fulfilled."[65] The United Methodist Church allows the possibility of post-mortem conversion in its funeral prayers for persons who did not profess Christian faith: "look favorably . . . upon those . . . who scarcely knew your grace. . . . Grant mercy also to those who have departed this life in ignorance or defiance of you."[66] Even the conservative Christian Reformed Church has a funeral prayer for those who lived openly sinful lives ("we place in your merciful hands N. . . . His/her life was filled with sin and struggle, but only you . . . perceive what mustard seed of faith . . . was hidden in his/her heart") and for those who were not known to be Christian ("we commend N. . . . to your merciful care, knowing that you . . . will do right").[67]

These inclusive petitions are hopeful signs—and I urge Roman Catholics and Eastern Orthodox (as well as Protestants, of course) to explicitly pray for the unsaved dead.

Concluding Remarks

Christians, McLaren says, must "accommodate (if not welcome) the new while preserving the old," must "incorporate the ancient with the

---

64. Anglican-Orthodox Dialogue, *Dublin Agreed Statement*, Section III: "Worship and Tradition: The Communion of Saints and the Departed," Section 66. The prayer (cited in Ware, "One Body in Christ," 189–90) states: "O Christ . . . who hast descended into hell and shattered the eternal bars, revealing the way of ascent for those who dwell in that lower world . . . accept intercessory propitiation on behalf of those held fast in hell . . . and send down on them relaxation of their torments." While not a salvation prayer *per se*, it does assume that the suffering of the unsaved can be relieved.

65. Episcopal Church, *Book of Common Prayer*, 383–93. Also see United Methodist Church, *United Methodist Book of Worship*, 43–44 and 495.

66. United Methodist Church, *Service of Death and Resurrection*, 83.

67. Vander Zee, *In Life and Death*, 203–4.

avante garde." Ressourcement and *semper reformanda* must be held in tension. The church, the Roman Catholic Bishops say, must witness to unchanged faith while accommodating new understandings.[68] As Webber challenges us: "the Holy Spirit calls the Church to examine its faithfulness to God's revelation in Jesus Christ, authoritatively recorded in Scripture and handed down through the Church."[69] An ancient-future faith blends tradition and revision, developing fresh doctrinal insights and liturgical expressions that stand in continuity with long-established Christian belief and practice. To Protestants I say: retrieve past practice—revise recent tradition by returning to older tradition. Begin praying for the dead—if you already do so in the burial office, add prayers of intercession regularly in public worship, and include all the departed. To Roman Catholics and Eastern Orthodox I say: revise existing practice—refine long-standing tradition. Continue praying for the dead—but expand the scope of your prayers to include the unsaved.

Our prayers should match the doctrines we confess. The demand for coherence, Terrance Tiessen says, means "that people's beliefs should be internally consistent (i.e. that they should agree with themselves) and that their actions should be consistent with their theology."[70] If and how we pray for the dead must fit our theological and eschatological convictions—and *vice versa*. If we believe that the culmination of all things is not experienced immediately at death then consummation prayers are appropriate. If we believe that those in God's presence continually increase in love, then growth prayers are appropriate. If we believe that those who die in a state of grace but unready for God's presence are gradually transformed after death then purification prayers are appropriate. And if we believe that opportunities for repentance continue beyond death then salvation prayers are appropriate. To believe any of these things but not pray for them is to make faith and practice inconsistent.

In the second volume I defend consummation, growth, purification, and salvation prayers. In the remainder of this volume I turn to the logical presuppositions which prayer for the dead requires: assumptions about the efficacy of prayer and about the life that comes after death (about human nature and identity and about time and eternity).

---

68. McLaren, "One, Holy, Catholic and Fresh?" 16 and 19 and U.S. Conference of Catholic Bishops, *General Instruction*, 7 and 10.

69. Webber, cited in Husbands, "Introduction," 10.

70. Tiessen, *Providence and Prayer*, 14.

A PAUSE

The Goals of Explanation and Proof

A MORNING IN THE campus cafeteria, a big window with lots of light, students floating by with a cheery "good morning." My colleague Timothy and I are having coffee and discussing this book. "I'm afraid I come on too strong in some places," I confess. "And I think I sound more confident than I am. After all, my opponents will think 'we've answered everything you say.'" He looks thoughtful—then replies. "Maybe you need to sprinkle throughout the text reminders that, while you don't have conclusive proof, you are building a strong case for your positions." "Yes," I pause, rolling pungent coffee around my mouth. Timothy continues: "so what if those on the other side aren't convinced? Sometimes we just reach rock-bottom fundamental disagreements." Minutes later, as he stands to leave, he advises: "Take a look at Nozick's distinction between explanation and proof."

The remaining chapters in this book lay out the philosophical assumptions (concerning petitionary prayer, human nature, time, and eternity) and theological framework (concerning God's nature and purposes in creation and redemption) that lie beneath prayer for the dead. It is important to clarify what my goals in these chapters are. Robert Nozick distinguishes two purposes of intellectual investigation: explanation and proof. Robert Roberts and Jay Wood agree: intellectual activity aims at understanding and warranted true belief.[1]

One mode of philosophy and theology seeks explanation—it tries to "render [ideas] coherent and better understood."[2] The process of thinking aims to elaborate and sharpen ideas, concepts, and theories by delineat-

---

1. Nozick, *Philosophical Explanations*, 8, and Roberts and Wood, *Intellectual Virtues*, 33. In these paragraphs I draw on Nozick's "Introduction," 1–24.

2. Ibid., 8.

ing their contents and exploring their connections with other ideas—all with the goal of increasing understanding by grasping and drawing connections. In the remainder of this book I examine how praying for the dead is not an isolated idea but is linked to diverse questions beyond the practice itself. My goal is to piece together various ideas, to show how prayer for the dead fits with philosophical assumptions and theological doctrines that support it, to understand how these various ideas fit together in a coherent conceptual network. Prayer for the dead is embedded in a set of beliefs, and I attempt to expose its connections to these assumptions.

Intellectual investigation, however, has aims other than explanation—helping someone understand something better. It can also serve the purpose of defending particular conclusions; this mode of philosophy and theology offers proof by giving arguments that attempt to persuade the listener to believe certain things. I will defend specific views, attempting to build a cumulative case by giving reasons to support them. This does not mean, however, that other views of prayer, human nature, or time lack merit. "Even [if] one view is clearly best," Nozick says, "we do not keep only this first-ranked view, rejecting all others."[3] Even when strong, few philosophical or theological arguments force us to accept their conclusions; they have defects and thus are not perfect, foolproof, or knock-down. Alternative positions on difficult and controversial questions like the workings of prayer, the makeup of human nature, and the essence of time are admissible, even if the ones I commend are—to my mind—most adequate. Different thinkers will disagree about which views are admissible and about how they should be ranked in plausibility.

Philosophy and theology are both explanatory and persuasive activities, and so I have two motivations in forthcoming chapters. My goals are both explanation (helping the reader understand various theories that connect to and undergird prayer for the dead) and proof (getting the reader to believe various ideas by providing convincing arguments). I attempt to explain—to put certain beliefs in alignment with each other, to show how prayer for the dead goes along with other things in philosophy and theology. And I try to prove—to convince by reasoning that these assumptions and ideas should be accepted. The goal of proof, Nozick contends, is more coercive—the idea is to persuade, to construct arguments that are powerful enough to force listeners to accept certain

3. Ibid., 21–22.

positions. The goal of explanation, by contrast, is less coercive—the idea is to deepen and extend understanding of one's own (or an alien) belief system, to see how it fits together. In the following chapters I offer explanations I hope the reader will find illuminating and arguments I hope they will find convincing. My explanations and arguments are—to use Nozick's words—"put forward not as the sole correct view on their topics, but as members among others of admissible classes, with the hope that they will be ranked first, or at least highly likely." While I defend certain views—a non-deterministic theory of petitionary prayer, a materialist portrait of human composition, and a dynamic conception of time—as most intuitively plausible and rationally coherent, I do not attempt "to knock all other theories [of prayer, human nature, or time] out as inadmissible."[4] Even readers who do not think that I have succeeded at proof can approach my ideas as explanations.

---

4. Ibid., 23–24.

chapter 5

GOD, CAUSALITY, AND THE EFFECTIVENESS OF PRAYING FOR THE DEAD

I AM GRADING PAPERS at my desk when the phone call comes. "Dad, I'm feeling sick and can't continue with softball practice," my high-school-aged daughter Becky says. "Can you come pick me up at the field house?" I think for a moment, then reply: "I'll be there in a few minutes. But can you meet me at the main entrance instead?" "That's fine," she answers. This ordinary conversation has the earmarks of a personal relationship. It involves parties who act independently of each other; each can cause changes in the plans of the other, and each is open to adapting their own plans. Taken at face value, biblical prayer has this same character.

"Prayers for the dead," Charles Wright asserts, "are natural to those who believe . . . in the efficacy of prayer for others and . . . in the dead being in a state of conscious existence."[1] It assumes that

1. the dead can be helped
2. by our intercessions.

But what if statement 1 is false and the dead are beyond help? Or suppose 2 is false and they can be helped, but not by our prayers?[2] In either case

---

1. Wright, "Prayers for Dead," 1.
2. Perhaps they can only help themselves, be helped by God, or be helped by us doing things like securing indulgences.

praying would be pointless. Prayer for the dead must meet three conditions in order to be intelligible:

1. the real influence requirement—prayer makes a difference to what God does,
2. the personal existence requirement—the departed consciously exist as the very same people they were in life, and
3. the open future requirement—change of spiritual state is possible after death.

Each condition is individually necessary and all together are jointly sufficient for prayer for the dead to make sense. In this chapter I examine the logic of petitionary prayer—and in the next two, the nature of the life to come (which is conscious, personal, and temporal).

The Effective Prayer Requirement

The prayers for the departed that concern me are intercessions which ask God to do something; in fact, the word "prayer" comes from the Latin *precari*—"to ask earnestly."[3] If praying for my dead father makes no difference—if it cannot motivate God to act on his behalf—then it is useless. The *real influence requirement* states that prayer can change God's mind about what God will do and thus can shape how things go in the world. "What we pray and how we pray," Tyron Inbody says, "depends on what we understand God to be and how we understand God to work in the world and in our lives."[4] Petitionary prayer only makes sense with a certain kind of God (one who is personal and responsive) and in a certain kind of universe (one that is non-deterministic).

Petitionary Prayer in the Bible

A philosophy of petitionary prayer, Charles Taliaferro contends, should be shaped by how it is portrayed in the Bible.[5] "Call to me and I will answer you" (Jer 33:3), God says; "call on me [and] I will deliver you"

---

3. Taliaferro, "Prayer," 677. Whenever I use the word "prayer" I mean "petitionary prayer"—and I use the terms "petition" and "intercession" interchangeably.
4. Inbody, "Power of Prayer," 63.
5. Taliaferro, "Prayer," 683.

(Ps 50:15). "What other great nation," Moses asks the Israelites, "has a god so near to it as the Lord our God is whenever we call to him?" (Deut 4:7). Walter Brueggemann observes that biblical prayer has a "cry out–response" structure. "This poor soul cried," the psalmist (Ps 34:4, 6, 17) says, "and was heard by the Lord, and was saved from every trouble." The person who prays experiences a problem; they pray—believing that God is sovereign and can change things and that God is caring and wants to intervene for good—and God hears and answers.[6]

The "ask–answer" pattern occurs in the national life of Israel. In Egyptian bondage the Hebrew slaves cry out; God hears and sends Moses the deliverer (Exod 2:23–24). At Sinai the Israelites rebel and God threatens destruction; Moses implores God to "turn away from your fierce wrath," and "the Lord changed his mind about the disaster that he planned to bring on his people" (Exod 32:12–14). When the Israelites fear to enter Canaan, God once more wants to destroy them. Moses again pleads and God again relents: "I do forgive—just as you have asked" (Num 14:17–20). The future was contingent—God could punish or not—and God wanted someone to change God's mind. The "ask–answer" pattern occurs as well in the personal experience of individuals. Abraham pleads with God to preserve the innocent in Sodom, and Lot and his family are saved (Gen 18:16–33). When the widow's son dies, Elijah prays and "the Lord listened . . . ; the life of the child came into him again" (1 Kgs 17:20–22).[7] Numerous other examples from Gideon (Judg 6:36–40) to King Hezekiah (Isa 37:12–20) could be given.

Christian Scripture[8] also emphasizes a God who answers prayer. Jesus practiced petitionary prayer—asking that Peter's faith not fail (Luke 22:32) and that his suffering be removed (Matt 26:39–42). Jesus taught petitionary prayer: "ask, and it will be given you," he says; "your Father in heaven [will] give good things to those who ask" (Matt 7:7,11). Jesus

---

6. Brueggeman, *Psalms and Life of Faith*, 78–82 and 136–48.

7. Brueggemann (*Threat of Life*, 43–44) says that Elijah "prays an imperative to God. His is a voice of deep, demanding faith . . . . God yields to Elijah. Elijah has compelled God to act. . . . The prayer, faith, courage and daring of Elijah have changed the world."

8. By "Christian Scripture" I am referring to what is usually called the New Testament. My concern with language about "Old" and "New" Testaments is that it can imply a historically supersessionist view that I am uncomfortable with. I appreciate that talking of the so-called "New Testament" as "Christian Scripture" is clumsy (because Christian Scripture also includes the so-called "Old Testament"), but I hope readers will understand my intentions.

urges perseverance in prayer (Luke 11:5–8; 18:1–8), and his healings and exorcisms are done in response to cries of distress from those in need (e.g., Matt 9:27–29). When asked, he stills the storm (Matt 8:23–27), brings a girl to life (Matt 9:18–19, 23–25), and rescues Peter from drowning (Matt 14:30–31).[9] Petitionary prayer was practiced in the early church. St. Peter prays for Tabitha's restoration from death (Acts 9:40); the believers pray for boldness (Acts 4:23–31) and for St. Peter's escape from jail (Acts 12:5–19). St. Paul prays for strangers (for healings on Malta, for example—Acts 28:8) and on behalf of his fledgling churches (e.g., Rom 1:9). He requests prayer from others—for release from prison, for example (Phil 1:19). He teaches that we should make requests to God (Phil 4:6)—as do St. Peter (1 Pet 5:7), St. James (4:2; 5:16–18) and St. John (1 John 3:21–22).

The biblical data suggest that prayer influences God's actions, changing the future and making it different that it would have been without prayer.

Theological Reflection on Petitionary Prayer

Petitionary prayer has two purposes: it changes our minds and it changes God's mind. Prayer affects the person praying; it attunes our hearts and minds to God and determines our fundamental orientation to the world. Beyond its human formation function, petitionary prayer has a divine-influence function: it sometimes causes God to act in ways that God would not have acted if not asked to do so. This claim—that prayer is effective—raises deep questions about what God is like and how God relates to creation.[10] The Church of England Commission on Christian Doctrine wonders:

> when we are praying for the departed, are we asking God to do things God has already determined either to do or not to do, so that our prayer can have no effect . . . one way or the other? Are we asking God to change God's mind as to the fate of . . .

9. Bueggemann, *Psalms and Life of Faith*, 82–83.
10. In what follows I draw on Basinger, *Case for Free Will Theism*; Basinger, "God Does Not Necessarily Respond to Prayer"; Basinger, "Why Petition?"; Brummer, *What Are We Doing When We Pray?*; Cohoe, "God, Causality and Petitionary Prayer"; Davison, "Petitionary Prayer" (both sources); Mavrodes, "Prayer"; Murray, "God Responds to Prayer"; Murray and Meyers, "Ask and It Will Be Given"; Smith, "Philosophical Reflection on Petitionary Prayer"; Smith and Yip, "Partnership with God"; Stump, "Petitionary Prayer"; Taliaferro, "Prayer"; Tiessen, *Providence and Prayer*.

particular souls? Are we assuming that, in default of our prayers, God will not do the good things for which we are asking? Or that unless we pray God will not do these good things as effectively or as quickly, so that our prayers have power to intensify or speed up God's action?[11]

How should we understand petitionary prayer in general—and petitionary prayer for the dead in particular?

Defining Effective Prayer

Petitionary prayers ask God to intervene for good in the lives of people. St. James (5:16) claims that "the prayer of the righteous is powerful and effective"—it causes God to act. Daniel and Frances Howard-Snyder point out that the very nature of petitionary prayer assumes real influence. "Our words do not constitute the speech-act of petitioning if we think that our words won't make any difference to whether [God] does what we ask." If my prayer is "I ask that you heal my friend, but I know that what I ask makes no difference to what you do"—then my words are not a *petition*, which are by definition requests that attempt to influence others to act.[12]

To be effective, a request must make a distinctive causal contribution to an event happening. There are three types of effective prayer.

1. *Strongly effective prayer* is a necessary condition for God acting—it determines whether or not God acts at all.[13] Sometimes a request gives us a reason to do something we would not otherwise have done. I may

---

11. Archbishops' Commission, *Prayer and Departed*, 17–18.

12. Howard-Synder, "Puzzle of Petitionary Prayer," 46.

13. A *necessary* cause C is the circumstance in whose absence an event E cannot occur. If C is a necessary cause of E, then E will not happen unless C happens. When prayer is necessary, our not asking stops God from acting—in the same way that I might not paint the bathroom unless Jenna asks. By contrast, a *sufficient* cause C for the occurrence of an event E is the circumstance (or set of circumstances) in whose presence the event must occur. If C is a sufficient cause of E, then when C happens so does E. It might be thought that prayer is never a sufficient cause since our asking cannot force God to act; God is a sovereign King, not a puppet who we micromanage. But prayer can indeed be sufficient for God's acting since God can decide to do something if it is requested—just as my son David's asking might be reason enough for me to stop writing and go bicycling with him (all things being equal—that there is no gunman in the street, for example). See Copi and Cohen, *Introduction to Logic*, 450–51 and Brummer, *What Are We Doing When We Pray?* 74–82.

throw out some old shirts, which I prefer to keep, because my wife Jenna asks me to—and God (to use Scott Davison's words) may "bring about the thing requested because of the prayer, so that had the prayer not been offered, the thing in question would not have occurred."[14] "You do not have," St. James asserts, "because you do not ask" (Jas 4:2). If—for example—Monica's prayers for the salvation of her wayward son, Augustine of Hippo, are strongly effective, then without them he would not have been saved.

2. *Moderately effective prayer* is contributive to God acting—it determines, not whether God acts, but how and when.[15] Requests may exert influence by giving us reason to do differently something we were already going to do. I am planning to take Jenna to the evening symphony—but when she asks to go to the afternoon matinee instead, I agree. "It is possible," Eleonore Stump says, "that God would have saved Augustine without Monica's prayers but not in the same amount of time or not by the same process."[16] David Crump points out that when the ancient Jews recited the *kaddish*—"may God establish God's Kingdom in our lifetime . . . speedily and soon"—they "were keenly aware that they asked God to perform works God had already begun, works God fully intended to complete. . . . Nevertheless, prayers could influence the outcome of God's plan—that was, after all, the essence of the petition. . . . Human behavior was . . . capable of influencing God's timing and the particulars of its fulfillment."[17] Some aspects of God's action are contingent and can be affected by prayer.

3. *Weakly effective prayer* is additive to God's motivation—it provides an extra reason for God to do something God would have done anyway. I am planning to get a haircut this weekend, but when Jenna asks, it gives me additional reason—above and beyond other reasons I might have—to do so. In fact, each time Jenna repeats her request I have a

14. Davison, "Petitionary Prayer," *SEP*, slightly modified. Elsewhere ("Petitionary Prayer," *OHPT*) he calls this the "counterfactual dependence" theory of prayer. If a person had not prayed for some item, then it would not have happened. Both necessary and contributive prayers meet this counterfactual condition.

15. A *contributive* cause C shares responsibility for an event E happening. If C is a contributory cause of E, then changing C changes E. Contributive prayers influence the particulars of how and when God acts to bring something about—just as my child's request is necessary not to whether he gets supper, but to whether he gets spaghetti instead of soup and eats at 5:30 rather than 6:30.

16. Stump, "Petitionary Prayer," 89.

17. Crump, *Knocking on Heaven's Door*, 112 and 130.

new reason to act—as I do when I receive the same request from multiple sources (if my daughter Sarah also asks me to get a haircut).[18] Prayers may move God to act—Caleb Cohoe says—"even in some cases where their objects would have been secured without prayer."[19] David Chapman observes that "a significant proportion of Christian prayer involves our asking God to do what we believe God wills to do anyway."[20]

The real influence requirement insists that prayer for the dead is effective—that it makes a difference by moving God, in one way or another, to act on their behalf.

The Problem of Petitionary Prayer

Petitionary prayer raises several difficult questions. C. S. Lewis identifies one: "the thing you ask for is either good . . . or else it is not. If it is, then a good . . . God will do it anyway. If it is not, then God won't. In neither case can your prayer make any difference." In rebuttal, Lewis points out that "if this argument is sound . . . it is an argument not only against praying, but against doing anything whatever." The goal of every human action is either good or bad—if it is good God will bring it about without our involvement and if it is bad God will prevent it whatever we do. "Why wash your hands? If God intends them to be clean, they'll come clean without your washing them. If God doesn't, they'll remain dirty . . . however much soap you use. Why ask for the salt? Why put on your boots?" Since we know that our actions produce results that God does not provide on God's own, perhaps our prayers are effective as well.[21]

Lewis' *reductio ad absurdum* argument, while insightful, does not resolve the apparent logical inconsistency between the effectiveness of prayer and God's perfect character. A God who can and wants to act for good will simply do so—while a God who withholds what we need until we pray seems less than perfect. The problem of petitionary prayer is an aspect of the problem of evil: if God is completely good and powerful, then evil should not exist—nor should prayer be necessary for God to

---

18. See Howard-Snyder, "Puzzle of Petitionary Prayer," 50. I owe this point to my colleague Timothy Linehan. It may be that repeated, multiple-origin prayers are necessary for strongly and moderately effective prayer.

19. Cohoe, "God, Causality and Petitionary Prayer," 37.

20. Chapman, "Rest and Light Perpetual," 46.

21. Lewis, "Work and Prayer," in *God in Dock*, 105–6.

do what is best.²² One horn of the dilemma is the *pointlessness of prayer problem*—if God is already acting to do what is good then prayer cannot make a difference. The other horn is the *diminished character of God problem*—if God will not act effectively until a request is made then God's goodness or power are compromised. Deterministic and non-deterministic theologies resolve this problem differently.²³

Petitionary prayer and deterministic theology

Deterministic theology, Oliver Crisp says, has two defining claims: divine immutability (God is an absolute being who cannot change) and divine determinism (God ordains all that comes to pass, including human actions).²⁴ God is not affected by anything outside of God; God cannot be influenced by God's creation in any way. The future is actual, not potential—there is only one possible course of events. Everything that happens is fixed down to the last detail, being determined by God to occur as it does. Human beings have compatiblistic freedom. A person's action is free if it is caused by their beliefs and desires and is not caused by some external form of control. Actions, on this view, can be completely determined yet still be free.

In deterministic theism petitionary prayer cannot affect God's actions since God cannot change. Whether God brings about some state of affairs cannot require prayer, for that would make God dependent on something outside of God. And since the future is totally settled and nothing is open-ended, prayer cannot influence what happens.

Theological determinists give two reasons why we should pray. First, petitionary prayer is a discipline of personal transformation. It creates moral and spiritual change by aligning our attitudes and actions

---

22. The *problem of evil* consists of a trilemma: 1. God is completely good (and so wants to get rid of evil and suffering). 2. God is completely powerful (and so can get rid of evil and suffering). 3. There is evil and suffering in the world. The *problem of petitionary prayer* involves a parallel trilemma: 1. God is completely good (and so wants the world to be as good as it can be). 2. God is completely powerful (and so can make the world as good as it can be). 3. Our prayers are effective (God does not act independently to make the world as good as it can be, but waits for prayer).

23. This analysis is in some respects simplistic; I am ignoring many fine details since there are a number of deterministic and non-deterministic theisms. See Tiessen, *Providence and Prayer*, for an overview of several theories.

24. Crisp, "John Calvin and Petitioning God."

to God's will.²⁵ Second, petitionary prayer is the predetermined means through which predetermined ends occur. Thomas Aquinas claims that "divine providence not only disposes what effects will take place, but also the manner in which they will take place, and which actions will cause them.... We do not pray in order to change the decree of divine providence, rather we pray in order to [acquire] those things which God has determined would be obtained only through our prayers."²⁶ God's eternal and fixed plan includes both that Augustine be saved and that it happen through Monica's prayers.

Deterministic views of petitionary prayer are deeply flawed. First, they substitute a philosophical theology of God as absolute Being derived from Platonic and Aristotelian metaphysics for a biblical theology of God as supreme Person.²⁷ God is not like the pagan idols which cannot hear and act (Isa 41:7 and 44:18; Jer 10:5). Instead, Abraham's prayer for Sodom saves Lot and Moses' prayer for Israel averts God's wrath. Petition changes the future by influencing God to act differently than God would have without prayer. Determinist interpretations rob biblical language of its plain meaning.²⁸

Second, deterministic theologies make prayer useless since it has no direct effect on God but is simply the preordained means to accomplish what God has decreed to happen. As Ambrose of Milan notes: "if all things come to pass by the will of God, and God's counsels are fixed, and none of the things God wills can be changed, prayer is vain."²⁹ Vincent Brummer makes an important distinction: "to say that God brings about events *by means of* our prayers is not the same as to say that God brings about events *because of* our prayers."³⁰ John Sanders makes a similar point: in deterministic theologies "God may be said to do [something] 'because'

---

25. God, Calvin (*Institutes*, Book 3.20.3, Vol. 2, 174) says, "ordained [prayer] not so much for God's own sake as for ours." He lists several psychological effects of prayer (such as preventing a sense of self-sufficiency by making us aware of our dependence of God's provision of our needs).

26. Aquinas, *Summa Theologiae*, Vol. 39, 2a 2ae q 83 a2, 53.

27. Crump, *Knocking on Heaven's Door*, 284.

28. There are, of course, debates about when Scripture's meaning is plain and when its language is metaphorical. All interpreters read some texts literally and some metaphorically, so the question is where we draw the line. I take the passages cited above at face value.

29. Ambrose, cited in Brummer, *What Are We Doing When We Pray?* 39. Yancey (*Prayer*, 131) attributes this quote to Origen.

30. Brummer, *What Are We Doing When We Pray?* 59; emphasis added.

we prayed only in the sense that God has always decreed that God was going to do [it] after we prayed the prayer God also decreed." Since the prayers themselves are as much a part of God's predetermined plan as the answers are, God is the only one acting.[31] In deterministic theology our prayers—including petitions for the dead—can have no effect whatsoever on what God decides; it is by definition impossible. Non-deterministic theologies, by contrast, affirm the real influence of petitionary prayer.

Petitionary prayer and non-deterministic theology

Non-deterministic theism rejects both divine immutability and divine determinism. God is a personal being who is involved with history. God limits God's own power in order to respect libertarian freedom. An action is free if the person can either do or not do the action, if they can make a different choice than the one they actually make—and it is not determined in advance that we will or will not do a given action. The future is potential, not actual—there are many possibilities for how it might unfold. Peter Geach says that "what happens in the world . . . depends not only on God's will but on the wills of . . . millions of little first causes. . . . God's terrifying love of freedom has made the will of God's creatures the hinge of fate, on which it turns whether some door of possibility shall be open or be shut."[32] By granting us a central role in determining which path the world takes, God voluntarily gives up complete control over history. Being infinitely wise and resourceful, however, God is able to incorporate human choices—even those that oppose God's will—into God's plan. God, Geach suggests, is like a grand chess master who will realize God's intentions and win the game whatever moves we do or do not make.[33] While God's ultimate goals and moral character and commitments never change, God does adjust God's strategies in response to human actions.

In non-deterministic theology prayer is effective since God's actions are sometimes contingent on our requests. "You do not have because you do not ask" (Jas 4:2), St. James says, and Jesus' disciples could not exorcize a young boy because they did not pray (Mark 9:28–29). Lewis concludes:

---

31. Sanders, *God Who Risks*, 270. Crisp ("John Calvin and Petitioning God," 144)—a determinist—admits that determinism makes prayer pointless; in fact, he says, it makes prayer *necessarily* pointless.

32. Geach, *Virtues*, 53 and 60.

33. Geach, *Providence and Evil*, 57–58. I defend non-determinism in "Bonhoeffer and Open Theism."

"God made God's own plan . . . such that it admits a certain amount of free play, and can be modified in response to our prayers."[34] But this raises a concern. *Weakly* effective prayer does not threaten divine perfection since God has—before we pray—sufficient motive to act (to which our prayers add a new reason). But there is a problem with *strongly* and *moderately* effective prayer: since asking is necessary to whether or how God acts, our not praying can stop God from acting at all or from acting optimally. Stump defines the dilemma this way: "the assertion that . . . prayers are necessary [or contributive] . . . seems to impugn God's goodness, and the claim that they are altogether without effect . . . undercuts petitionary prayer."[35] Non-determinists seem to affirm real influence only to deny divine perfection.

The answer to this dilemma parallels the greater good strategy for resolving the problem of evil.[36] Evil is permitted by God in order to realize better goods (such as protecting human freedom, building moral character, and preserving natural laws). In the same way, there are important things that can only be achieved if God does not act unless we pray. The primary good God achieves by doing things if we ask is human-divine partnership—it makes us "God's fellow workers" (1 Cor 3:9 *NIV*) in accomplishing God's purposes. "God's policy is to involve us," John Goldingay says, and "prayers of intercession are part of the way we are involved in running the world."[37] In prayer we collaborate with God, contributing to how and when—sometimes whether—God acts. By praying for Israel Moses shapes a future that would not have been the case had he remained silent. Because God has chosen to act in partnership with us, there are things that God can and would like to do but which are withheld if we do not pray—the demon-possessed boy was not healed because Jesus' disciples did not pray. "An order of created things which includes creaturely causation and petitionary prayer," Cohoe says, "is better than one in which God brings all things about immediately."[38]

Another good of petitionary prayer is that it makes us responsible for meeting the needs of other people. "God rests our neighbor's good

---

34. Lewis, "Work and Prayer," in *God in Dock*, 106.
35. Stump, "Petitionary Prayer," 89.
36. The greater good strategy for resolving the problem of evil adds a fourth premise—God has a good reason for allowing evil—to the argument and the contradiction between the first three is blunted.
37. Goldingay, "Logic of Intercession," 262 and 264.
38. Cohoe, "God, Causality and Petitionary Prayer," 45.

upon our [actions]," George Buttrick points out, so "why not upon our prayers?"[39] George Mavrodes agrees: "part of the divine purpose for the world is that we should grow into . . . a community of mutual love . . . in which each of us does good things for the others, including the good of praying for the others."[40] Praying is an act of love for and a means of service to other people; it lets us seek their welfare and make a difference in their lives. "Intercession," Goldingay says, is priestly action that "involves standing in the place of people who need to have their position represented."[41] God "leaves part of the job of making the world a better place up to [us]," Lawrence Masek adds, "and prayers for others allow [us] to exercise this power."[42]

Prayer with real influence does not diminish God's character since a world where God does not act until we pray is better than a world where God acts independently, whether we pray or not. God sometimes refrains from acting in ways that God can and would like to in order to achieve the important good that Nicholas Smith calls "expanded moral agency in partnership with God."[43] Since it is better, all things considered, that God sometimes not act unless asked to, non-determinist theologies can affirm that prayer is effective—that it influences the timing and specifics of how God's intentions are accomplished—without diminishing God's perfect character.

Concluding Remarks

There are, of course, reasons to be skeptical of petitionary prayer. What about unanswered prayers—like St. Paul's repeated plea that God remove his "thorn in the flesh" (2 Cor 12:7)—which, in Bill Newcott's words, "seem to sail off into some cosmic dead letter file?"[44] And what about answered prayers—is it ever possible to know that particular prayers have been effective in influencing God to act? What evidence, Davison

39. Buttrick, *Prayer*, 112.
40. Mavrodes, "Prayer," Section 2.
41. Goldingay, "Logic of Intercession," 268.
42. Masek, "Petitionary Prayer," 274 and 280. Allen ("On Not Understanding Prayer," 2) comments: "if we could not ask God then the ways in which our moral concern could . . . express itself would be greatly restricted. . . . One can at least help through prayer." This is especially true of praying for the dead.
43. Smith, "Philosophical Reflection on Petitionary Prayer," 5.
44. Newcott, "Paradox of Prayer," 50. See Craig, *No Easy Answers*, chapter 2.

wonders, could we have that an "apparent answer to prayer would not have happened anyway, even if nobody had prayed for it?"[45] However we answer these questions—we know that some prayers are not answered but do not know that any are—the biblical model and mandate is clear.

God, Karl Barth asserts, "does not act in the same way whether we pray or not. Prayer exerts an influence upon God's action.... That is what the word 'answer' means.... The fact that God yields to human petitions, changing God's intentions in response to human prayer, is not a sign of weakness. God ... has so willed it."[46] We pray for the departed to a God who—Dietrich Bonhoeffer says—"is no timeless fate, but waits for and responds to sincere prayer."[47] The eschatological future is indefinite—its timetable and details are yet to be determined by God and can be influenced by prayer. St. Peter (2 Pet 3:12) commands us to be persons who are "waiting for and *hastening*"—the Greek word *speudontas* means "to speed" or "urge on"—the final events, the coming of the day of God. David Payne comments: "this is a striking suggestion, implying that human beings can in some way speed up God's plans."[48] What goes for consummation goes generally: since God's will has not been completely fulfilled for any of the dead, their fates can be influenced by prayer. Just as we can affect how and when the last things occur, so growth in heaven may not occur as intensely as it can with prayer, purification in purgatory may not happen as easily or quickly as it would with prayer, and salvation in hell may be resisted and delayed longer than it might with prayer. Prayers for the dead make a difference.

We pray for the departed expectantly. As the Archbishops' Commission concludes, "we [are not] pleading with a reluctant God to change God's ... purpose concerning them. Rather, we express a simple, trustful confidence in the loving care and mercy of a heavenly Father.... Prayer for the departed is not, any more than any other prayer, an attempt to ... suggest to God some action that it was not already God's will to take."[49] Christopher Cocksworth agrees: "we are not saying to God 'we doubt your willingness to do this and feel that you need some encouragement

---

45. Davison, "Petitionary Prayer," *OHPT*, 294.
46. Barth, cited in Yancey, *Prayer*, 143.
47. Bonhoeffer, *Letters and Papers*, 46.
48. Payne, "2 Peter," 1569.
49. Archbishops' Commission, *Prayer and Departed*, 19.

from us. . . .' In fact, we are saying the opposite . . . : 'do as you have promised.'"⁵⁰

While I believe that theological determinism cannot make sense of petitionary prayer, determinists may feel differently. And so, regardless of our theology we should intercede for others. It might be thought, however, that prayer *for the departed* is pointless—perhaps because they do not consciously exist as the very same people between death and resurrection. I turn to that topic next.

---

50. Cocksworth, *Prayer and Departed*, 21.

chapter 6

HUMAN NATURE, PERSONAL IDENTITY, AND PRAYER FOR THE DEAD

My college Philosophy of Death class was debating whether or not there is an afterlife. "I think there is," said Joe. "We are made up of two parts. When we die our souls and our bodies separate; the body is buried in the ground while the soul goes to heaven or hell." Jennie did not agree: "science shows that to be conscious we have to have a working brain—and so the mind is part of the body. When we die our brains stop functioning, consciousness ends—and that's it." To structure the discussion, I labeled their views. "Joe," I said, "you're a survival dualist. You believe that we survive death, and so you are a dualist—while the body dies another part lives on. And Jennie, you're an extinction materialist. You think that we are physical bodies without souls, so you expect to become extinct at death when your consciousness is destroyed. The mind dies with the body because every mental experience depends on something happening in the brain." Death results in one of two conditions (personal survival or personal extinction) and there are two main theories of human nature (dualism and materialism). The standard pairings of afterlife scenarios and anthropological views are survival dualism and extinction materialism. Having explained this, I continued: "it might surprise you both to learn that there is a third alternative: survival materialism. It claims that consciousness requires a body but does not rule out life after death."

Henry Swete states that those "who [1] believe in the efficacy of prayer and [2] have grasped the continuity of human life before and after death, are moved . . . to remember in their prayers the souls of friends and relatives who, though dead to the world, are still alive in the sight of God."[1] Prayer for the departed assumes that they can be helped by our intercessions, and the previous chapter defended the effectiveness of petitionary prayer. But while efficacy is necessary for prayer for the dead to be sensible, it is not sufficient since it is possible that the dead cannot be helped. In order for prayer to be beneficial, the *personal existence requirement* must also be met. It includes two separate conditions.

1. The *conscious experience requirement* states that the dead are aware—they think and feel.
2. The *preserved identity requirement* states that the dead exist as the very same people they were in life.

If I am praying for my dead father then he must exist, be conscious, and be my dad—otherwise prayer *for him* is pointless.

What Scripture teaches about the life to come is imprecise and the philosophical issues concerning human composition and personal identity are complex. In this chapter I describe the major positions—aiming to identify views which are compatible with prayer for the departed, consistent with Scripture, and philosophically defensible.[2]

Afterlife Possibilities

Four broad afterlife scenarios are possible:

1. permanent extinction
2. multiple reincarnations
3. permanent disembodied existence as a soul
4. resurrection as a body.

The first three positions contradict Scripture (as well as the creeds and tradition). The Bible clearly teaches life after death (Rev 14:13), so option 1 is ruled out.[3] The Bible claims that we have only one earthly life, not a

---

1. Swete, "Prayer for Departed," 500, order reversed.
2. The philosophical discussions in the next two chapters aim to be brief, clear, and accurate—which means making some contentious statements and ignoring nitty-gritty details for the sake of brevity and accessibility.
3. This eliminates the existential eschatology of Paul Tillich and Rudolf Bultmann

series of lives (Heb 9:27), so option 2 is eliminated. The Bible indicates that the life to come is bodily (1 Cor 15:35–56), so option 3 must be rejected. That leaves option 4 as the Christian hope. Resurrection can occur immediately at the moment of death or at some point after death (creating a gap in time, an intermediate state, between death and resurrection). There are three possibilities concerning the nature of an intermediate state: non-existence, disembodied existence, and embodied existence. Four afterlife scenarios, then, are consistent with option 4:

A. immediate resurrection with no intermediate state

B. non-existence during the intermediate state

C. disembodied existence as a soul during the intermediate state

D. physical existence in a body during the intermediate state.

Let us see what prayer for the departed requires.

The Conscious Experience Requirement

Consider these points.

1. The purpose of prayer for the dead is to help them.

2. In order to be helped, they must have interests. To have an interest is to have a stake in something and to gain or lose depending on what happens to that thing.

3. In order to have interests an entity must be conscious. Tables and tulips have no interests—they have no good of their own and cannot be helped or harmed for their own sake. But persons do; certain interests are central to our well-being and we flourish or languish as those interests are advanced or set back.[4] In order for the dead to have interests, they must be conscious.

---

in which immortality is about new life here and now—and the process eschatology of Charles Hartshorne in which immortality is being eternally remembered by God. All deny a real afterlife. Permanent extinction (annihilation) of *the unsaved* is a theological possibility.

4. See Feinberg, *Harm to Others*, chapter 1. I discuss these themes further in "Grace We Are Owed," "Broad Inclusive Salvation," and "Earning, Deserving."

4. To be conscious is to have inner awareness—subjective mental states that feel a certain way.[5] Persons have a rich mental life consisting of perception, reasoning, memory, emotion, planning, choosing, communication, and self-awareness. The mind or self is the subject of conscious experience.

If the dead have no thoughts or feelings—and thus no interests—then nothing can be done to benefit them, and our prayers can do them no good. We must determine, then, how Scripture describes and whether philosophy allows survival involving retention of identity and personality.

Biblical Teaching on Life after Death

The Bible has no detailed theory of the afterlife—but the basic picture is of a conscious intermediate state and future resurrection.[6] This is a logical implication of combining two sets of texts—future consummation texts and continuing existence texts—into what Tom Wright calls a two-stage hope: "life after death" (the intermediate state where we go at death) followed by "life after life after death" (the final state where we exist following consummation).[7]

---

5. McGinn (*Eternal Questions*, Lectures 9 and 10) identifies three characteristics of consciousness. 1. Subjectivity: there is something that it feels like for me when I taste coffee. 2. Intentionality: conscious states are *about* things. If I hear thunder, my awareness is directed toward something—thunder. 3. Transparency: we know directly, immediately, and infallibly what our mental states are. I have privileged access to and knowledge that I am seeing yellow or feeling pain. Consciousness is a subjective, intentional, and transparent phenomenon.

6. My review of biblical material draws on Anderson, "On Being Human"; Anderson, *Theology, Death and Dying*, chapters 4, 5 and 6; Bloesch, *Last Things*; Casey, *Afterlives*; Cooper, "Biblical Anthropology"; Cooper, *Body, Soul and Life Everlasting*; Green, *Body, Soul and Human Life*, chapter 5; Green, "Bodies—That Is, Human Lives"; Green, "Eschatology and Nature of Humans"; Murphy, *Bodies and Souls*, chapter 1; Nichols, *Death and Afterlife*, chapters 1 and 2.

7. Wright, *Resurrection of Son of God*, 129-30 and *Surprised by Hope*, 36. The Roman Catholic International Theological Commission ("Some Current Questions," 220-21) agrees: "the whole Christian tradition, without any important exceptions, has ... conceived ... eschatological hope as embracing two stages. Between the death of people and the consummation of the world ... a conscious element of people subsists."

Future consummation texts

Option A—immediate resurrection—denies an intermediate state; because it contradicts the Bible's future consummation texts it is ruled out as an afterlife scenario.[8]

Future consummation texts portray the culmination of history as an event which will occur after, not at the point of, our death. In ancient Judaism the dead, righteous and wicked alike, enter *sheol*—translated as "hell," "the grave," or "the pit"—a dim, shadowy underworld cut off from fellowship with God (Pss 88:4-12 and 115:17; Isa 38:18-19 and 14:10).[9] The book of Job offers no hope; *sheol* is "the land of gloom and deep darkness" where the dead go, "never to return" (10:21; cf. 14:11-12; 2 Sam 14:14; Eccl 3:18-21; 9:7-10).[10] While some post-exilic psalms (e.g., 16:10; 49:15) suggest salvation from *sheol*, the expected deliverance is not specified. Eschatological hope was this-worldly; it concerned the historical existence of the nation, not the afterlife of the individual. After the exile, hope in communal survival faded and was replaced by ideas of personal survival.[11] The book of Daniel (12:2) gives the first clear ref-

---

8. Option A states that resurrection to the final state takes place immediately after the death of individual persons. Final eschatological events are collapsed into and experienced at the moment of death, leaving no intermediate state between death and resurrection. Divine judgment and the return of Christ to the world at the end of history become judgment of and the coming of Christ to individuals when they die. Death and final consummation are one and the same event. On this view, Ratzinger (*Eschatology*, 252, 110-11) explains, "a person, by his dying, enters . . . into the end of the world, . . . into Christ's return and the resurrection of the dead. There is, therefore, no 'intermediate state' . . . . 'Being with the Lord' and resurrection from the dead are the same thing" since resurrection happens in death." Karl Barth (see Verhey, *Christian Art of Dying*, 204) and Brian Hebblethwaite (*Christian Hope*, 211) as well as conservative scholars Murray Harris (*Raised Immortal*) and Joel Green (*Body, Soul and Human Life*, 140-48) deny an intermediate state and defend resurrection at the moment of death. Resurrection in death became popular among German Roman Catholic theologians in the 1970s who were uneasy with classical dualist anthropology and believed that the soul cannot exist without a body. Immediate resurrection ignores collective and cosmic aspects of eschatology; in fact, it denies any *future* consummation. It is vigorously contested by Ratzinger and the classical view was reaffirmed in 1979 by the Congregation for the Doctrine of the Faith.

9. See Wachter, "Sheol."

10. Job's statement of vindication—"after my skin has been . . . destroyed, then in my flesh I shall see God" (19:25-27)—envisions a return to bodily health in this life not resurrection beyond the grave.

11. The shift from a national hope to an individual hope had causes external to Jewish faith. Exilic Jews were influenced by Babylonian religion which taught bodily

erence: "many of those who sleep in the dust of the earth shall awake, some to everlasting life, and some to shame and everlasting contempt." 2 Maccabees 7—where seven faithful Jews are martyred—states that God will not abandon the righteous dead in *sheol*, but will bring them back to life.[12] In the prophets eschatological events are described as the "Day of the Lord"—a dramatic future intervention of God in history that will include both judgment and restoration. Jesus' teaching about the kingdom of God—the parables of growth and of waiting, for example (Matt 13:24–33; 24:1–30, 45–51)—indicates that it is fully completed in the future. Jesus points to the future when "many will come from east and west and will eat . . . in the kingdom of heaven" (Matt 8:11). The Beatitudes (Matt 5:3–12) refer to a still-to-come *eschaton*—as do the second petition in the Lord's Prayer (Matt 6:10) and the eschatological discourses concerning the end of history (Matt 24–25; Mark 13; Luke 21). In the Epistles the "Day of the Lord" is synonymous with "the day of our Lord Jesus Christ" (e.g., Phil 1:6,10)—the second coming of Jesus to judge the world and consummate a kingdom of righteousness.

Future resurrection texts describe it as something that does not happen at death. Jesus states that resurrection is in "that age"—that is, the age to come (Luke 20:34–35)—and agrees with Martha that the dead "rise again . . . on the last day" (John 11:24). "The hour is coming," Jesus says, "when all who are in their graves will . . . come out" (John 4:28–29; cf. Matt 25:31); this suggests resurrection of everyone at a single future time. St. Paul correlates the resurrection with the *parousia*; it will occur "at [Christ's] coming," "at the last trumpet" (1 Cor 15:23,52)—a symbol in Jewish literature for God's triumphant appearance at the end of time (cf. Rom 8:18–23; Phil 3:20–21; 1 Thess 4:16). Resurrection is general;

---

resurrection, judgment, and reward and punishment. Hellenistic understandings also affected Jewish thought; the Wisdom of Solomon combines Greek belief in an immortal soul with Hebrew belief in bodily resurrection and intertestamental literature mentions disembodied souls in an intermediate state (see Cooper, *Body, Soul and Life Everlasting*, 91 and Nichols, *Death and Afterlife*, 29). The shift also had causes internal to Jewish faith. In this life the wicked often prosper while the righteous suffer (Ps 16; 49; 73)—and personal survival, with destiny determined by earthly conduct, is a natural implication of Jewish belief in a just God. There was also growing awareness that God's life-giving act of creation suggests a life-giving act of resurrection (see Nichols, *Death and Afterlife*, 33)—that God loves creation and this love is present everywhere, even in *sheol* (Ps 139:7–8). God's own character and covenant require life beyond death.

12. The Sadducees' question about the seven brothers references this story and attempts to reduce belief in life after death to absurdity (Matt 22:23–33). See Verhey, *Christian Art of Dying*, 189.

"we will all be changed" (1 Cor 15:51), everyone at the same time—not individually and immediately at death, but as part of the transformation of the cosmos.

These texts indicate resurrection and consummation at the appearing of Christ and rule out option A—individual and immediate consummation at death.

Continuing existence texts

Option B denies personal existence in the intermediate state (the dead either do not exist now at all, or if they do, are unconscious). Because it contradicts the Bible's continuing existence texts—which, as we shall see, imply uninterrupted conscious survival between death and consummation—it, too, is irrelevant as an afterlife scenario.[13]

Ancient Judaism did not see death as extinction since a remnant of the dead person exists, with no vitality, in the darkness of *sheol*. The Hebrew word *rephaim*—which means "weak ones" or "dead ones" and is often translated as "shades"—refers to the inhabitants of *sheol*. Since death means cessation of life in all aspects, the *rephaim* generally exist in a dreary state of inactivity. But the dead are not unconscious; they can see, reason, and speak (Isa 14:9, 16; Ezek 32:21). King Saul's encounter with Samuel's ghost (1 Sam 28) suggests that the *rephaim* retain something of their earthly personality and at times can be roused to a conscious, active state.[14] The fact that they continue to exist underlies the prohibition against communication with the dead (Lev 19:31; 20:6).

---

13. Option B—Christian mortalism—is the idea that the soul of the dead is unconscious until reawakened at the resurrection. This tradition, which goes back to the church fathers, has survived in some circles up to today (see Brown, *Ransom of Soul*, 9). Martin Luther, in order to completely undermine purgatory, defended unconsciousness between death and resurrection (as did some sixteenth-century Anabaptists). In addition, he believed that Christ would return and resurrection would occur soon, so placed little emphasis on the intermediate state. See Thiselton, *Life After Death*, 69 and Kerr, *Compend of Luther's Theology*, 238. John Calvin's first theological writing—*Psychopannychia*, meaning "wakefulness of the soul"—denies soul-sleep. Merricks ("Resurrection of Body" and "How to Live Forever") and Reichenbach (*Is Man Phoenix?*) defend extinction and recreation.

14. See Cooper, *Body, Soul and Life Everlasting*, 65 and Liwak, "Rephaim." For an overview of how the Israelites and their neighbors treated the dead see Hallote, *Death, Burial and Afterlife*.

By the time of Jesus belief in individual survival was common. The Pharisees accepted an intermediate state in which the righteous and wicked inhabit different realms (*paradise* and *gehenna*), followed by a future resurrection and judgment to one of two destinies. The Essenes, an apocalyptic sect, envisioned a climactic end to history when God raises the dead and rewards the godly with life in the messianic kingdom. Only the Sadducees denied resurrection and saw *sheol* as permanent (Acts 23:8).

Jesus claimed that Abraham, Isaac, and Jacob are conscious in *sheol* since God "is God not of the dead, but of the living; for to him all of them are alive" (Luke 20:38)[15]—and he was transfigured with Moses and Elijah who were in existence between death and resurrection (Matt 17:1–13). Jesus assured the good thief that he would enter *paradise* that very day (Luke 23:43)—immediately after death, not in a distant future.[16] In Jesus' parable of the rich man and Lazarus (Luke 16:19–31) both men are conscious—either in an intermediate state (the resurrection has not yet occurred since the rich man still has brothers alive on earth) or after immediate resurrection (since the characters are embodied and already experiencing punishment and reward).[17] Then there is Jesus' own experience between death and resurrection. He was not raised immediately, but after three days—so he entered some kind of intermediate state. And it seems that he was not extinct; Scripture hints that he was in *hades*—in *paradise* encountering the good thief and in *gehenna* freeing those held captive (1 Pet 3:18–20).[18]

St. Paul, as an educated Pharisee, likely believed in a conscious intermediate state (Acts 23:6–8). In 2 Corinthians 5 he states that when

15. While Jesus' argument concerns the resurrection, I believe that we can infer from it conclusions about consciousness in an intermediate state.

16. The word *paradise* is ambiguous; it can refer to either the intermediate resting place of the dead or the final resurrection of the righteous—but in either case, affirms continued existence after death. See Verhey, *Christian Art of Dying*, 188.

Luke 23:43 has no punctuation in Greek, and so the comma can be placed after, not before, the word "today"—being rendered as "I tell you the truth today, you will be with me in *paradise*" (as in the New World Translation). Green (*Body, Soul and Human Life*, 163) says "it is grammatically possible that 'today' could be read with 'truly I tell you.'" This, however, is not the best reading given "its function as an adverb to denote when the criminal will join Jesus in *paradise*."

17. See Green, *Body, Soul and Human Life*, 160–61 and Jeremias, "Abyss" and "Hades." The parable does not intend to teach details about the afterlife; Jesus simply uses stock Jewish imagery to frame his main concern—the law of caring for the poor.

18. Cooper, *Body, Soul and Life Everlasting*, 142.

"the earthly tent we live in is destroyed, we have a building from God, . . . eternal in the heavens. For in this tent we groan, longing to be clothed with our heavenly dwelling—if . . . when we have taken it off we will not be found naked. . . . [W]e wish not to be unclothed but to be further clothed, so that what is mortal may be swallowed up by life" (vv. 1–4). Some interpret this as describing three states of existence: the earthly state (being clothed), the disembodied intermediate state (being naked), and the resurrection state (being re-clothed). Others see a simple contrast between the mortal earthly body and the immortal resurrection body; it is unlikely, they claim, that St. Paul envisioned existing as a disembodied soul in an intermediate state.[19] Still other scholars suggest immediate resurrection since the new body is "put on over" (the Greek word is *ependyein*) the old body with no interval of nakedness. He "leaves us with the impression," William La Due says, "that the soul is joined by [an afterlife] body of some sort as soon as it has left its earthly body behind."[20] St. Paul assures the Thessalonians that the dead will be raised to share in Christ's kingdom after a period of sleep (the Greek word *koimethentas* does not imply unconsciousness, but is used in intertestamental texts to refer to persons in the intermediate state who are conscious and active).[21] He describes post-mortem existence in the presence of God, "with Christ" and "at home with the Lord" (2 Cor 5:6–8; Phil 1:23). This implies conscious fellowship with God directly at death.[22] In St. John's glimpse of heaven (Rev 6:9–11) the souls of the martyrs await vindication and resurrection. To some this indicates a conscious intermediate state; they are, Allen Verhey notes, "not envisioned as sleeping but as waiting, watching, hoping, praying for the final triumph of God's cause."[23] Others see it as simply a mystical vision.

Biblical texts are open to differing interpretations, so we must be cautious about drawing specific metaphysical conclusions from their

19. Anderson, "On Being Human," 190.

20. La Due, *Trinity Guide*, 6. Also see Cooper, *Body, Soul and Life Everlasting*, 157.

21. Cooper, *Body, Soul and Life Everlasting*, 151. The word "sleep" (also used in 1 Cor 15:20) is simply a common synonym for "death."

22. These verses, Reichenbach (*Is Man Phoenix?*, 185; cf. 85) says, are compatible with unconsciousness between death and resurrection. St. Paul "is not speaking about objective time [as recorded by the clock and calendar], but rather subjective time [as experienced by a person]. Though the time between death and resurrection . . . is objectively long, subjectively it is experienced as immediate . . . . Thus St. Paul can say that to die is to be with (to experience) Christ (at the next conscious moment)."

23. Verhey, *Christian Art of Dying*, 206.

imprecise language. They do, however, suggest conscious existence immediately at death and thus seem to rule out option B—temporary nonexistence. And they suggest an interval between death and resurrection, thus ruling out option A—immediate consummation. Two scenarios, then, are compatible with biblical teaching: *disembodied* existence (option C) and *embodied* existence (option D) during the intermediate state. I now turn to see whether philosophical reflection rules out either of these views as impossible.

Philosophy and the Conscious Experience Requirement

There are two aspects to human beings—physical bodies and mental experiences—and our bodies and minds work together.[24] Our bodies are physical; they are made of matter that occupies space and they possess the properties of physical objects (such as shape, size, and color). What we do with our bodies is public and observable. The mind is the center of consciousness—it is both a set of mental states and abilities (perceptions, thoughts, and emotions) *and* the entity, the subject, that has or experiences them. Our minds are non-physical; they are not made up of matter and do not occupy space or possess physical properties. What is in our minds is private and internal. Philosophers have proposed a variety of views concerning the relationship between the mind (mental states and processes) and the body (particularly the brain and its states and processes). In this brief overview I discuss three theories of human nature: we are souls (the dualist view), we are bodies (the materialist view) and we are persons constituted by bodies (the constitution view).[25]

24. My review of philosophical theory draws on Barcalow, *Open Questions*, chapter 3; Barry, *Philosophical Thinking about Death and Dying*; Belshaw, *10 Good Questions*; Davis, *Risen Indeed*, chapters 5 and 6; Kagan, *Death*; Rachels and Rachels, *Problems from Philosophy*, chapter 6; Taliaferro, "Human Nature, Personal Identity and Eschatology;" Walls, *Heaven*, chapter 4, and *Purgatory*, chapter 4. For multidisciplinary Christian perspectives on human nature see Brown, *Whatever Happened to Soul?*; Green, *What about Soul?*; Green and Palmer, *In Search of Soul*.

25. There are three main positions. *Materialism* says that persons are entirely physical; there are no non-physical components to a person. We are complex physical organisms, so mind and brain are the same reality; everything is physical, including the mind. *Idealism* says that persons are entirely non-physical; our minds are non-physical and our bodies are merely sensations in our minds. I do not consider idealism a serious theory of reality, although it has been defended by the likes of George Berkeley. *Dualism* says that persons consist of both physical bodies and non-physical minds. We are made up of two different kinds of reality. There are many ways to be a

1. Theory one—*dualism*—sees human beings as souls. Dualism, Richard Swinburne says, claims that human beings "consist of two parts—a body which is a material substance, and a soul which is an immaterial substance and to which the conscious life of thought and feeling belongs." While there are differences between mind and soul, in this paragraph I use the terms interchangeably—the soul is a non-physical entity that has the powers of mind.[26] Dualism sees body and soul as different kinds of things—separable parts which normally function in unity. Plato believed that an immaterial soul pre-exists the body, which is its earthly prison; at death the soul enters a disembodied afterlife. Aristotle described human nature as a composite of body and soul (the latter of which makes the body alive, is the source of human consciousness and abilities, but perishes at death).[27] René Descartes observed that in addition to various experiences, there is the being, the self, who has them—"I think therefore I am." Body and mind are connected together in this life, but when the body dies, the soul (which contains the conscious mind) continues to exist. Thomas Aquinas believed that the soul is the organizing principle that assembles material elements together into a living body and exercises its

---

materialist or dualist. Varieties of *materialism* include behaviorism (mental states are dispositions to behave), identity theory (mental states are brain states—minds and brains are the same thing), functionalism (mental states are causal intermediaries that relate perceptual stimuli with behavioral effects), and eliminativism (mental states do not exist).Varieties of *dualism* include interactionism (minds and brains influence each other), parallelism (minds and brains run in parallel series but without affecting each other), and epiphenomenalism (brains affect minds but minds do not affect brains). See Double, *Beginning Philosophy*, chapter 5; Rauhut, *Ultimate Questions*, chapter 6; and the scholarly essays in Timmons and Shoemaker, *Knowledge, Nature and Norms*, chapter 3.

26. Swinburne, *Is There a God?*, 70. The terms "mind" and "soul" refer *both* to a set of mental states *and* to the subject of these mental states. The concept of the soul can be difficult to grasp. The standard philosophical definition is that the soul is a simple immaterial substance—simple (not made of parts), immaterial (not made of matter) substance (an individual thing that has certain powers—it contains consciousness and psychological abilities: thinking, perceiving, feeling, remembering, planning, and choosing). This paragraph follows Murphy, "Nonreductive Physicalism," 24. See Appendix Note 1 for arguments for and against dualism.

27. For Aristotle, form is not matter and the soul is the form of the body, so it is not material—it does not exist apart from the body and yet is essential for the existence of a living human being. For Plato the soul is an entity, while for Aristotle it is more a life principle that provides characteristic human powers—vegetative powers of the soul (growth and reproduction) are shared with plants and animals; sensitive powers of the soul (sensation and emotion) are shared with animals; rational powers (intellect and will) are uniquely human. See Murphy, *Bodies and Souls*, 12–15.

functions through the body. Death separates the soul from the body, leaving a conscious but incomplete human being in the intermediate state.[28]

Contemporary emergent dualism says that the soul is not directly created by God but arises naturally through biological evolution (and individually through fetal development). As neurological structures develop from simple to complex, consciousness emerges—first in animals, then, at a higher level and with self-awareness, in human beings. William Hasker argues that organisms with complex brains generate both conscious states *and* subjects (or selves) having those conscious states.[29] What makes all these views dualist is the idea that human beings consist of physical brains and non-physical souls (which, as the conscious essence of a person, survive death). The relationship of body and mind is one of interaction. What is important with regard to the intermediate state is that a body is not necessary for consciousness.

Dualism, once philosophically dominant, is now a minority view. Materialism—now the popular view in philosophy and psychology—asserts that human beings are entirely physical organisms and that there is no immaterial soul. I consider two main versions—identity materialism (which I simply call materialism) and constitution materialism (or constitutionism).[30]

2. Theory two—*materialism*—sees human beings as bodies. Materialism, in Peter van Inwagen's words, asserts that "we are identical with our bodies."[31] Every mental event, every thought and emotion, is the

28. Aquinas, *Summa Theologiae*, Vol. 3, 1a q12 a5, 125. "The soul is united to the body by nature and separated from it against its nature and *per accidens*. Therefore, the soul, when stripped of the body and as long as it is without the body, is imperfect." Roman Catholic magisterial teaching (International Theological Commission, "Some Current Questions," 224) reaffirms this "anthropology of duality." Also see Eberl, "Do Human Persons Persist?"

29. Emergence is the idea that when elements of a certain sort are assembled in the right way, something new with a new set of powers comes into existence. Arranging iron molecules in a particular way, for example, makes a magnetic field emerge. See Hasker, *Emergent Self*; "Persons as Emergent Substances;" and "On Behalf of Emergent Dualism."

30. Materialism, as a general worldview, states that physical matter is the only reality and all phenomena are the result of matter. Christians, obviously, must be dualists regarding ultimate reality: God is immaterial and creation is material, and God does not need a body in order to think or interact with the world. My discussion of dualism and materialism is restricted to anthropology and the nature of human persons.

31. Van Inwagen, "I Look for Resurrection," 9. See Appendix Note 2 for arguments for and against materialism.

product of brain activity. Brain function is necessary for the mental states which depend on it; damage from a stroke or chemicals such as alcohol affect consciousness and mental activity. In the unborn consciousness does not appear until the brain reaches a high level of complexity, and no cerebral cortex function—as in persistent vegetative state—means no conscious awareness at all.[32] Mental events, then, are identical to—or at least require—brain processes; where the brain goes, the person goes. The fact that we use different words to refer to mental events and brain events does not mean that there are different entities involved; there is only one reality, one set of events, described in two different ways (just as Marilyn Monroe and Norma Jean Mortensen are one person). What is conscious and has mental properties is not an immaterial soul but a physical body—a brain. The relationship of body and mind is one of identity; a body is necessary for consciousness.[33]

3. Theory three—*constitutionism*—sees human beings as persons. Persons have a rich, conscious mental life—a psychological essence consisting of thoughts, feelings, and memories. According to constitutionism, Lynne Rudder Baker says, human beings are persons who are constituted by, but not identical to, physical bodies—just as a Styrofoam cup is constituted by a particular piece of Styrofoam but is not identical to it.[34] The cup and the piece of Styrofoam have different persistence

---

32. A persistent vegetative state is a condition of complete and permanent unawareness of the self and the environment. While autonomic brainstem activity continues, cerebral cortex functions supporting consciousness do not.

33. In this brief discussion I have, of necessity, blurred some very important distinctions between varieties of materialism such as identity theory, functionalism and property dualism. There are significant differences between substance dualism (brain and mind are independent entities) and property dualism (there is no substance except for the physical brain—but the brain has special non-physical, or mental, properties). Mental events are non-physical properties of physical brains. Property dualism, while apparently a blend of materialism and dualism, is actually a version of materialism since mental events cannot exist without the physical brain.

34. Baker, *Persons and Bodies*; "Material Persons;" "Christians Should Reject Mind-Body Dualism;" and "Persons and Metaphysics of Resurrection." Also see Corcoran, "Constitution View of Persons." Baggini (*Pig That Wants to Be Eaten*, 113) notes that the fact that consciousness *depends on* the brain does not mean that consciousness *is identical to* the brain. "Compare the situation with a musical score. It can exist in something physical: sheet music, a computer file, perhaps even the brain of a musician. But it would be wrong to conclude that a score there *is* any of these objects. The score is, in essence, a kind of code which needs to be inscribed *somewhere* to continue to exist. But it is the code, not the somewhere, which makes it what it is." In the same way, beliefs, memories and personality make up who we; this set of traits is written in the

conditions—the changes they can undergo without ceasing to exist. The Styrofoam existed before the cup did—and I can make the cup go out of existence by crushing it, but the Styrofoam remains.[35] In the same way, body and person are not identical since they have different persistence conditions: the body can exist without the person (human embryos are pre-persons and human organisms in persistent vegetative state are post-persons) and the person can exist without the body they now have. To put it another way—the same function (computing numbers) can be performed by different systems (an abacus, slide rule, or calculator). Similarly, what makes someone a person is not what they are made of but how they function—that they think, remember, choose, and are self-aware.[36] *Consciousness* can take place in different physical systems. "Just as computers of different constructions can run the same software program," David Papineau says, "creatures with different physiologies can share the same kind of conscious experience. This is why humans and octopuses can both feel pain, even though they are physically quite different." In the same way, *human consciousness* can also exist in different bodies. The relationship of body and mind is one of constitution; a body of some type is necessary for consciousness, but a particular body is not.[37]

---

brain, but that does not mean that we are our brains.

35. The Styrofoam cup example comes from my colleague Timothy Linehan. Constitutionism is a hybrid view. It is the same as dualism in having a non-material aspect—personality—that exists apart from the body and so can transfer between earthly and afterlife bodies. It is the same as materialism in requiring some kind of physical body as necessary to support consciousness. This theory reaches deep into metaphysical concepts such as substance, change, parts and wholes—see Appendix Note 3.

36. Functionalism is the view that mental states are causal intermediaries between perception and behavior; they are defined in terms of the causal roles they play, not their material make-up. They are like computer software rather than hardware. Functionalism is consistent with dualism, but most functionalists are materialists or constitutionalists.

37. Papineau, *Consciousness*, 86. Murphy ("Nonreductive Physicalism" and *Bodies and Souls*) suggests that mental events causally supervene on—or occur in addition to—physical events. If I let my neighbor know when I am home by turning the porch light on, then the message "I am home" supervenes on the light being lit. Supervenient properties can be made real in multiple ways; the message "I am home" can also be sent by putting my window shades up. If a supervenient property (like the message "I am home") can be realized—or made real—in multiple ways, then it and its current manifestation (the lit porch light) are not identical. In human persons mental events supervene on brain events (consciousness requires a body of some kind to support it) but are—in philosophical jargon—"multiply realizable" (we can inhabit

Both materialism and constitutionism claim that human beings are purely physical organisms; there is no non-physical soul and consciousness requires a body. Constitutionism is clearly consistent with postmortem survival since at death God can transfer consciousness—the essence of a person—to a different afterlife body. Materialism is usually taken as incompatible with survival since at death, when the brain stops functioning, consciousness is destroyed—but in fact it does allow life after death (as I explain shortly).

Dualism, materialism, and constitutionism are all—with varying degrees of plausibility—philosophically possible.[38] I turn next to consider what the Bible suggests about the makeup of human beings—whether consciousness exists in immaterial souls or requires a physical body. While Christian tradition is dualist, many contemporary Christian scholars are materialists.[39]

Biblical Teaching on Human Composition

In Hebrew Scripture, the word *nephesh*—often translated "soul"—does not refer to a specific part of a person, an immaterial entity, but to the whole human being. In many cases *nephesh* is translated as "person" or

---

different bodies than we do). Mental events depend on, but are not identical to, brain processes.

38. Philosophy of mind is an active field in contemporary philosophy, but no one really knows how to explain consciousness and solve the mind-body problem. No theory can be conclusively proved or disproved by scientific evidence or philosophical argument. Some philosophers opt for a mysterian position, claiming that consciousness lies beyond human comprehension (just as knowledge of calculus lies beyond the abilities of dogs)—see, for example, McGinn, *Problem of Consciousness*.

39. Some, such as Cullmann (*Immortality of Soul or Resurrection of Dead?*), claim a strong distinction between holistic Hebrew Scripture (which portrays human beings as animated bodies) and dualistic Greek philosophy (which sees human beings as embodied souls). They suggest that dualism is not a Judeo-Christian idea, but was imported into theology from Hellenist philosophy by the ancient church (which sacrificed St. Paul's focus on resurrection of the body to Plato's emphasis on immorality of the soul). This view, however, may be too simplistic. Greek views of human nature were diverse: Plato was a dualist (the soul is naturally immortal and exists disembodied after death), but Aristotle was not a dualist in this sense (the soul, according to Aristotle, is intrinsically united to the body and cannot exist without it). In addition, the Bible and Jewish tradition had some concept of the soul and of an intermediate state between death and resurrection. Dualism was not simply read into Scripture. See Cooper, *Body, Soul and Life Everlasting*, chapter 1 and Murphy, *Souls and Bodies*, chapter 1.

"self." The psalmist prays "guard my life" (Ps 25:20, *NRSV* and *NIV*, not "keep my soul," *KJV*), and "my *nephesh* cries out" (e.g., 55:17; 88:1) simply means "I cry out." A second word *ruach*—"wind" or "breath," often translated "spirit"—refers to the vital energy that animates living creatures and turns dead matter into living matter (e.g., Gen 2:7). To some this indicates that human beings are composed of two different elements; to others it shows that we are single, integrated wholes with embodied existence. John Cooper, a dualist, concedes: "soul and spirit, *nephesh* and *ruach*, seem either to refer to the whole psychophysical person or . . . to the energizing life-force given by God. Neither use refers to an immaterial entity."[40]

In Christian Scripture, the Greek word *psyche*—often translated "soul"—does not normally mean a disembodied spirit, but a whole person. According to Eduard Schweizer, *psyche* "does not carry . . . any clear distinction between a non-corporeal and a corporeal state. . . . The reference is not to a part of [the individual] that has survived death, but to the total existence of a [human being]."[41] Often it simply means "life" or "self"; King Herod sought the infant Jesus' *psyche* (Matt 2:20)—and Jesus says that those who lose their *psyche* will find it (Matt 10:39). Sometimes it seems to refer to a soul existing apart from the body; Jesus tells his hearers to "not fear those who kill the body but cannot kill the *psyche*" (Matt 10:28)—if it is possible to kill one but not the other, then they must be distinct elements. The parallel text, however, makes no body-soul distinction: "do not fear those who kill the body" (Luke 12:4–5). The command to "love . . . God with all your heart, . . . soul, and . . . mind" (Matt 22:37) means to love God with our entire being; it is not suggesting different parts of a person. "The word *psyche* seems . . . to refer," Wright says," like the Hebrew *nephesh*, not to a disembodied inner part of the human being but to . . . the person or . . . the personality."[42] A second word *pneuma*—often translated "spirit"—also has multiple meanings. "The spirits of the righteous made perfect" are currently in heaven awaiting resurrection (Heb 12:23; cf. Rev 6:9; 20:4)—but it is not clear whether the reference is to an immaterial entity or the whole person. St. Paul's

---

40. Cooper, *Body, Soul and Life Everlasting*, 48; cf. 50–55. See Seebass, "Nephesh" and Fabry, "Ruach." In intertestamental literature the anthropological terms *nephesh* and *ruach* can refer to a disembodied soul in an intermediate state (see Cooper, *Body, Soul and Life Everlasting*, 91 and Nichols, *Death and Afterlife*, 29).

41. Schweizer, "Psyche," 654–55.

42. Wright, *Surprised by Hope*, 152.

flesh-spirit contrast (e.g., Gal 5:17) does not divide people into two metaphysical parts but identifies two spiritual orientations—a self-centered nature and a God-loving nature. In St. Paul's prayer that "spirit and soul and body be kept sound and blameless" (1 Thess 5:23), *pneuma* means the whole person in a particular respect—in relation to God—not a component part.[43] Christian Scripture, James D. G. Dunn says, has an aspective view of human nature (emphasizing specific dimensions of a person's life), rather than a partitive view (defining essential parts of a person's makeup).[44]

The scholarly consensus is that biblical anthropological terms seldom, if ever, refer to an immaterial soul that survives death apart from the body. They have functional rather than ontological meaning and refer to the whole embodied person or some aspect of the person—thoughts, feelings, intentions, desires—not to distinct entities within a person.[45] We are not part physical body and part non-physical soul, Wright concludes: "the idea that every human possesses an immortal soul, which is the 'real' part of them, finds little support in the Bible."[46]

Scripture, it seems, is compatible with both dualism and materialism. I turn next to the nature of personal identity.

The Preserved Identity Requirement

Prayer for the departed requires that they exist as the very same people they were in life (having the unique characteristics that make them who they are). The Bible indicates that they do. King Saul encountered Samuel—one and the same in life and death. Daniel's prophecy (12:2) and Jesus' teaching assume that the same persons that lived on earth experience judgment, reward, and punishment. The rich man and Lazarus

---

43. See Schweizer, "Pneuma."

44. Dunn, cited in Murphy, *Bodies and Souls*, 21.

45. Anderson, "On Being Human," 178. Even if we reject the idea that a special part is responsible for unique human abilities, the word "soul" can still be used as long as we understand that it refers to the functional abilities of a complex physical organism, not a separate immaterial substance that inhabits the body. The term "soul" should be seen, Hick (*Death and Eternal Life*, 43–46) and Anderson ("On Being Human," 177) say, as a value term referring to distinctive human abilities, to the personal, interpersonal and spiritual dimensions of the self, not an independent part.

46. Wright, *Surprised by Hope*, 28. While Scripture contains no detailed anthropology, the church combined Aristotle's teaching of body-soul unity in this life with Plato's notion of disembodied existence in the intermediate state.

both remember their former lives (Luke 16:19–31), and the "sheep" and "goats" recall helping or ignoring the needy (Matt 25:31–46).[47] Moses and Elijah appear with the transfigured Jesus and are recognized by the disciples (Matt 17:1–13). The risen Jesus assures his followers "see that it is I myself" (Luke 24:39)—the same person and body, but transformed. St. Paul affirms that after death we—the very people who exist now—will be in conscious fellowship with or separation from God (Phil 1:21, 23). He reassures the Thessalonians that they will be reunited with their dead loved ones (1 Thess 4:13–18).

I should say something more about resurrection since it has implications for how we understand personal identity and the intermediate state. In 1 Corinthians 15, St. Paul gives his clearest teaching.[48] Resurrection, for Jews, meant *bodily* resurrection—the Athenians rejected St. Paul's preaching because he challenged disembodied Platonic souls (Acts 17:32). The earthly body will be changed into, not replaced by, the afterlife body. It will be, Thomas Oden says, "not a different body but a different form of the same body" we had in this life—like an upgrade of computer hardware, the new is like the old, only better. The resurrection body is an enhanced body.[49] There is continuity; the resurrection body is connected to and emerges from the earthly body as full-grown plant is related to seed (v. 37). There is also discontinuity; the earthly body is "perishable" and frail as a "physical body," while the resurrection body is "imperishable" and glorified as a "spiritual body" (vv. 42–44; cf. Phil 3:21). The phrase "spiritual body" does not mean that resurrection bodies are immaterial (there is no such thing as a non-physical body; bodies are by definition physical) but that they are sinless, animated by and obedient to God's Spirit, rather than to sinful desires.[50]

The Bible supports the preserved identity requirement. I turn, then, to philosophical analysis.[51] Survival requires continuity of the self; in

---

47. For why responsibility requires identity across time see Appendix Note 4.

48. There are two sources of information on the resurrection body: Gospel descriptions of Jesus' resurrection appearances (which suggest both continuity and discontinuity between Jesus before his resurrection and after it) and St. Paul's teaching in 1 Corinthians 15. Some in Corinth denied there was a resurrection to come, and others saw it as disembodied immortality.

49. Oden, *Life in Spirit*, 402 and Alcorn, *Heaven*, 116. See Davis, "Physicalism and Resurrection," 248.

50. See Wright, *Surprised by Hope*, 155–56. Bynum, *Resurrection of Body*, gives a comprehensive history of Christian thought on resurrection.

51. My review of philosophical theory draws on Barcalow, *Open Questions*, chapter

order for an earthly person and an afterlife person to be one and the same, there must be some kind of continuity between them. First, we should distinguish numerical and qualitative identity. Two things are *numerically* identical if they are one and the same object; they are *qualitatively* identical if they are exactly alike.[52] A thing can change qualitatively and yet remain the same numerically; despite losing a hubcap, my car today is the same one I bought ten years ago. Similarly, changes of body and personality represent different stages in the life of one continuing person. Second, we should distinguish accidental from essential properties. A property is a way a thing can be or not be—for example, being yellow, being born in 1957, or being mean-tempered. *Accidental* (or contingent) properties are those which a thing does have but need not have in order to be what it is, characteristics it can lose without ceasing to exist. *Essential* (or necessary) properties are those which a thing must have, without which it cannot be the thing it is; if it loses them it ceases to exist. My motorcycle painted a new color is still the same motorcycle, but adding two more wheels makes it another kind of vehicle. In the same way, I survive losing all my hair, but not all my memories or psychological traits.

An earthly individual is identical with an afterlife individual if they are numerically identical and share the same essential properties, which constitute their identity. The three theories of identity correspond to the three theories of human nature. *If we are souls*, then an earthly individual is identical with an afterlife individual if they have the same soul. If the body dies but the soul continues to exist, then the individual survives. *If we are bodies*, then an earthly individual is identical with an afterlife individual if they have the same body. This does not mean that the body must retain all the same material constituents, since our bodies are constantly losing old particles and gaining new ones (but are connected by overlapping stages that belong to one and the same individual). If after death the body continues to exist, then the individual survives. *If we are persons*, then an earthly individual is identical with an afterlife individual if they have the same memories and personality. Once again, this does

---

4; Barry, *Philosophical Thinking about Death and Dying*; Kagan, *Death*; Rachels and Rachels, *Problems from Philosophy*, chapter 5; Rauhut, *Ultimate Questions*—all of which draw on Parfit, *Reasons and Persons*. Also see the scholarly essays in Timmons and Shoemaker, *Knowledge, Nature and Norms*, chapter 2.

52. Items can be 1. numerically identical but qualitatively distinct (my father—one continuing person—was a young boy in 1925 and an old man in 2000) and 2. numerically distinct but qualitatively identical (such as two different copies of one book).

not mean that every single psychological element stays exactly the same; we lose old beliefs and gain new desires—and as long as these changes are gradual and have the right pattern of overlap, they do not threaten identity. If the body dies but the personality continues to exist, then the individual survives.[53]

Which is the real me—soul, body, or personality? "What is essential to being me," Emmett Barcalow answers, "is a specific cluster of thoughts, feelings, beliefs, desires, emotions, values, preferences, interests, experiences and memories"—my psychological essence. This means that I continue to exist as long as my consciousness, my memories and personality, continues. We can see this by creating fictional stories in which soul, body and personality come apart, leaving one without the others.[54]

1. *Soul without personality* does not preserve identity. Suppose every weekend God programs my soul with a different personality so that I remember nothing of my previous life and have none of the same psychological traits: then my identity is lost and I do not survive.[55] The possibility of retaining a soul but not being the same person indicates that soul is not the essence of identity—and that personality is.

2. *Body without personality* does not preserve identity. First, suppose a *different* person in the same body. Jill is in a car crash; after weeks in a coma, Jill's body wakes up—but it is not Jill since the recovered individual has total amnesia and an entirely different personality. Jill's body survives but she—the person—does not. Second, suppose *no* person in the same body. Jack, injured in the accident, is permanently unconscious; he continues to have body functions without personality functions. Jack's body

---

53. Kagan, *Death*, 129–31 and 165. It is certainly possible for a coma victim to wake up with a different personality yet the same memories—and it is not obvious that this is a different person. While memory and personality traits are separate conditions, for simplicity's sake I treat them as one criterion.

54. Barcalow, *Open Questions*, 119. Philosophers often use thought experiments which are not actually possible—science fiction stories, for example—to clarify concepts and determine whether a claim is theoretically possible. Locke (*Essay Concerning Human Understanding*, II, xxvii, 15) imagines a prince waking up in a cobbler's body while the cobbler's mind is transferred into the prince's body. Who is the individual with the cobbler's body but the prince's memories and personality? If the body is what matters, it must be the cobbler—but if personality, the prince. See Kagan, *Death*, 113–15.

55. Consider what happens when a flash drive is reformatted—all data is erased and gone forever. If death is reformatting, then all personality traits are lost once and for all and all that remains is the substance, the device, that held the personality. For more on why soul without personality lacks identity see Appendix Note 5.

survives but he—the person—does not. Situations in which the person does not survive but the body does indicate that body is not the essence of identity—and that personality is.[56]

3. *Personality without soul* preserves identity. Suppose every weekend God replaces my soul with a different one, programming it with my personality: then my identity is preserved and I survive. The possibility of switching souls while remaining the same person indicates that soul is not the source of identity—and that personality is.[57]

4. *Personality without body* preserves identity. Imagine a brain recorder that scans how Bert's brain (and thus his personality pattern) functions; this information is stored and downloaded into a second brain—Ernie's—which is reconfigured to exactly match the first. If we transfer Bert's psychological properties to Ernie's body and Ernie's to Bert's, then they switch bodies; Bert (the consciousness with his memories and personality) now has Ernie's body and *vice versa*.[58] The possibility of switching bodies while remaining the same person indicates that body is not the source of identity—and that personality is.

Soul without personality *is not* me and body without personality *is not* me—so neither soul nor body is sufficient for continued existence across time. But personality without soul or body *is* me—so personality is both necessary and sufficient. The essence of a person is how they think, feel, and act. Since the real me is my personality, my continued existence requires continuation of my mental life—I survive death so as long as

---

56. A permanently comatose body once constituted a person, but no longer does—and a fetus does not yet constitute a person, but someday will. This does not mean, of course, that abortion is permissible. The fetus, while not yet a person, will become one. Because of its potential—the fact that it has a valuable future—abortion may be wrong even though the fetus is not a person. Bodies in persistent vegetative states, however, have no potential for recovering consciousness—and, lacking a valuable future, may be rightly disconnected from life supports like feeding tubes keeping them biologically alive.

57. The personality view faces the duplication problem. What if God replaces my body and soul with two new bodies and souls, imprinting each with my personality. It is hard to believe that they would both be the same person. For a discussion of this problem, see Appendix Note 6.

58. This example comes from Law, *Philosophy Gym*, 243. Locke (*Essay Concerning Human Understanding*, II, xxvii, 17) argues that wherever my consciousness and personality, I go. He imagines someone's little finger being separated from their body; should "consciousness go along with the little finger, and leave the rest of the body, it is evident the little finger would be the person, the same person; and self would then have nothing to do with the rest of the body."

my psychological essence survives. If a *Star Wars* movie is dubbed from VHS to DVD and the tape destroyed, the movie still exists—and if at death God transfers my psychological essence to an afterlife body, then I continue to exist. Identity of a person is identity of consciousness and personality—so I can change bodies and still be me. I can survive the death of my body; I cannot survive the destruction of my mind. Personality is what provides continuity between earthly and afterlife individuals.[59]

The Metaphysics of the Intermediate State

We now have the pieces necessary to construct views of the intermediate state that are compatible with the personal existence requirement—and thus with prayer for the dead. There are three such views:

1. survival dualism—we are souls and the intermediate state is disembodied;

2. survival materialism—we are bodies and the intermediate state requires embodiment in the same body;

3. survival constitutionism—we are persons and while the intermediate state must be embodied, it can be in a different body.

All survival theories require persistence of personality.

Dualism and the Intermediate State

Dualism implies a disembodied intermediate state. During this life consciousness and personality depend on the brain, but after death the soul separates from the body and continues in conscious existence, being re-embodied at resurrection. Aquinas claims that disembodied souls retain the powers of memory, intellect, and will—and Henry Price argues that

---

59. This example comes from Baraclow, *Open Questions*, 119. It might be wondered why the transfer of psychological essence must occur *at death*. There seems to be no obvious problem with temporal discontinuity between a pre-death person and an afterlife person (so long as God keeps the information that is them). Since God's memory of them can plug the temporal gap, so to speak, materialists and constitutionalists do not need an intermediate state body to preserve identity. Such temporally gappy existence, while possible, makes prayer for the dead more problematic. For a discussion of this issue, see Appendix Note 7.

souls can know of each other's existence, communicate telepathically, and have dreamlike perceptions of their surroundings.[60]

Dualism seems to allow personal survival in the intermediate state. But disembodied existence raises many questions. While the person may be able to engage in mental activities (thoughts, feelings, and memories in a world of dream-images) they will not be able to do bodily actions, experience physical sensations, perceive the environment, or interact with others. We should distinguish, Nancey Murphy says, two views of personality. The *intellectualist* view sees it as a set of intellectual abilities (reasoning, will, and memories). The *holistic* view says that while necessary, these are not sufficient for personality; who we are also includes moral dispositions and interpersonal relationships.[61] Consider, for example, afterlife sanctification. Swinburne claims that the soul can grow morally into goodness by becoming aware of inconsistencies among its beliefs and desires and making the necessary adjustments.[62] But intellectual reflection, while necessary for developing virtue and eliminating vice, is not sufficient. John Hick points out that turning away from self-centeredness involves facing situations of moral choice in how we treat people. This requires communication and interaction with others in a common environment—and this, in turn, seems to require a body.[63] Murphy, too, thinks that "embodiment is necessary for social life. . . . A body is the soul's only means of relating to other souls. . . . If there are disembodied consciousnesses, they are strictly solitary. . . . Our bodies constitute the very possibility of engagement with one another in this world or any other."[64] While a disembodied soul can perhaps maintain the intellectual component, it cannot preserve holistic personality.

---

60. Aquinas, *Summa Theologiae*, Vol. 3, 1a q12 a5, 125 and Price, "Survival and Idea of 'Another World.'" Also see Hick, *Death and Eternal Life*, chapter 14.

61. See Murphy, *Bodies and Souls*, 132–37.

62. Swinburne, *Evolution of Soul*, 284. Also see Walls, *Purgatory*, 111.

63. Hick, *Death and Eternal Life*, 459–63 and chapter 14. "It takes bodies," Roberts (*Exploring Heaven*, 113) says, "to effect qualities of character; minds that make moral decisions don't exist without them." Godfrey (*Philosophy of Human Hope*, 87) agrees that "it seems difficult to conceive of . . . choice of principle over inclination except in terms of space and time and body. Virtue therefore seems to require body." Price's notion of souls inhabiting some kind of "soul space," communicating telepathically and thus developing morally is not incoherent—but is, for the reasons I have given, implausible. A body is essential for holistic and full relationships with others.

64. Murphy, *Bodies and Souls*, 139–40. Also see Verhey, *Christian Art of Dying*, 212. For various models of resurrection see Appendix Note 7.

Materialism and the Intermediate State

In order to affirm an afterlife materialists must accept either immediate bodily resurrection or an embodied intermediate state. But since immediate resurrection contradicts Scripture, the only viable materialist option consistent with prayer for the dead is an embodied intermediate state. Between death and resurrection, Douglas Connelly says, "we don't simply float around . . . as ghostlike spirits. [We] . . . function within temporary bodies of some kind."[65]

The strongest materialist position claims that the earthly body and the intermediate state body must be numerically identical. As Peter van Inwagen puts it: "if I am a material thing, then, if a man who lives at some time in the future is to be [me], there will have to be some sort of material and causal continuity between this matter that composes me now and the matter that will then compose that man."[66] It is not enough that the afterlife body contain the same particles as the earthly body; there must also be continuous and direct causal connection, without a time gap, between the two bodies. To meet these requirements, van Inwagen proposes survival by body-snatching. At the moment of death God removes the earthly body and replaces it with a perfect physical duplicate. The body that is buried is a lookalike—while the original body is immediately reanimated by God as an intermediate state body. By preserving numerical identity between the two bodies, the body-snatching scenario ensures that the afterlife body is a continuation of the earthly body. Another materialist proposal is survival by body-splitting. Kevin Corcoran and Dean Zimmerman suggest that at the moment of death God divides the earthly body into two identical streams—a living intermediate-state body and

---

65. Connelly, *Promise of Heaven*, 38. Green (*Body, Soul and Human Life*, 140–48) and Rahner (*Theological Investigations*, Vol. 17, 114–24), for example, reject an intermediate state, which they assume can only be disembodied, and argue that resurrection must take place at the moment of death for materialist reasons since there is no soul existing without a body. Cooper (*Body, Soul and Life Everlasting*, 116) asserts that without dualism there is no conscious intermediate state, no personal existence between death and resurrection—and Davis (*Risen Indeed*, 89) claims extinction-recreation as the only materialist scenario for post-mortem survival. These positions all assume false alternatives—either dualism (and a disembodied intermediate state) or materialism (and temporary non-existence or immediate resurrection). They ignore the possibility of an embodied intermediate state.

66. Van Inwagen, "Dualism and Materialism," 486. Also see "Possibility of Resurrection," 114–21. I adapt van Inwagen's proposal, which concerns the resurrection body, to the intermediate state body.

a dead corpse. This ensures that the afterlife body is causally connected to and materially continuous with (and so numerically identical to) the earthly body.[67]

Neither the body-snatching nor body-splitting proposals are offered as explanations of what actually occurs after death. They are simply meant to demonstrate that materialism can allow an embodied intermediate state—and thus meet the personal existence requirement of prayer for the dead.

Constitutionism and the Intermediate State

Body-snatching and body-splitting assume that God must use the actual matter of the earthly body in fashioning the intermediate state body. Constitutionism, a less radical materialist view (on which human beings are wholly physical, but not identical with their bodies), rejects the "same matter" requirement. Since it only needs psychological continuity, the same person (who is numerically identical) can exist in different bodies (which are numerically distinct). For constitutionism the intermediate state must be embodied, and we survive death by body-switching. "At some future time," Chad Meister says, "the mind will be transferred into a different material medium.... If one's mind is reduced to a software package and reinstalled in another physical system after death, one survives."[68] Since what is necessary to being the same person is psychology, we continue to exist as long as an intermediate state body can be created and programmed with the same personality. We survive, David

---

67. See Corcoran, "Persons and Bodies"; "Physical Persons"; "Constitution View," 167; Zimmerman, "Compatibility of Materialism and Survival." I adapt their proposals, which concerns the resurrection body, to the intermediate state body. Zimmerman, I should note, is a dualist who argues that materialism is compatible with afterlife survival.

68. Meister, "Death and the Afterlife," 298, slightly modified. Polkinghorne (*Faith of Physicist*, 163 and *God of Hope*, chapter 9) suggests that we are patterns of psychological information (like a digital file on a flash drive), not substantial physical entities (the device that holds the information). Afterlife existence occurs through body-switching: "the pattern that is me will be remembered by God and ... recreated by God when God reconstitutes me" physically in the intermediate state. Wright (*For All Saints*, 72 and *Surprised by Hope*, 162) agrees that at death God will download our software into new hardware. In this life the earthly body provides the hardware for consciousness and personality; in the next life intermediate state and resurrection bodies will provide physical hardware for the same psychological software. For more on body-switching, see Appendix Note 8.

Winter says, "as personalities expressed in a new kind of body. . . . Just as a message is still the same message, whether it's spoken in words or flashed in Morse code, so . . . we shall be the same persons, whatever the material form in which our personalities may be expressed."[69] One and the same person can be constituted by an earthly body in this life and by intermediate and resurrection bodies in the next—with personality carrying identity across these different bodies. If God can create a new body and give it my psychological essence, then it will be me—and I will know I am myself, just like when I woke up this morning.

Concluding Remarks

Where are the dead now? There are three possible afterlife scenarios concerning an intermediate state (and consistent with bodily resurrection).[70]

1. *There is no intermediate state.* The dead are immediately resurrected. This view, however, eliminates prayer for the dead and lacks biblical warrant. The eschatological pattern of Christian Scripture and church tradition is intermediate state and resurrection.

2. *There is an unconscious intermediate state.* The dead are either extinct or exist but are unaware. The notion of soul sleep, however, has no support in Scripture and is incompatible with prayer for the dead.[71]

3. *There is a conscious intermediate state.* The dead are aware between death and resurrection. This option is compatible with both future consummation and continuing existence texts—which taken

---

69. Winter, *Hereafter*, 30.

70. Cocksworth, *Prayer and Departed*, 12.

71. In the most technical sense, it is not true that scenarios 1 and 2 are incompatible with prayer for the dead. Both scenarios claim that—experientially—we go directly to the final state, either immediately at death (1) or after a period of non-existence (2). 2 allows consummation prayer but 1 does not—and as long as change is still possible in the final state, then growth, purification, and salvation prayers are possible on both scenarios 1 and 2. On scenario 2, God could, as it were, "store up" our prayers for the dead and set about answering them after resurrection. This assumes that transformation beyond the start of new creation is possible—a notion that is not obviously unbiblical (since Revelation 21-22 seems to suggest purification and salvation of those in the Lake of Fire after the consummation of the kingdom—see MacDonald, *Evangelical Universalist*, 114–32). Perhaps prayers made now speed up the deliverance of those in the Lake of Fire after judgment day. Thanks to my editor, Robin Parry, for pressing me on this point. For further explanation, see Appendix Note 9.

together imply a conscious intermediate state where the dead rest in peace and a final state when they rise in glory.

If I am right about all I have said in this chapter, then prayer for the dead is best explained by conscious existence as the same person between death and resurrection. If we are souls then we can exist in the intermediate state without any body at all. If we are bodies then in the intermediate state we must have the particular body we have now; God can preserve it through snatching or splitting. If we are persons then the intermediate state allows a different body (we can exist without *this* body but not without *a* body); God can provide one through switching. Prayer for the dead is consistent with all three theories: dualists can pray for the dead, materialists can pray for the dead, constitutionists can pray for the dead. All affirm the personal existence requirement.

My own view is that human beings are embodied consciousnesses. We are by nature physical creatures; we never exist without a body, which is an essential aspect of who we are. In order to survive death a person must be constituted by a body.[72] We have, then, two afterlife bodies. "In the interim state," Donald Bloesch says, "the human spirit is not disembodied.... At the moment of death we are clothed with an incorruptible body. When Christ comes again, we will be re-clothed with a glorified body that is eternal."[73] Randy Alcorn agrees: God must "grant us some physical form that will allow us to function as human beings while [we are] 'between bodies,' awaiting our resurrection.... Intermediate bodies... serve as bridges between our present bodies and our resurrected bodies."[74] Jerry Walls worries that intermediate state bodies lessen the force of death and weaken the significance of future resurrection. But Alcorn insists that intermediate bodies "in no way minimize the absolute

---

72. What kind of experience, Macquarrie (*Christian Hope*, 113) asks, can a disembodied soul have? Certainly not a full personal life since it has no sense perception or relationships with other people. "It is difficult," Russell (*History of Heaven*, 10) states, "to conceive of human intellect and will, reason and affect, existing without... a body." This observation goes back to the church fathers. Evodius of Milan was a moderate neo-Platonist who objected to the early Augustine's radical neo-Platonism on the grounds that, even in the afterlife, the soul must be accompanied by some material "vehicle" that allows experience (see Brown, *Ransom of Soul*, 73, 135).

73. Bloesch, *Last Things*, 127–31; cf. 36, 123, 139–40. We might question Bloesch's division of the incorruptible body and the glorified body from each other since for St. Paul they are the same resurrected body. Bloesch's point that we have two afterlife bodies, however, remains plausible.

74. Alcorn, *Heaven*, 57.

necessity . . . of our future bodily resurrection." Whether or not they are numerically identical, each afterlife body is qualitatively distinct from the others—and the intermediate state body is not transformed in the way the resurrection body will be.[75] I suspect that earthly and afterlife bodies need not (as a matter of necessity) but will (as a matter of fact) be continuous in form (but not necessarily in matter). Jesus' earthly and resurrection bodies, while not identical, shared a real connection—and St. Paul teaches that the afterlife body has a developmental relationship to the earthly body: the second emerges from and is a refinement of the first.[76] Frederick Buechner suggests that God will bring back to life "a new and revised version of all the things which made [a person] the particular human being he was and which he needs . . . a body to express: his personality, the way he looked, the sound of his voice, his peculiar capacity for creating and loving, in some sense his face."[77] Personal identity involves the same physical body and psychological traits; while only the latter is strictly necessary, both are important aspects that make us who we are.

The departed can benefit from prayer since they consciously exist as the very same people they were in life. It might be thought, however, that praying for them is pointless because they are in a static state of bliss or pain. If their situation is unchangeable, then prayer for them is useless—even if they are consciously aware. In order that prayers for the dead make sense, afterlife experience must involve dynamic development. I turn to that topic next.

---

75. Walls, *Heaven, Hell and Purgatory*, 125–27 and Alcorn, *Heaven*, 59; also 113. Hoekema (*Bible and Future*, 105), while not subscribing to this view, lists many scholars who accept an embodied intermediate state. Friedrich Schleiermacher, for example, held that persons in the intermediate state already possess new bodies (La Due, *Trinity Guide*, 24). Also see Walls, *Purgatory*, 98–100.

76. Winter, *Hereafter*, 58–66.

77. Buechner, *Wishful Thinking*, 43.

chapter 7

TIME, ETERNITY, AND PRAYER FOR THE DEAD

WE GATHER AT THE bonfire in the field next to the church. It is five o'clock in the morning—and we have met for my favorite service, the Great Vigil of Easter, celebrated by Christians since the fourth century. After the *paschal* candle is lit we process into the sanctuary where, for an hour, as light dawns and day breaks, we listen to the record of God's great acts of redemption in history—creation, the deliverance of Noah and Isaac, the exodus from Egypt, the restoration of Israel after exile, Christ's resurrection from death. Then we look forward, asking God to "carry out . . . the plan of salvation" until "all things are . . . brought to their perfection" and "each of us to the fullness of redemption." History has a direction—it has come from somewhere past and is going to something future. The Eucharistic prayer each Sunday recounts, more briefly, this temporal narrative—it recites salvation history from creation to new creation, and we affirm the mystery of faith in Christ: "we remember his death [past], we proclaim his resurrection [present], we await his coming in glory [future]." The priest prays: "in the fullness of time, put all things in subjection under your Christ, and bring us to that heavenly country where . . . we may enter the everlasting heritage of your sons and daughters."[1] This is the biblical narrative—a history begun and to be consummated in time, a reality that is open-ended and oriented toward the future. The world was created good, is broken by sin, and is being—and finally will be—made right.

1. Episcopal Church, *Book of Common Prayer*, 288–91 and 368–69.

Prayer for the departed assumes that they can be helped by our intercessions. Chapter 5 argued that prayer in general is effective, having real influence on the accomplishment of God's purposes. Chapter 6 argued that the dead consciously exist right now as the very people they were in life—and so can, in theory at least, be helped. These two requirements, while necessary, are not sufficient to make prayer for the dead sensible. The departed could be conscious but in a static state of joy or sorrow. The point of prayer, after all, is to help them—and help implies that their situation can be improved, made better than it is. Suppose I am praying for my dead father. Even if prayer in general is effective and even if my dad consciously exists as the same person, if his situation is complete and nothing can change, then prayer for him is pointless. If, however, he is awaiting something more and experiencing ongoing development, then prayer makes sense. And so a third condition must be met: the *open future requirement* asserts that history remains unfinished and that the dead are in a progressive state. Prayer for the dead requires, in the words of John Hick, "a dynamic view of immortality, in which the person continues . . . to move, as a free creature, . . . towards . . . perfect fulfillment . . . in the ultimate Kingdom of God."[2] Change is an inherently dynamic concept, and so the open future requirement entails the *temporal becoming requirement*: time, both before and after death, flows. Only if events occur in succession are development and change possible. All the dead await final consummation—in the meantime, the blessed continue growing in God, the imperfect are morally transformed, and the unsaved can repent and return to God. If prayer for any of the dead is effective, then their futures must be open to change rather than static and irrevocable.[3]

The Incomplete Future and the Dynamic Afterlife

The past and the future differ in the sense that the past is actual (a closed set of facts) while the future is potential (an open set of possibilities). Past events cannot be changed and are forever fixed, but there are numerous

---

2. Hick, *Death and Eternal Life*, 220. Walls (*Purgatory*, 102) agrees: prayer for the departed "requires subjects that retain not only consciousness, but are able to undergo . . . spiritual growth."

3. Traditional theology holds that spiritual development of the saved dead is open while spiritual destiny of the unsaved dead is closed. I reject this view—claiming that the future is open for all the dead.

ways future events may happen. Theological determinists reject this asymmetry of past and future. The future is just as real as the past. Everything that will happen is settled down to the last detail and is either predestined or foreknown by God to occur as it will.[4]

Prayer for the dead requires an open future. The open future requirement includes two separate conditions:

1. the *incomplete future* requirement: final consummation is future for both the living and the dead, and

2. the *dynamic afterlife* requirement: the post-mortem condition of the dead is progressive, not static.[5]

Both are necessary if prayer for all the dead is to be intelligible.

First, consummation prayer (for the completion of God's purpose in history) requires an incomplete future; there must be actual future events that have not happened yet. There are three possibilities for when eschatological events occur.

1. Eschatological events are realized individually *in this life*. In the existentialism of Paul Tillich and Rudolf Bultmann, immortality is about new life here and now—not a real afterlife. Eschatology concerns present, not future events; it takes place as we encounter God in moments of radical decision and live authentically now.[6]

2. Eschatological events are realized individually *at the moment of death*. In the consummation-in-death view of Karl Barth and Ladislaus Boros, there is no intermediate state between death and resurrection. Divine judgment and the return of Christ to the world

---

[4]. The future may be settled either by divine decrees or by human choices. In the former case, God determines all that will occur—in the latter case God knows what we will freely choose to do in the future. Determinists and non-determinists both accept an *incomplete* future (since eschatological events have not happened yet)—but determinists deny and non-determinists affirm an *open* future. Determinists see the future as closed: future events are necessary—they must occur in one particular way. Non-determinists see the future as open: future events are contingent—they may occur in many different ways.

[5]. These two conditions are distinct. It is possible to affirm 1 (eschatological events are not already complete but lie in an objective future) but deny 2 (afterlife time does not flow but is static). It is also possible to affirm 2 and deny 1—and to deny both 1 and 2.

[6]. See LaDue, *Trinity Guide*, chapter 2.

at the end of history are judgment of and the coming of Christ to individuals when they die.[7]

If eschatological events are completely realized in this life or at death, then there is nothing left to hope for. The Bible clearly teaches life after death, however, so option 1 is ruled out—and its future consummation texts eliminate option 2. That leaves

3. Eschatological events are realized collectively *in a future beyond death*.

Consummation at the end of history entails an intermediate state between death and resurrection. An intermediate state is, by definition, temporary; it means that things are not in their ultimate state. In two-stage eschatology the future is *consummation-incomplete*. Final consummation will only be completed when Christ returns, the dead are raised and judged, evil defeated, and God's kingdom established on earth. Consummation prayer requires that these events be future, that they are yet to occur, for both the living and the dead.[8]

Second, growth, purification, and salvation prayers require that the post-mortem condition of the dead be dynamic, not static. Death either constitutes a closed future (a passive state of being in which change cannot occur) or an open future (an active process of becoming in which change happens). If spiritual development and destiny become complete and final at death then prayer for the departed is pointless—but if futures

---

7. Barth eliminates an intermediate state by eliminating time, by taking the resurrection of the dead out of time. Instead, the dead are immediately raised to new life in God's eschatological kingdom (see Verhey, *Christian Art of Dying*, 204–6). Boros, too, affirms that the transformation of the body happens immediately at death, for the dead are not in time (see La Due, *Trinity Guide*, chapter 3). Ratzinger (*Eschatology*, 107–8) explains this view: human beings "enter through death ... into the fulfillment of history"—and so "on the other side of death history is already complete. The end of history is ever waiting for the one who dies" because "the person who dies steps into the presence of the Last Day and of judgment, the Lord's resurrection and *parousia*." "The end of time is itself no longer time. It is not a date which happens to come extremely late in the calendar but rather non-time, something which ... is outside of time.... Death itself leads out of time into the timeless.... Death signifies leaving time for eternity with its single 'today' .... The end of time is timeless."

8. *World history* is divided into two phases: pre-eschatological history (which occurs before the last things) and eschatological history (the transcendent future beyond the last things). *Individual histories* have three stages: one earthly stage (life in this world before death) and two afterlife stages (an intermediate stage and a final stage).

after death are open to change then it is not. Two types of change must be possible if prayer for *all* the dead is to make sense.

1. The saved must be capable of spiritual development, which is not finalized at death. Their futures are *incomplete*: in the afterlife they continue moving in the same direction as their orientation towards God in earthly life. The post-mortem future is open-ended for
    a. the blessed who increasingly participate in God's life (their futures are *growth-incomplete*) and for
    b. the imperfect who gradually develop holy love (their futures are *purification-incomplete*).
2. The unsaved must be able to change their spiritual destiny, which is not settled at death. Their futures are *open*: they can change direction, reversing their orientation to God. They can repent and escape from hell (their futures are *salvation-open*).[9]

Growth, purification, and salvation prayers require that individual histories be unconcluded and capable of development and alteration after death.

Prayer for the dead entails the temporal becoming requirement. A *static state* view of the afterlife claims that it is timeless. Individuals exist in one eternal unchanging moment that is always the same; at death they reach final closure in spiritual development and destiny. A *dynamic process* view, by contrast, claims that the afterlife is temporal. It involves progress and change—unending movement toward God for the saved and unending chances of salvation for the unsaved. The Episcopal Prayers of the People ask God "that your will for [the dead] may be fulfilled."[10] For none of the departed has God's purpose been completed: none have been resurrected in God's new creation. In addition, those in heaven have not yet stopped growing in their relationship with God, those in purgatory lack mature love and are not fully united with God, and those in hell are separated from God.

In examining whether there is an incomplete future and whether the afterlife is dynamic I identify positions that are compatible with prayer

---

9. Some scholars think that hell is temporarily salvation-open, that is, only prior to Christ's appearing. The particular judgment experienced at death is revocable until final judgment—which is irrevocable. Other scholars see hell as permanently salvation-open, with repentance remaining possible even after final judgment. In volume two chapter five I opt for the latter view.

10. Episcopal Church, *Book of Common Prayer*, 389.

for the departed and consistent with both reason and revelation. These questions—the nature of time and eternity and of God's relationship to them—are among the most difficult in philosophy. While perfect understanding and definitive proof are hard to have, and while some readers will dispute my conclusions, I attempt to offer a coherent explanation of and to build a strong cumulative case for the dynamic temporality view of time.

Philosophical Theories of Time

Reality is either timeless (beyond time) or temporal (within time). The static timelessness view says that all events exist in an eternal present without temporal succession. The dynamic temporality view sees both earthly life and the afterlife as processes of change in which events follow one another in time. Prayer for the dead requires salvation history to be incomplete and the life beyond death to be temporal, with developing events and choices.[11]

The Nature of Time

Time is, most basically, an ordered sequence of events, one after another—as Karl Rahner puts it, "a chain of individual occurrences stretching forward and backward."[12] John McTaggart distinguishes two forms that this linear succession can take: the A-theory of dynamic temporality and the B-theory of static timelessness.[13] In the A-theory time flows dynamically—like watching a movie being played through a projector, where frame follows frame in a changing stream of sequential images. The viewer sees new images appear and replace others, which cease to exist. In the B-theory, however, time exists statically—like looking at a movie film unrolled on the floor, where earlier frames are located before

---

11. Traditional theology holds that world history is dynamic and eternal life is static. I reject this view—claiming that both earthly and eschatological time is dynamic.

12. Rahner, *Theological Investigations*, Vol. 19, 172.

13. McTaggart, "Unreality of Time." My review draws on Conee and Sider, *Riddles of Existence*, chapter 3; Craig, "Time, Eternity and Eschatology," Dowden, "Time;" Dyke, "Metaphysics of Time;" Le Poidevin, "Experience of Time;" Markosian, "Time;" Rahner, *Theological Investigations*, Vol. 19, chapter 13; Sklar, "Time;" Smart, "Time;" Smith, "Time, Being and Becoming."

later ones. The images laid out this way are totally motionless relative to the viewer.

The A-theory claims that the fundamental feature of time is ordering of events in terms of past, present, and future. The passing of time is an objective aspect of reality. Time flows in a dynamic process; like driving forward on a road, events change from future to present to past.[14] Things come into existence and go out of existence; the Vietnam War was future in 1900, present in 1970, and past in 2000. The A-view of time is tensed; all of reality exists in one of three modes—some events are past, some are present, some are future. Past, present, and future are genuine properties of events. Since tensed facts are real, propositions have different truth values at different times; the statement "the United States is at war in Vietnam" was false in 1900, true in 1970, and false again in 2000.[15] In the tensed theory, time is dynamic and reality undergoes change.

The B-theory claims that the fundamental feature of time is ordering of events in terms of earlier than, simultaneous with, and later than. Reality itself does not involve change, but is a simple block of time in which events are temporally and eternally positioned relative to each other, but are not objectively located in the past, present, or future. As Richard Bauckham and Trevor Hart say, "there is no temporal movement, only a temporal series of relationships or a temporal arrangement of events" forever fixed in a static eternal present.[16] Propositions have one

---

14. The source from which time springs, Moltmann (*Coming of God*, 26, 283–287) says, is the future. Time is directional—it flows out of the future into the present; future becomes present, and present past.

15. There are three tense forms, and to assign a tense to a fact is to indicate the particular time—past, present, or future—of the action or event. To say a fact is tensed is to say that it is past, present, or future. The present, Wolterstorff ("God Everlasting," 83) claims, is the most basic mode of temporality; past and future are defined in terms of present—the past was present and the future will be present. The present moment is the instant of becoming, without duration, where future becomes past. According to one version of the A-theory—presentism—only present time exists; the past no longer exists and the future does not yet exist. According to another version—the growing universe model—both past and present are real, but the future is not; the future is mere potential (an open set of possibilities) while past and present are actual (a closed set of facts). Reality changes in size, getting bigger at each moment, as more and more events, once future, become present and then past. According to a third version—eternalism—past, present, and future are equally real.

16. Bauckham and Hart, "Shape of Time," 42. The Vietnam War does not have the tensed property of being past, only the tenseless property of being later than other events. The intrinsic, tenseless relation of events as earlier than, simultaneous with, and later than are absolute and unchanging. Whether the Vietnam War is occurring

unchanging truth value: "the Civil War is earlier than the Vietnam War" is always true. The B-view of time is tenseless, and time does not flow. The passing of time—the experience of future events becoming present and then past—is a subjective perception of the mind seeing reality from a particular position in time; no temporal position is objectively "now" (just as no geographical location is objectively "here"—though it may be subjectively experienced as "here" by a particular person inhabiting it). The Vietnam War is future for a person living in 1900, present for a person living in 1970, and past for a person living in 2000. The B-theory implies that all events in time are equally real. History is spread out, like a road seen from a mountain; all events are, objectively speaking, occurring "now."[17] In this tenseless theory, time is static and change from future to present to past is not objectively real.

The B-theory, in which events are ordered in static tenseless relationships, misses the essence of time as temporal becoming. If this is what time is like, then prayer for the dead is problematic. The A-theory, in which events are ordered in dynamic tensed relationships, in which time flows and change occurs, makes best sense of such prayer. The dead are in time, awaiting consummation and experiencing growth in love, purification from sin or repentance toward God.

God and Time

How is God related to time, including eschatological events?[18] Scripture declares that God always exists, at every moment of time, without beginning or end (Ps 90:1–4 and 102:25–27; Rev 22:13). God's endless existence can be understood either as eternal timelessness (God exists

---

now depends on being located at a certain time (between 1955 and 1975).

17. In the B-theory time is like space, Dyke ("Metaphysics of Time," Section 2) explains: "all times are equally real, no matter where they are located, just as all places are equally real no matter where they are located." As Aquinas (cited in Brenner, "Aquinas on Eternity," 17) says "God knows the flight of time in God's eternity, in the way that a person standing on top of a watchtower embraces in a single glance a whole caravan of passing travelers." The A-theory, by contrast, claims that time is different from space; while all places are equally real, all times are not—the present (and perhaps the past) is most real.

18. My review draws on Craig, "Divine Eternity"; Davis, *Logic and Nature of God*, chapter 1; Ganssle, "God and Time"; Helm, "Eternity"; Kneale, "Eternity"; Morris, *Our Idea of God*, chapter 7; Padgett, "Eternity"; Stump, "Eternity"; Swinburne, *Coherence of Theism*, chapter 12, and "God and Time"; Wolterstorff, "God Everlasting."

outside of time, the same from age to age, without sequence and change) or as everlasting temporality (God forever exists in and develops through time).

The traditional view is that God is timeless. God exists beyond time in an eternal now without temporal succession. God experiences all events at once (in a B-series of earlier and later), not in moment-by-moment sequence (without the flow, the before and after, of an A-series).[19] Augustine of Hippo defended divine timelessness: "in the eternal, nothing is transient, but the whole is present. . . . Your 'years' neither go nor come. Ours come and go . . . in succession. All your 'years' subsist in simultaneity, because they do not change."[20] Boethius of Rome, Anselm of Canterbury, and Thomas Aquinas also endorsed divine timelessness—as does C. S. Lewis: "to be God is to enjoy an infinite present, where nothing has yet passed away and nothing is still to come."[21] God is thought to be timeless because God as Creator is wholly other than creation. Plato distinguishes being (ultimate reality—the world of the timeless and unchanging forms, like the number 9, which has no past, present, or future) from becoming (lesser reality—the temporal world of change and impermanence in which things and people come and go)—and claims that eternal unchanging beings are superior to things that change.[22] Christian tradition followed Plato: time is what is transitory, eternity is what is permanent—creation exists in succession, God lives in simultaneity.

19. Craig (*God, Time and Eternity*, 137) points out that the B-theory is the metaphysical presupposition of divine timelessness and the A-theory of divine temporality. Quinn ("Eternity," 382) explains timelessness: "eternity is simultaneously present to every instant of time. Each part of time coexists with the whole of eternity, although this part may be past or future in relation to other parts of time. Hence every event in time is present to eternity; God sees each event actually occurring." Peterson et al. (*Reason and Religious Belief*, 62) agree: "all of time is present to God, all at once and changelessly, in God's eternal present."

20. Augustine, *Confessions*, chapters 11.11 and 16, 228 and 230. Augustine contrasts time (the fluid and constantly changing flow of experience) from eternity (the simple and unchanging ever-present moment).

21. Lewis, *Letters to Malcolm*, Letter 20, 109. Also see *Mere Christianity*, 146.

22. Plato, *Timaeus*, 37e6–38a6, 723–24. Several reasons are given for thinking that God is timeless. First, God is a simple being without parts. No sequence of distinct moments make up God's life; instead, God possesses all of God's life at once. Second, God is a maximal being. A timeless being who experiences its entire life all at once has a fuller life than a temporal being whose life comes in brief slices, some of which are gone forever while others are yet to come (Morris, *Idea of God*, 128–29). Third, God is an immutable being. Change implies imperfection, a move from better to worse or *vice versa*. Divine perfection allows no change—hence no temporal succession.

The problem with divine timelessness is that it limits both God's knowledge of and action in the world. First, a timeless God cannot know what is happening as it happens. God knows timeless truths (tenseless facts like "Elijah's prayer for the widow's son is earlier than St. Peter's prayer for Dorcas"—1 Kgs 17:20–22 and Acts 9:36–41) but does not know temporal truths (tensed facts like whether these prayers are past, present, or future).[23] The biblical God, however, has current and changing knowledge of creation. The psalmist (139:1–2) states that "you know my sitting down and my rising up" and "trace my journeys and my resting-places"—events that occur at different times. Knowledge of current events is necessarily temporal—so a timeless God cannot know what is happening *now*. God is not located at particular time segments and so cannot know that today is Wednesday, March 9, 2016. To have changing knowledge of a constantly changing world, God must exist through a sequence of different times and events in God's life must occur before and after each other. God's knowledge of temporal events, Nicholas Wolterstorff says, "is infected by the temporality" of those events.[24]

Second, it is difficult to make sense of a timeless God interacting with the world and human beings. While such a God—Richard

---

23. This argument assumes that tenseless propositions cannot be translated into tensed propositions without losing meaning. Tenseless propositions (that an event occurs at some time, say proposition 1—"the Vietnam War occurs between 1955 and 1975") differ from tensed propositions (that an event is happening now, say proposition 2—"the Vietnam War is now being fought"). 1, being tenseless, can be known at all times; it has a constant truth value; but 2, being tensed, can only be known at one particular time. 2 has variable truth value; it is false in 1900, true in 1970 and false again in 2000. If all God knows is that the Vietnam War happens after the Civil War, God does not know if (a) both are past, (b) both are future, (c) one is past and one is future, (d) one is present and one is past or (e) one is present and one is future.

24. Wolterstorff, "God Everlasting," 93. It is only possible to know that an event *is* happening when it is actually happening; no one can know that an event *is* happening before it begins or after it ends. God can only know that I am sitting when I am sitting or that I am rising when I am rising. God's knowledge grows as time flows and changes as history develops, as things come to be and pass away. This means that God's knowledge changes; God begins to know that the Vietnam War is happening when it begins and stops knowing that it is happening when it ends. "The concept of a timeless eternity makes God an unliving God without relationship. But the God of the biblical traditions," Moltmann (*Sun of Righteousness*, 63) says, "is a living God, who has relationships in time to God's temporal creations." God's relationship to creation requires temporality—a personal God who is engaged with a temporal creation and responds to temporal events, who deliberates, anticipates, remembers must be in time. Divine eternity, Cullmann (*Christ and Time*, 23) says, means "not the timelessness of God . . . but . . . the endlessness of God's time." God's eternity embraces the reality of time.

Swinburne says—has a frozen and impersonal existence,[25] the biblical God acts in a changing and temporal world. God intervenes at particular times in history—"when the fullness of time had come God sent his Son" (Gal 4:4), and God "will bring [final consummation] at the right time" (1 Tim 6:14–15). In order to act at specific times, God must know more than just the lexical ordering of events; God must know where in the sequence things currently are. In order to rescue the Israelites at the Red Sea, for example, God must know that they have left Egypt.[26] God also acts in succession; God answers Elijah's prayer before answering St. Peter's prayer, and God reveals truth progressively ("long ago God spoke to our ancestors . . . by the prophets, but in these last days he has spoken to us by a Son"—Heb 1:1–2). If there are "former things" and "new things" then there is temporal flow (Isa 42:9; 43:18–19; Rev 21:1,4–5).

In particular, Wolterstorff notes, God must be temporal in order to respond to the free actions of human beings; "given that all human actions are temporal, then those actions of God which are 'response' actions are temporal as well."[27] Answers to prayer, for example, require temporal succession—first Hannah prays and then God acts (1 Sam 1). Or take God's actions of punishing and forgiving. These are intrinsically temporal; David's sin of adultery comes before God's judgment and David's repentance comes before God's pardon (2 Sam 11–12).[28] A God who is

---

25. Swinburne, *Coherence of Theism*, 221. Pruss and Rasmussen ("Time without Creation," 406) wonder whether the notion of God as Trinity fits comfortably with the idea of God as timeless. God's existence is not static and unchanging across infinitely many moments of time. Instead, God is Trinity—a communion of persons eternally bound together by the mutual exchange of love, an eternal *perichoresis* (divine dance) of Father, Son, and Spirit in which new thoughts and expressions of love occur. This giving and receiving, which characterizes God's inner life prior to creation, involves movement and change; this requires dynamic temporality and is incompatible with static timelessness. Internally—as well as externally—God's life is temporal.

26. B-theorists will contest this—claiming that God can know that at such and such a point in the sequence [i.e., when the Israelites reach the Red Sea] God will bring it about that the sea parts. God need not be located in the temporal stream to do that. In debates like this A-theorists and B-theorists reach rock-bottom fundamental disagreement that may not be amenable to further argument.

27. Wolterstorff, "God Everlasting," 93. Verhey (*Christian Art of Dying*, 205–6) agrees: "the account of God's being and activity in Scripture does not suggest a timeless God."

28. Swinburne, *Coherence of Theism*, 28. God's actions of warning and promising are also temporal. Through the prophet Jeremiah (18:7–10) God says: "at one moment I may declare concerning a nation . . . that I will . . . destroy it, but if that nation . . . turns from its evil, I will change my mind. . . . And at another moment I may declare

causally active in the world cannot, William Lane Craig says, "remain untouched by the world's temporality."²⁹

God's eternity is not timeless simultaneity but infinite temporality—temporal sequence and endless duration. God does not experience time all at once; instead, God experiences time as a sequence of changing events. God exists within A-series time and God's inner life is sequential; God experiences the flow of events and has life phases that are past, present, and future. God experiences time differently from human persons; "with the Lord one day is like a thousand years, and a thousand years are like one day" (2 Pet 3:8; Ps 90:4).³⁰ Nonetheless, in Hick's words, God "is a temporal reality undergoing continual change."³¹

Eschatology and Time

How do theories of time and eternity relate to eschatology? Recall that the open future requirement includes two separate conditions.

1. The incomplete future requirement states that eschatological events are future—there is a real future ahead for both the living and the dead. This is a necessary condition of consummation prayer.

2. The dynamic afterlife requirement states that post-mortem existence is dynamic—the condition of the dead is one of development

---

concerning a nation . . . that I will build . . . it, but if it does evil . . . then I will change my mind." Stump ("Eternity"), who defends timelessness, concedes that "there are things an atemporal God cannot do—such as remembering or planning ahead." So does Leftow ("Eternity," 257): "a timeless God does not remember, forget, feel relief or cease to do anything. For a timeless God has no past, and one can remember or forget . . . only what is past. A timeless God does not wait . . . , hope, foreknow . . . or deliberate. For a timeless God has no future. . . . If timeless, God does not change . . . God's attitudes or plans."

29. Craig, "Divine Eternity," 155. As noted, defenders of timelessness reject the argument that because God's knowledge and activity is in time, therefore God is in time. See Stump, "Eternity;" Stump and Kretzman, "Eternity" and Wolterstorff, "God Everlasting."

30. St. Peter means that in view of God's eternal existence, a thousand years are nothing—and so the *parousia* is not delayed by divine standards, only by human expectations. We cannot conclude from this verse that God is outside time.

31. Hick, *Death and Eternal Life*, 220. Thiselton (*Life After Death*, 210) agrees: instead of "a Greek and Thomist view of timeless perfection and 'essence,'" we should opt for "the biblical view of the living God, who is always on the move and . . . never static."

and change. This is a necessary condition of growth, purification and salvation prayers.

Each condition is most naturally associated with an A-view of time.

The incomplete future requirement

"Without . . . temporality," Karl Barth says, "the content of the Christian message has no shape."[32] God's purpose is essentially temporal: salvation history has a forward direction beginning with creation and moving toward an ending in consummation. Oscar Cullman distinguishes the Greek symbol which is a circle, from the biblical conception of time, which is linear.[33] George Florovsky summarizes: "the category of the future was quite irrelevant in the Greek version of history. History was conceived as a rotation, with an inevitable return to the initial position, from which a new repetition of events was bound to start again." Time was a closed circle, an unending repetition not leading to a goal or end—and salvation consisted in entering timeless eternity. "On the contrary, the biblical view opens into the future, in which new things are to be . . . realized. And an ultimate realization of the divine purpose is anticipated in the future . . . a state of consummation." Time, he continues, is "a teleological process, inwardly ordained toward a certain final goal. A *telos* is implied in the very design of creation. . . . History has to have an end, at which it is 'fulfilled' or 'consummated.'"[34] Time is a linear A-series of events that moves toward the completion of God's plan.

So when are eschatological events completed? Assuming they are not fulfilled in this life, there are—to repeat—two possibilities. As John Cooper puts it, they are either

---

32. Barth, cited in Swinburne, *Coherence of Theism*, 225.

33. Cullmann, *Christ and Time*, chapter 2.

34. Florovsky, *Creation and Redemption*, 244 and 246. Ratzinger (*Eschatology*, 51–52) agrees: "Scripture's understanding of time is linear. What time is may be known by looking at the ladder whose steps are: yesterday, today, tomorrow. Because it is a line of ascent, it offers the space in which the fulfillment of a divine plan may take place. In other words, salvation occurs within time." This means that God's "eternity . . . must be seen . . . as infinite temporality."

1. realized immediately at death (they "are ever-present realities which become real for us when we transcend time at the moment of our death") or

2. realized at some future point after death ("the second coming of Christ and the renewal of creation are events in future earthly history which Christ will bring about by once again leaving eternity and breaking into time").[35]

What, Tom Wright asks, is the chronology of life after death? "Do those who die go into a different time-sequence, so that they go straight to the ultimate destination at once? Or do they rest . . . , while waiting, so that we all arrive at the end together?"[36]

Consummation at death faces serious difficulties. As argued in chapter 6, it contradicts the Bible's future consummation texts, which portray the culmination of history as occurring after, not at, death. Immediate consummation is also theologically problematic, Joseph Ratzinger points out. First, it means that "on the other side of death history is already complete." But it is contradictory to claim that history is "simultaneously completed and still continuing." History cannot be unfolding for the living and ended for the dead—"and therefore to declare that history is already cancelled and lifted up into an eternal Last Day after death is impossible." Second, final consummation of all history in death undermines the very concept of eschatology. On this picture, Ratzinger asks, "what future can history and the cosmos expect? Will they ever come to their fulfilled wholeness, or will an everlasting duality separate time from an eternity that time can never reach?" Immediate consummation dehistoricizes the *eschaton*. Eschatological events, then, must be objectively future, not realized at death. "History really continues," Ratzinger says, "it remains a reality, even from a vantage point beyond death."[37] As Wright puts it, the dead "wait for something more: for the new world . . . and bodily resurrection."[38] The biblical writers, Cooper adds, "clearly believed that Christ's return and the advent of the new heaven and earth are future

---

35. Cooper, *Body, Soul and Life Everlasting*, 210.

36. Wright, *Following Jesus*, 112.

37. Ratzinger, *Eschatology*, 110, 188, 253, and 188. This follows the definition of Pope Benedict XII in *Benedictus Deus* (1336): the resurrection of the body does not take place simultaneously with the personal state of heaven, purgatory or hell, which occur immediately after death.

38. Wright, *Following Jesus*, 112.

historical events, not realities already actual in the transcendent eternal now."[39] Even when wars and other signs occur, Jesus says, "the end is still to come" (Mark 13:7).

An incomplete future fits best with an A-view of time.[40] Eschatology, by definition, concerns the *last* things, the *future* of individuals and the cosmos, the *end point* of a series of events. There is "a period of time between death and resurrection," Cooper says, and this "presupposes that the dead remain on the same time-line as the living, that eschatological time is historical time."[41] The fact that final consummation is collective means that eschatological events are not completed individually at death. As Origen of Alexandria points out:

> the apostles [in heaven] have not yet received their joy: they are ... waiting for me to participate in their joy.... Abraham is still waiting to attain perfection. Isaac and Jacob and all the prophets are waiting for us in order to attain the perfect blessedness together with us.... You will have joy when you depart from this life if you are a saint. But your joy will be complete only when no member of your body is lacking to you. For you too will wait, just as you are awaited.[42]

St. John (Rev 6: 9–11) confirms that the fulfillment of God's purposes is not complete, since the martyrs are still waiting for final redemption. "They are at rest; they are conscious," Wright says, "but they are not enjoying the final bliss which is to come in the New Jerusalem.... Until all God's people are safely home, none of them is yet fulfilled."[43] The fact that evil remains in the world also proves that consummation is future. When the last day arrives suffering and injustice will disappear from creation: "death will be no more; mourning and crying and pain will be no more, for the first things have passed away" because God is "making all things new" (Rev 21:4–5; cf. Isa 25:7–8). The A-view of eschatology resolves the problem of evil: since time flows and real change occurs, evil will be entirely past when creation is put to rights.

---

39. Cooper, *Body, Soul and Life Everlasting*, 211.
40. This follows Craig, "Time, Eternity and Eschatology."
41. Cooper, *Body, Soul and Life Everlasting*, 211.
42. Origen, cited in Ratzinger, *Eschatology*, 185–86. In this passage Origen comments on Hebrews 11:39 (the heroes of faith "would not, apart from us, be made perfect") and 1 Corinthians 12:12–27 (we are one body with many members so no part can say to another "I have no need of you").
43. Wright, *For All Saints*, 24.

In addition to being future, eschatological events follow one another in chronological sequence—the return of Christ, general resurrection, final judgment, heaven and hell. St. Paul indicates that they will occur "each in his own order: Christ the first fruits, then at his coming those who belong to Christ. Then comes the end, when he hands over the kingdom to God the Father, after he has destroyed every ruler and every authority and power" (1 Cor 15:23–24). Since eschatological events are both objectively future and chronologically sequenced, they are best explained by A-time. These events remain ahead for the living and the dead—and for God as well. They lie in a future part of God's life and will be experienced by God in sequence as they happen. Since his resurrection and ascension, the writer to the Hebrews (10:12–13) says, Christ "has been waiting"—and continues to wait—"until his enemies would be made a footstool for his feet."

B-series time, by contrast, has troubling implications for eschatology. If all events are equally present then time has no direction and history is not moving forward. In B-time the last things—*parousia*, resurrection, and judgment—are, Craig says, "fixed in their tenseless temporal locations and not in any sense approaching so as to be differently regarded than past events."[44] And since God is timeless, God has no eschatological future; as Lewis puts it, for God "nothing is still to come."[45] God experiences all events—the resurrection of Jesus and the general resurrection, the first Advent and the second—as equally present. B-time also means that evil is never banished from creation but remains eternally present— the Holocaust is forever as real as the New Jerusalem. In Hick's words, since "evil is eternalized together with good.... there is no final resolving of evil."[46]

"We *look* for the resurrection of the dead and the life of the world *to come*," the Nicene Creed says, for the time when Christ "*will* come again in glory." Cullmann emphasizes that "the coming consummation

---

44. Craig, "Time, Eternity and Eschatology," 609. He (608-9) allows that "eschatology is meaningful . . . on the B-theory, since that theory . . . affirms temporal asymmetry, though it denies . . . temporal becoming." And yet "one gets a less robust eschatology on a B-theory than on an A-theory."

45. Lewis, *Letters to Malcolm*, Letter 20, 109. Leftow ("Eternity," 257) agrees: "a timeless God does not wait." While timeless beings have no future, beings with future parts—with temporal phases of any kind—exist in time. God has life episodes, some which are past and no longer exist, others which are future and do not yet exist. See Leftow, "Eternity (Addendum)," 359.

46. Hick, *Death and Eternal Life*, 221.

is a real future, just as the past redemptive deed of Jesus Christ . . . is . . . a real past."[47] The first Advent, John Robinson says, is "the first half of a single process that will be completed in the future" at the second Advent. There will be, Ratzinger adds, "an end to history . . . , a truly 'Last Day.'"[48] Consummation prayer requires that eschatological events are future for the dead. As John Bramhall says, "though [the souls of the faithful departed] be always in an estate of blessedness, yet they want the consummation of this blessedness. . . . Then what forbids Christians to pray for this . . . consummation of blessedness? So we pray, as often as we say 'thy Kingdom come,' or 'come Lord Jesus, come quickly.'"[49] Because the future is consummation-incomplete, we ask (in Wright's words) for "the fulfillment of God's complete purposes"—that God "bring the whole creation to a joyful completion and the fulfillment of God's eternal Kingdom."[50] Such prayers make good sense with A-series time but seem problematic on a B-series.

The dynamic afterlife requirement

The afterlife is either an eternal timeless moment or an eternal process of development—as Hick says, "participation in eternity, beyond all temporal successiveness" or "dynamic life, presupposing change and time."[51] The traditional view is that the life to come is static and timeless, a changeless state of joy or pain; only purgatory requires temporal succession, since entry to heaven follows purification.[52] As Aquinas says, the eternal joy of

---

47. Cullmann, *Christ and Time*, 15.

48. Robinson, *In the End, God*, 70 and Ratzinger, *Eschatology*, 51–53 and 166. The Roman Catholic International Theological Commission ("Some Current Questions," 217–18) also rejects "atemporalism"—the view that time does not exist after death. St. John's "way of speaking about the souls of the martyrs [Rev 6:9–11] does not . . . remove them from all reality of succession . . . . Similarly, if time should have no meaning after death . . . , it would be difficult to understand why St. Paul used formulas referring to the future in speaking about . . . resurrection [e.g. 1 Thess 4:13–18]."

49. Bramhall, cited in Archbishops' Commission, *Prayer and Departed*, 79.

50. Wright, *For All Saints*, 24 and Archbishops' Commission, *Prayer and Departed*, 51.

51. Hick, *Death and Eternal Life*, 207.

52. Brown (*Ransom of Soul*, 107–8, 113) points out that purgatory changed the idea of the other world by inserting time—sequence and a suspension of timelessness—into eternity. Purgatory requires delay—a twilight zone between time (this world) and eternity (heaven) for souls that do not directly enter God's presence where

the saints is "a share in the divine eternity, transcending all time" and "is not marked off into past, present, and future."[53] Death means the end of existence in time, removal from the reality of succession—"we transcend the flux of historical becoming," as Ratzinger puts it, "and participate in the true present."[54] If the afterlife is a static state of timelessness, without change or progress, then growth, purification, and salvation prayers are pointless.

First, the afterlife is temporal because God acts gradually rather than instantaneously. As John Polkinghorne points out, "part of the continuity that we may expect to hold between the two halves of God's great creative-redemptive act is that the patient God who acts through temporally unfolding processes in the old creation, will continue to act in a similar fashion in the unfolding fulfillment of the new creation." "The universe is a world of temporal process," he adds, "and if we believe in the consistency of the Creator, we should not expect that its successor will be so radically different that it is ... a world of timeless existence. It too will surely have its developing history." Given God's nature, the life to come "will not be a timeless world of 'eternity,' but a temporal world whose character is everlasting."[55]

Second, the afterlife is temporal because human beings are inherently temporal creatures—successive entities—whose life is one of development and growth. Actions and experiences take place in succession one after another, and relationships with other people are progressive and changing. "We cannot conceive a timeless life," Moltmann says, "for the life of the living is life in time."[56] "Is it even logically possible," Ratzinger

---

time ceases.

53. Aquinas, *Summa Theologiae*, Vol. 33, 2a2ae q18 a2, 33. Eternity after death is not, Rahner (*Theological Investigations*, Vol. 19, 170-71) says, "the unlimited continuation of time ... , the running on of time with one section coming after another." Eternity is "a never ending time running on into infinity ... , a continuation of time into eternity." Such a view of the afterlife would make heaven boring for the saved and salvation possible for the unsaved—both of which Rahner questions as "dangerous and pernicious" implications. Pannenberg (cited in Polkinghorne, *God of Hope*, 117-18) claims that since "temporality is a piece with the structural sinfulness of our life," ultimate fulfillment will require "an end of time."

54. Ratzinger, *Eschatology*, 174, slightly modified. The idea that "time shall be no more" comes from the *KJV* mistranslation of Revelation 10:6—which actually means "there will be no more delay" (*NRSV* and *NIV*) in God bringing final consummation.

55. Polkinghorne, *God of Hope*, 120, 15-16 and 117.

56. Moltmann, *Sun of Righteousness*, 63. "It is not conceivable," Russell (*History of Heaven*, 10-12) says, that "human beings ... could exist without ... time. ... Even

asks, "to conceive of [persons], whose existence is achieved exclusively in the temporal, being transposed into sheer eternity?" We "cannot simply move across from the condition 'time' into the condition . . . timelessness."⁵⁷ Knowing God in heaven, developing moral dispositions in purgatory, and repenting of sin in hell require a temporal reality in which the dead experience change and have lives occurring in succession.

1. *Growth prayers* for the blessed require the afterlife to be growth-incomplete: spiritual perfection is not finished at death. Traditional theology sees heaven as—in John Casey's words—"a state of eternal stillness," a timeless spiritual existence characterized by static contemplation of God. Growth prayers, however, require heaven to be "a state of eternal progress."⁵⁸ Heaven is not, John Meyendorff says, "a static contemplation of divine 'essence,' but a dynamic ascent of love, which never ends, because God's transcendent being is inexhaustible, and always contains new things to be discovered."⁵⁹ Participation in the infinite nature of God can never be completed, and so the saints experience continuously deepening awareness of and communion with God. At death, Lewis says, we begin "Chapter One of the Great Story . . . which goes on forever: in which every chapter is better than the one before."⁶⁰ Heaven's events—worship, activity, relationships—are essentially temporal. I develop this position in volume two chapter 3. Here I am simply identifying a growth-open heaven (which cannot be timeless but requires a succession of moments) as a necessary assumption of growth prayer: "grant that, increasing in

---

glorified bodies cannot function without time, for it takes time to sing a hymn or even to think a thought."

57. Ratzinger, *Eschatology*, 109 and 182. Timelessness, he claims, confuses the very meaning of eternity. "Can an eternity which has a beginning be eternity at all? Is it not necessarily non-eternal, and so temporal, precisely because it had a beginning? Yet how can one deny that the resurrection of a human being has a beginning, namely, after death?"

58. Casey, *Afterlives*, 349.

59. Meyendorff, *Byzantine Theology*, 219. Against the Platonic notion that perfection is unchanging and static (like a statue), Polkinghorne (*God of Hope*, 143) suggests that perfection is dynamic and progressive (like music). It is necessary "for finite embodied beings to participate in unfolding temporal process, as much in the new creation as in the old. Dynamic becoming is the form of perfection appropriate to creatures of our kind." And so "eschatological fulfillment will . . . be an everlasting unfolding of salvific encounter with God, rather than a timeless moment of beatific illumination" (132).

60. Lewis, *Last Battle*, 211.

knowledge and love of thee, they may go from strength to strength in the life of perfect service in thy heavenly Kingdom."[61]

2. *Purification prayers* for the imperfect require the afterlife to be purification-incomplete: moral development is not concluded at death. To enjoy the fellowship of the Trinity eternally we must be able to love perfectly. As Lewis says, before entering joy the imperfect must "be cleaned first" in a "process of purification" and prayer for them "presupposes that progress [is] still possible."[62] Since complete holiness does not happen during this life, either God abruptly transforms us into morally perfect people without our cooperation at death or a process of moral renewal, in which we take part, continues after death.

Instant transformation by a unilateral act of God is problematic since it would disrupt personal identity. We are temporal beings, and so remaining the same person across time requires that changes occur gradually. If God instantly gives imperfect believers holy characters, then the individual who lived on earth and the one who exists after death would not be the same person. Character transformation involves habituation in which we develop virtues by repeated actions done across time. Aquinas suggests that length of time in purgatory differs according to the degree of ingrained sin.[63] I return to these matters in volume two chapter 4. Here I am simply indicating that a purification-open purgatory (which cannot be timeless but requires a succession of moments) is necessary for purification prayer to make sense: "grant to the departed purification from all their sins, that they may obtain that holiness which fits them for heaven."[64]

3. *Salvation prayers* for the unsaved require the afterlife to be salvation-open: spiritual destiny is not settled at death. Again there are two possibilities: death either involves an open future (in which forgiveness is still available) or a closed future (in which all chance of reconciliation with God is ended). Traditional theology affirms a closed future—once

---

61. Episcopal Church, *Book of Common Prayer*, 489.

62. Lewis, *Letters to Malcolm*, 20, 109–10.

63. Aquinas, *Summa Theologica* Vol. 3, Supplement to the Third Part, Appendix 1 q2 a5–6. "Some venial sins cling more persistently than others, according as the affections are more inclined to them, and more firmly fixed in them. And since that which clings more persistently is more slowly cleansed, it follows that some are tormented in purgatory longer than others, for as much as their affections were steeped in venial sins."

64. Modification of the traditional Roman Catholic prayer for the souls in purgatory.

a person is dead, no change of spiritual destiny is possible, so hell is inescapable. If a person has not known about or has rejected God on earth, there is no second chance after death; life choices are irrevocable. Christians across the centuries, however, have questioned this teaching, arguing that death is not a decisive break and that posthumous salvation is possible. In order for the unsaved to escape hell, a change of spiritual direction after death must be possible. Both God's offer of grace and the sinner's ability to respond must continue beyond death; these two conditions constitute salvation-open death. Repentance and forgiveness, as noted earlier, are temporal concepts; human repentance must precede divine forgiveness—in the afterlife as in this life. In volume two chapter 5 I defend these claims. Here I am simply pointing out that a salvation-open hell (which cannot be timeless but requires a succession of moments) is a necessary condition of salvation prayer: "God of infinite mercy and justice, who . . . hatest nothing that thou hast made, we rejoice in thy love for all creation and commend all men to thee, that in them thy will be done."[65]

Biblical Data on Time and Eternity

Prayer for the dead requires

1. eschatological events that are future and incomplete and
2. an afterlife that is dynamic and fluid.

Edward Kettner observes that "there are no basic assertions in Scripture as to the nature of time. . . . The Christian doctrine of time must belong to philosophical rather than to biblical theology."[66] Nonetheless, let us see what the Bible says or implies about time, eternity, and eschatology.

Hebrew Scripture has no general word for time as an enduring dimension or for degrees of time—past, present, future; the concern, instead, is for the timing of events and particular points in time.[67] The most common words, *'eth* and *mo'edh*, refer to a definite moment—the point of time when something happens or is to be done, the right or favorable moment. In the prophets it is used of the time when God will intervene

---

65. Archbishops' Commission, *Prayer and Departed*, 55; cf. 20.
66. Kettner, "Time, Eternity and Intermediate State," 93.
67. See Jenni, "Time" and Rietz, "Time" as well as Barr, *Biblical Words for Time*; Cullmann, *Christ and Time*, chapter 1; Robinson, *In the End, God*, 55–67.

in history (e.g., Jer 51:6; Hab 2:3). Christian Scripture has two words for time. *Chronos* means time in general—it refers to quantitative time, a chronological succession of moments measured by a clock or calendar. *Kairos* means an appropriate point of time—it refers to qualitative time, a special moment within *chronos* when significant events happen. It is the time in history when God acts—"the time is fulfilled" Jesus announced when beginning his ministry (Mark 1:15). *Kairos* often has eschatological reference: "the time is near" (Luke 21:8; Rev 1:3; 22:10), Christ will appear "at the right time" (1 Tim 6:15) and the kingdom will be established at "the times . . . that the Father has set" (Acts 1:7). *Kairos* relates to the fulfillment of a goal or *telos*. Biblical faith is oriented toward the future: God is a God of purpose and history is a process with a goal—final consummation for individuals and all of creation. Unfolding time is necessary to bring this purpose to fulfillment.[68]

Consummation prayer requires that eschatological events are future, that history is consummation-incomplete. As we saw in the last chapter, the life to come has two stages: a temporary, penultimate state (which Donald Bloesch calls the "near hereafter") and a permanent, ultimate state (the "far hereafter").[69] The Bible's future consummation texts teach that there is a final culmination of all things beyond the intermediate state. God's ultimate will for human beings—resurrection in a recreated earth—remains future for the dead; it is unfinished and awaits completion at the return of Christ.

Growth, purification, and salvation prayers require that post-mortem existence be dynamic, with individual histories unfinished at death. The Bible says very little about whether the experience of the departed is static or allows change in spiritual development and destiny. The main reasons for believing one or the other are theological; our views of heaven, purgatory, and hell are integrated with other things we believe about the nature of time, eternity, and salvation. Consider growth prayers, which require the afterlife to be growth-incomplete. In one sense the saints reach closure in heaven through experiencing unending satisfaction and contentment: "in your presence there is fullness of joy; in your right hand are pleasures forevermore" (Ps 16:11). But in another sense

---

68. Robinson (*In the End, God*, 30–33) points out that the term "final" has a double meaning: chronological finality (being last in a time-series, occurring after everything else as a concluding moment—related to *chronos*) or teleological finality (the fulfillment of a purpose—related to *kairos*).

69. Bloesch, *Last Things*, 136.

they never reach closure since eternity is an open-ended process of being "transformed . . . from one degree of glory to another" (2 Cor 3:18). In its images of heaven as a fertile garden (the restored Eden) and a bustling city (the New Jerusalem), the Bible does not suggest a static, contemplative afterlife but a dynamic, active one. Or take salvation prayers, which require the afterlife to be salvation-open. The finality of death seems to be taught in Scripture. Take, for example, Hebrews 9:27: "it is appointed for mortals to die once, and after that the judgment." This verse, however, simply does not say that there are no more chances for salvation after death. It does say that we live and die once and that judgment comes after death, but it does not say what the purpose or result of judgment is—that God's love stops reaching out to the unsaved or that they cannot repent, in time, beyond the grave.

Scripture clearly teaches a cosmically-incomplete future. And while it does not indicate whether the afterlife is growth-incomplete or purification-incomplete for the saved or salvation-open for the unsaved, there is good theological reason to think each true based on what the Bible does say. As Jerry Walls points out, "there is no direct way to settle some issues by straightforward biblical exegesis of isolated texts." But, he insists, "this hardly means that there is no way to argue matters theologically or to arrive at a biblically-grounded view on issues [related to time and eternity]. For the question remains whether the doctrines cohere with things that are clearly taught in Scripture, or can even be inferred from them as a reasonable theological conclusion."[70]

Concluding Remarks

"Christians look forward in two ways," Dorothy and Gabriel Fackre comment, "long-range and short-term: Last Things and Next to Last Things. . . . Last Things, the final Future, have to do with the end of the world. . . . Next to Last Things have to do with the future that lies ahead of us—in both this world and the next—before God's grand Finale."[71] The future age, Cullmann insists, "is an actual future, that is, a future in time."[72] Eschatological events are incomplete. "We eagerly wait," St. Paul writes (Gal 5:5), "for the hope of righteousness." The martyrs in heaven

---

70. Walls, *Purgatory*, 56, modified.
71. Fackre, *Christian Basics*, 125–26.
72. Cullmann, *Christ and Time*, 65.

ask "how long?" and are told to wait a little longer for final vindication (Rev 6:9–11). "Do not remember the former things," God instructs, "I am about to do a new thing" (Isa 43:18–19; cf. 42:9). Because the last things are incomplete and lie in an objective future, we can pray for the end of history—the consummation of the work of love God began at creation.

Individual post-mortem histories are also incomplete—and so the afterlife is an eternal process of development, not an eternal timeless moment in which all events are statically present.[73] Time is a feature of the life of the world to come; it is characterized by progressive change and successive unfolding—and this requires an infinite series of chronological moments, of events following one another. As Moltmann says, it is an open system of temporal becoming: "there will be time and history, future and possibility in the Kingdom of glory. . . . Instead of timeless eternity we would . . . do better to talk about eternal time."[74] Prayer for the departed assumes a temporal life after death—endlessly extended time, not timelessness.

If death brings completion and finality—if it is a decisive moment of consummation when love of God is finalized, instant sanctification occurs and opportunity for salvation ends—then prayer for any of the dead has no use. If, however,

1. eschatological events lie in an objective future and are yet to be realized, and
2. the afterlife is dynamic and open to moral and spiritual change,

then prayer for them makes sense. If prayer for the dead is effective, then A-series time appears necessary since for none of the departed has God's will been completely fulfilled and because temporal becoming is the dimension in which change occurs.

Both the living and the dead are beings in time with lives characterized by succession. God, too, is temporal; God anticipates the *eschaton* and enjoys both a growing relationship with the saved dead and a changed relationship with the repentant dead. The entire life to come is dynamic; it always remains a process of temporal becoming and never becomes a state of timeless being. Even after the final reconciliation of all

---

73. Nichols, *Death and Afterlife*, 171. Eternity is either "everlasting time or the transcendence of time altogether" (179).

74. Moltmann, *Future of Creation*, 126.

things and people to God is complete, we will continue for all eternity to grow more and more into God's love.[75]

The Bible does not settle debates about the nature of time and eternity, and we must be cautious about the metaphysical conclusions we draw from its figurative and poetic language. There are deep mysteries, which we see dimly, about the transition from time to eternity. Nor do my arguments settle the matter decisively. Theologians of the past who thought of God as timeless had no difficulty affirming divine acts in history. While I find their account of how this works to be inadequate, it seems overly bold to simply declare them mistaken. That said, theology, history, and eschatology work very well on an A-theory, but seem to have problems on a B-theory. The A-theory of time and the temporal becoming view of eternity are simpler philosophically and more sensible theologically. In fairness, while I have raised questions about B-theories and eschatology, these matters are far from completely clear. I am fully aware that B-theorists will have responses to the concerns I have expressed—and it may be that the B-theory of time can account for real eschatological change, since there are competent defenders of this view. Perhaps the necessary conditions of prayer for the dead—an incomplete future and dynamic afterlife—can be met on either an A-theory or a B-theory, with either a timeless or a temporal God. But I have my doubts. When all is said and done, it seems to me that A-time is more intuitively appealing and rationally warranted. In some matters—like those of the last three chapters—decisive proof is hard to find. And yet, as Socrates pointed out centuries ago, "although it is very difficult if not impossible . . . to achieve certainty about these questions," it is our duty "to select the best and most dependable theory which human intelligence can supply."[76] Prayer for the dead may not require A-time or be inconsistent with B-time—but B-time

---

75. In both the intermediate and final states purification and repentance continue until all people are fully united with God. *Final* judgment simply means the last in time; it does not mean that opportunities for salvation are closed. An analogy: after repeatedly warning my misbehaving daughter to act properly, I finally send her to her room until she can be nice. My final decision does not mean a closed future for her. In the same way, final judgment does not imply closed destiny or completed development. Clement of Alexandria (cited in Ramelli, *Christian Doctrine of Apokatastasis*, 125) says that "the necessary corrections, inflicted out of goodness by the great Judge . . . , through several preliminary judgments, and again through the definitive judgment, compel 'those who have hardened too much' [Eph 4:39] to repent." Repentance can occur even after final judgment.

76. Plato, *Phaedo*, 85c, in *Last Days of Socrates*, 139.

does not easily lend itself to such prayers, while A-time accommodates them elegantly and coherently.

In the last three chapters I have argued that, in order to make sense, prayer for the dead requires three sets of assumptions—one concerning prayer, the other two concerning the state of the departed.[77]

1. Petitionary prayer is effective; it has real influence and makes a difference to what God does.

2. The dead consciously survive as the very same people they were in life.

3. The dead await eschatological events, which are incomplete—and post-mortem existence is a dynamic process of progressive change.

Each of these three conditions is individually necessary and all together are jointly sufficient for prayer for the dead to make sense. Having argued that prayer for the dead is logically coherent, I next outline a basic theological context for such prayers.

---

77. William Temple (cited in Archbishops' Commission, *Prayer and Departed*, 90) points out that "the objection to prayers for the dead rests on two assumptions, one of them unfounded and the other definitely false. The first is the assumption that at death all is irrevocably settled; whatever be the state of the soul at that moment, in that state it must unalterably remain. Neither in revelation, nor in reason is there a shred of evidence for this once prevalent delusion. We cannot doubt that growth in grace and power and love continues after death." This assumption concerns the nature of the afterlife—which requires and involves an incomplete and open future. The second concerns the nature of petitionary prayer generally: "the other assumption which leads men to object to prayers for the dead is the belief that we should only pray for such blessings as we fear may not be granted unless we pray for them. But this is flatly contradictory to the teaching of Christ. We are to pray for all good things because it is our Father's will to give them. . . . We do not pray for them because God will otherwise neglect them. We pray for them because we know God loves and cares for them."

chapter 8

CREATIVE LOVE CHRISTIANITY
A Theological Framework for Prayer for the Dead

I REMEMBER THE DAY I met God again for the first time, the day God stopped being—in Philip Gulley and James Mulholland's words—"a harsh judge . . . eager to punish and destroy all who do not satisfy God" and became "a gracious loving father waiting long through the night, with the light lit and the door open."[1] I left graduate study in philosophy more sure that there is a God but less sure that Christian faith is true. My doubts were compounded by a toxic church that refused to tolerate ambiguity and uncertainty. When I confided in my pastor, he scolded me for not being a believing Christian. Reciting 1 Corinthians 11:27–28, he told me that as one out of fellowship with God I was not to take Holy Communion. His words reinforced the image of God I had acquired in childhood—a God who cares but is to be feared, the deity sarcastically described by Brian McLaren: "God loves you and has a wonderful plan for your life . . . but will fry your butt in hell forever unless you do or believe the right thing."[2] Deeply wounded, but not knowing how to separate God's voice of love from the church's voice of condemnation, I let bread and cup pass me by—and soon stopped attending church altogether.

---

1. Gulley and Mulholland, *If Grace is True*, 46.

2. McLaren, *Last Word*, xix, slightly modified. Many people do not perceive the gospel as good news because Christian faith has been distorted by the idea that God's love is conditional: if we meet the conditions, loving God enough and in the right way, then God will love us—but if not, then God will reject and punish. In my case I got this view much more from churches than my parents.

I knew that in order to recover faith I had to find a more open congregation. Sunday, 2 February 1992 I visited an Evangelical Covenant Church for the first time. It was Communion Sunday, and Pastor Rob read the words of invitation: "come to this sacred table . . . not because you are strong, but because you are weak; not because you have any claim on the grace of God, but because in your frailty and sin you stand in constant need of God's mercy and help."[3] I was included—and with tears running down my face took the Sacrament for the first time in several years. That day was the turning point when I saw God change: I began to hear the welcoming "good news" gospel based on grace and love instead of the threatening "bad news" version based on law and requirements.[4] My healing and renewal had begun.

The Episcopal Church Prayers of the People include this petition: "we commend to your mercy all who have died, that your will for them may be fulfilled."[5] But what is God's will for the dead? For that matter, what is God's will for the living—or for human beings at all? Prayer for the dead raises the most basic of theological questions, matters that go to the center of God's purpose in creating spiritual beings and redeeming sinful humankind. "To understand the end," Tom Wright advises, "begin with the beginning," with "the plans of the creator God for creation as a whole."[6] The idea at the heart of Christian faith, Jeffrey Burton Russell says, is simple: "God pours out the cosmos with love and invites it to share God's joy."[7] We are made for the divine life of love, in this world and the next—and when relationship is broken God does everything possible to bring us back into communion. All of theology is framed by this relational understanding of God's purpose of love.

---

3. Evangelical Covenant Church, *Covenant Book of Worship*, 162.

4. See Borg, *Heart of Christianity*, 75–77. I do not, of course, want to oppose grace and law.

5. Episcopal Church, *Book of Common Prayer*, 389.

6. Borg and Wright, *Meaning of Jesus*, 197. Thomas (*Introduction to Theology*, 122) says that everything in theology flows from how we answer the question "why did God make human beings?"

7. Russell, *Paradise Mislaid*, 5. Throughout this chapter I draw on Pinnock and Brow, *Unbounded Love*.

God's Nature is Relational: Trinity and Incarnation

In "creation-based eschatology," Dermot Lane says, origin and destiny are connected—where we have come from (*genesis*) determines where we are going to (*telos*).[8] Our understanding of creation, however, depends on the true beginning—the nature and character of God.

Relational Trinity

God's purpose for creation and humanity is rooted in God's nature, the very essence of which is self-giving love (1 John 4:8, 16). God is not an undifferentiated unity—an absolute and solitary unmoved mover existing alone in infinite perfection. Rather, God is Trinity—a community of persons existing in an eternal relationship of mutual love. It is the reciprocal giving and receiving of love between the three persons that binds Father, Son, and Holy Spirit together. The idea of God as persons in communion is seen in Andrei Rublev's icon of the Holy Trinity, where three individuals are seated at a table in silent conversation. The head of each figure is inclined to the others, and their eyes are joined, creating a sense of attentive engagement, intimate fellowship, and oneness. God's innermost being is this everlasting partnership of love. As David Hart puts it: "God is Trinity, and always gives and goes forth toward the other." God is a set of relationships, "an eternal venture of love . . . whose fullness is the joy of an eternal self-outpouring."[9] The sharing of love, Clark Pinnock and Robert Brow emphasize, "is not just something that God decides to do, not just an occasional attribute. Loving is what characterizes God essentially."[10] Love is an essential property that defines the identity of God, not an accidental quality that God just happens to have.

---

8. Lane, *Keeping Hope Alive*, 12 and 15.

9. Hart, cited in Walls, "Heaven," 400.

10. Pinnock and Brow, *Unbounded Love*, 45. Baggini (*Pig That Wants to be Eaten*, 23) notes that when Christians say God is love, the "is" is one of identity, not attribution. God does not just have the quality of love (like my car has the quality of blueness); God *is identical with* love (like water is identical with H2O). Ramelli (*Christian Doctrine of Apokatastasis*, 664) points out that for ancient theologians like Origen and Augustine "God's goodness is far from being simply a kind of psychological trait (encompassing kindness, mercy, and the like), but it is an ontological reality, *the* . . . ontological reality, namely, that the Divinity is the supreme and absolute Good, the fullness of Good."

C. S. Lewis writes: to say "God is love" means that "the living, dynamic activity of love has been going on in God forever.... God is not a static thing... but a dynamic, pulsating activity, a life, almost a drama. Almost... a kind of dance."[11] This is how the Eastern Fathers understood the mutual indwelling of the divine persons. Ruth Duck says that the Greek word *perichoresis*—meaning "cyclical movement" or "reciprocity"—describes "the unity of the inner life of God, in which the three persons of the Trinity intermingle in a ceaseless flowing of love and shared life."[12] The mutual self-giving of Father, Son, and Spirit is, in Brian Wren's words, an "endless dance of love and light"—"communing love in shared delight."[13] The starting point of Christian faith is the dynamic, warm friendship shared by the persons of the Trinity from all eternity—the fact that "God is Life Together," as Dorothy and Gabriel Fackre put it.[14]

Relational Incarnation

The ceaseless flow of love, Duck says, "opens out toward creation."[15] God is revealed in the history of Israel, but we see the relational nature of God most clearly in Jesus Christ.[16] Jesus is "the exact representation" of God (Heb 1:3 NIV), "the exact imprint of God's very being (NRSV)"—"whoever has seen me," he says (John 14:9), "has seen the Father." This means that Jesus thinks, feels, and acts in the way God does. The God he reveals is a God of love. Jesus shows this, Marcus Borg says, by advocating compassion in a world concerned with purity.[17] The focus on purity was

11. Lewis, *Mere Christianity*, 151–152.
12. Duck, *Praising God*, 35–36.
13. Wren, cited in ibid., 36.
14. Fackre, *Christian Basics*, 10. Swinburne (*Was Jesus God?*, chapter 2) offers a philosophical argument for why a perfectly good God would exist as Trinity—an argument first made by Richard of St. Victor. Perfect love must be shared with another person, and perfect love between two people requires love for a third. God is perfect love, and therefore exists in three persons.
15. Duck, *Praising God*, 36.
16. Lane (*Keeping Hope Alive*, 126, slightly modified) contends that "the revelation that took place in the life of Jesus transforms the concept of God from classical antiquity with its emphasis on transcendence, immutability, impassibility and omnipotence.... The revelation of God in Jesus must be allowed to break up and reform the [Platonic and] Aristotelian understanding of God."
17. Borg and Wright, *Meaning of Jesus*, 71–72 and 238. "It is in the conflict between ... holiness and compassion as qualities of God ... that we see the central conflict in

reflected in laws that separated clean from unclean, righteous from sinner—thus creating a social world with hierarchy and divisions. Jesus, by contrast, emphasized compassion—his teachings (e.g., Luke 15:11–32), healings (e.g., Matt 8:3; Luke 8:43–48) and open table fellowship (e.g., Luke 7:36–50) broke rules of exclusion and turned social convention upside down by welcoming all into the kingdom (Matt 21:31). Gary Wills comments: "no outcasts were cast out far enough in Jesus' world to make him shun them—not Roman collaborators, not lepers, not prostitutes, not the crazed, not the possessed." Where Jewish religion "tried to create a restored community by keeping people out," Wright says, "Jesus created his by healing them and bringing them in."[18] He is the supreme demonstration of God's inclusive love and compassion—in Dietrich Bonhoeffer's words, "being for others."[19]

God's Purpose Is Relational: Creation

"The God of the Bible is best conceived as the supreme *person*," David Crump points out, "not the supreme *being* found in so much Christian theologizing."[20] God's relationality is both internal and external. Inwardly God is a communion of persons eternally bound together by the mutual exchange of love. Outwardly, Timothy Jackson states, "the primary moral attribute of the biblical God is steadfast love (*hesed, agape*), a willing of the good for all creation."[21] The first detailed self-description God gives to humankind is in Exodus 34:6–7:

> The Lord passed before [Moses], and proclaimed, "The Lord . . . , a God merciful and gracious, slow to anger, and abounding in steadfast love and faithfulness, keeping steadfast love for the thousandth generation, forgiving iniquity and transgression and sin, yet by no means clearing the guilty, but visiting the iniquity

---

the ministry of Jesus. The dominant social vision was centered in holiness; the alternative social vision of Jesus was centered in compassion" (Borg, *Meeting Jesus Again*, 49 and 13).

18. Wills, *What Jesus Meant*, 32 and Borg and Wright, *Meaning of Jesus*, 45–46. Borg (*Meeting Jesus Again*, 58) says "whereas purity divides and excludes, compassion unites and includes."

19. Bonhoeffer, *Letters and Papers*, 501.

20. Crump, *Knocking on Heaven's Door*, 284; emphasis added.

21. Jackson, *Priority of Love*, 72.

of the parents upon the children and the children's children, to the third and the fourth generation."

This declaration comes, Robert Gordon says, "as near as [Hebrew Scripture] anywhere achieves to providing a confessional definition of God" that concerns God's attitude to human beings.[22] God's love and forgiveness are inexhaustible—and while God rightly punishes sin, judgment is limited compared to mercy. The prophet Isaiah (30:18 *NIV*) declares that "the Lord longs to be gracious to you; he rises to show you compassion." The word translated as "waits" (*chakkah*) is a strong word in Hebrew; it suggests, Sharon Baker says, "thirsting with a strong craving," "longing with unquenchable thirst, with a desire so strong that it consumes every thought."[23] St. John (1 John 4: 8,16) also indicates that God's very nature "is love." Leon Morris comments: "this means more than 'God is loving.' It means that God's essential nature is love. God loves . . . because it is God's nature to love."[24] To repeat: love that actively seeks our well-being is not a qualifying property of God, but God's very essence.

Karl Barth describes the humanity of God as "God's relation to and turning towards humankind." God exists, "not in a vacuum as a divine Being-in-itself" but *pro me* ['for us']—"as the partner of humankind."[25] God created human beings for the purpose of friendship with God. Viewers of Rublev's icon feel themselves invited to join the three persons around the table, to share in their intimate communion. God is an eternal dance, and we are invited to join the loving dance of the Trinity as new partners.

The Bible is a love story—and this relational understanding of God's purpose stretches from God walking in the garden with our first parents (Gen 3:8) to God's presence in the new creation (Rev 21:3). God befriended Abraham (2 Chr 20:7; Isa 41:8, Jas 2:23) and talked with Moses

---

22. Gordon, "Exodus," 184. This "catalogue of God's attributes . . . runs through [Hebrew Scripture] like a refrain," Verhey (*Christian Art of Dying*, 281) notes.

23. Baker, *Razing Hell*, 72 and 146.

24. Morris, "First John," 1267.

25. Barth, cited in Macquarrie, *Christian Hope*, 62, slightly modified. Where the "closed Trinity" is exclusive and enclosed within itself, Moltmann (*Sun of Righteousness*, 151 and 157) says, the "open Trinity" is inclusive, inviting and open "in the overflow of love." In Protestant theological debates the Reformed *a se* God (who God is in Godself—remote and transcendent, a completely self-sufficient Being) has been set against the Lutheran *pro me* God (who God is for us—personal and involved). See my "Bonhoeffer and Open Theism."

"face to face, as one speaks to a friend" (Exod 33:11). God's desire is found in the formula of promise given to the Israelites—"I will be with you, and you shall be my people, and I will dwell in the midst of you" (Exod 29:45; Lev 26:11–12; 1 Kgs 6:13; cf. 2 Cor 6:16). *Yahweh* will be close and near—temporarily in the cloud and fire of the tabernacle (Exod 25:8) and permanently in the Temple on Mount Zion (2 Sam 7:5; Ps 68:18). As Wright points out, "the Temple was where Israel's God . . . had promised to come and dwell, to live in the midst of God's people."[26] The nation's union with God is described as marriage—with *Yahweh* as husband and Israel as wife (Isa 54:5–8; Hos 1–3). When the promise seemed canceled, the prophets repeat it—"my dwelling-place shall be with them; and I will be their God, and they shall be my people" (Ezek 37:27; cf. Isa 12:1–6; Jer 32:38; Zeph 3:15; Zech 2:10–11 and 8:3).

In the incarnation "the Word became flesh and lived among us" (John 1:14) in *Emmanuel*—"God is with us" (Matt 1:23). Wright says that "Jesus is . . . the Temple-in-person, the place where Israel's God has come to dwell in fulfillment of God's ancient promise."[27] Jesus described his followers as "friends" (John 15:15), those with whom the Trinity will "make our home" (John 14:23), and declared that after his ascension he would stay with us in the Holy Spirit who will "be with you" (John 14:16; cf. Matt 28:20). Jesus prays for the indwelling of human beings in the triune God, that as he is in the Father so his people may "be in us" (John 17:21; cf. 1 John 4:16). "The intimate relationship that Jesus himself had enjoyed with the Father," Wright comments, "is now open to all his followers."[28] This communion is compared to marriage with Christ as bridegroom and church as bride (Eph 5:22–33; Rev 19:6–7; 22:7). The end of history is described in terms of the promise: "the home of God is among mortals. He will dwell with them; they will be his peoples, and God himself will be with them" (Rev 21:3). God's eternal kingdom is depicted as a banquet shared with intimate companions (Matt 22:1–10; Luke 14:15–24; Rev 19:9). The theological narrative of Scripture from Genesis (Adam and Eve at home with God) to Revelation (the eschatological feast of union

---

26. Wright, *After You Believe*, 83–84. The concept of *shekinah* from Israel's postexilic theology means the presence of God in history among Israel (see Moltmann, *Sun of Righteousness*, chapter 11).

27. Ibid., 113. Moltmann (*Sun of Righteousness*, 30) agrees: "with Christ, God's indwelling takes on a body, a face and a name."

28. Wright, *Surprised by Hope*, 278.

between Christ and the church), Nathan Bierma concludes, "is the story of God-with-us."[29]

We are called to take part, Paul O'Callaghan says, "in the current of love that is the very life of the Blessed Trinity."[30] The Greek Fathers used the term *theosis* to describe God's relational purpose for humanity—participation and integration into God's life. Gregory of Nyssa states: "our very being as human is an invitation to respond in love to divine love, to share in the life of the Holy Trinity together with all other persons and the whole of creation" (2 Pet 1:3–4).[31] As creatures, we cannot become God metaphysically; we never take on God's incommunicable attributes (such as eternality). We can, however, become like God morally by developing the relational qualities that make up God's communicable attributes (such as compassionate love). We are filled with God's life as we take on the characteristics of the divine nature.[32]

Human Nature Is Relational: Anthropology

"We are brought into being," the Fackres say, "to fulfill [the] dream of life together with God and one another."[33] Because we are made to share the loving life of God, we have several basic traits.

First, we are essentially *spiritual* beings—creatures who are oriented to God and who find our supreme end in communion with God. Desire for God is an elemental part of human nature, which is shot through with deep spiritual longings. Augustine of Hippo expresses this thought in his prayer: "you have made us for yourself, O Lord, and our hearts

---

29. Bierma, *Bringing Heaven Down to Earth*, 110. "The story of the Bible is the story of God-with-us, from its inception and then rupture in Genesis, to God's attempt to recover it with Abraham and the Israelites throughout the [Hebrew Scriptures], to the arrival of *Immanuel*—which is Hebrew for "God with us"—in the person of Jesus in the Gospels, to the descent of the Holy Spirit, God's indwelling, on Pentecost, until the final descent and perfection of God-with-us . . . at the end of Revelation, for all eternity."

30. O'Callaghan, *Christ Our Hope*, 178.

31. Gregory, cited in Bakken, *Journey into God*, 85.

32. See Fairbairn, *Life in Trinity*, 7, 35, and 54. It is important to distinguish God's natural attributes (those traits which define God's metaphysical nature—spirit, eternal, omnipotent) from God's moral attributes (those traits which define God's moral character—with love being the most fundamental and with justice being grounded in love).

33. Fackre, *Christian Basics*, 3.

are restless until they rest in you." While we seek happiness in natural pleasures, they inevitably disappoint because what fulfills our nature is relationship with God.[34] This is why, Lewis says, we cannot find something other than God which will make us happy. "God made us: invented us as a man invents an engine. A car is made to run on gasoline, and it would not run properly on anything else. Now God designed the human machine to run on Godself. . . . God cannot give us a happiness and peace apart from Godself, because . . . there is no such thing."[35] "The chief end of man," the *Shorter Catechism* of the *Westminster Confession* declares, "is to glorify God and to enjoy God forever."[36] We are made to be brought into God's life, to find happiness in relationship with God; human flourishing culminates in the eternal, face-to-face vision of God.

Karl Rahner points out that all persons have a natural inclination toward God woven through their makeup. God "stamps . . . [human] nature" with "a tendency towards God, which . . . always completely permeates . . . [human] existence." This natural desire for God is both the gracious gift of God and a basic characteristic of human nature; it is not restricted to a rare few, but exists in the hearts of all people.[37] Every person enters the world graced by God; "human beings are always and everywhere, in all times and places, oriented and directed to . . . God."[38] This inherent gravitation of our being toward God may be experienced as vague spiritual impulses, as a hunger for meaning and purpose. Believers and non-believers alike are spiritual beings who long, often unconsciously, for intimacy with the God for whom they are meant and in whose love they find their *summum bonum*—their highest good.

Second, we are essentially *relational* beings. The core truth of God's being is the core truth of our own, Paul Wadell notes.[39] We are not solitary individuals but persons-in-relationship as God is Persons-in-Relationship. To be made in God's image is to be made for life together with God and one another. "Among living creatures," Andrew Schmutzer points

---

34. Augustine, *Confessions*, 3.

35. Lewis, *Mere Christianity*, 54. Also see *Problem of Pain*, 94 where Lewis argues that suffering destroys our illusions that we can find happiness in temporal things.

36. *Westminster Confession*, Shorter Catechism, 3.

37. Rahner, *Theological Investigations*, Vol. 6, 392–93. See Duffy, *Graced Horizon*.

38. Rahner, cited in Lane, *Keeping Hope Alive*, 22; cf. 23 and 38. *First grace* (being made for relationship with God) is given in creation, while *second grace* (salvation from sin) is offered through Christ. Original blessing is more basic than original sin.

39. Wadell, *Happiness*, 116.

out, "humankind is the 'great exception.' Humankind is theomorphic (i.e. having the form of God)." We are modeled on the divine, the social Trinity, and the *imago dei* has to do "primarily with the power to form . . . relationships."[40] Bonhoeffer agrees: "the likeness, the analogy of humankind to God is *analogia relationis*"—analogy of relationship.[41] Relationships are intrinsic to our identity as persons, and when we are in relationship with others God's very essence is reflected in us.

Third, we are essentially *free* beings, deciding and choosing beings. The goal of life is participation in the communion of the Trinity and so the ultimate good is being in proper relationship with God. But we must choose this voluntarily. While God wants fellowship with us, love cannot be forced; we must willingly reciprocate God's love by our own decision. Personal relationships of any kind require free will, and so God has endowed human beings with libertarian freedom—the ability to choose between genuine alternatives. "The happiness which God designs for" human persons, Lewis says, "is the happiness of being freely, voluntarily united to God and to each other. . . . And for that we must be free."[42] We can accept or reject God's love; we can love God and neighbor or love ourselves—we must choose whom we will serve (Deut 30:19; Josh 24:15).

The Betrayal of God's Purpose Is Relational: Sin

"God has created us to live in perfect communion and fellowship with God and with our neighbors," Owen Thomas says—and in the beginning human beings enjoyed relationship with God. But by free choice we refused God's love, and now "we are out of communion with God, alienated and estranged from God."[43] Because God is relational and because the human *telos* is relational, the doctrines of sin and salvation are best understood personally, not legally; family images, not courtroom images, should be central.[44] The *essence* of sin is not breaking rules; it is breaking relationship by failing to love God and other people properly. God is a father, not a judge[45]—Scott Hahn says—and we are runaways,

---

40. Schmutzer, "Theology of Sexual Abuse," 791 and 805.
41. Bonhoeffer, *Creation and Fall*, 65.
42. Lewis, *Mere Christianity*, 53 and 52.
43. Thomas, *Introduction to Theology*, 102.
44. Pinnock and Brow, *Unbounded Love*, 8.
45. Theological ancestors of this relational theology include Thomas Erskine and

not criminals.[46] The *effect* of sin is that friendship with God (Gen 3:8) has become exile and banishment (Gen 3:22–24)—life apart rather than life together. In addition, betrayal of relationship with God spread to betrayal between human persons.

Sin is *cor curvum in se*—a twisting in which we turn inward on ourselves and away from God and neighbor. Augustine describes sin as disordered love—the transferring of love from God to objects which are less good, failing to love God above all else and to love all things in God.[47] We are created for relationship, turned outward from oneself to others— but instead we have "turned towards . . . oneself."[48] Martin Luther agrees: "our nature has been . . . deeply curved in upon itself."[49] Bonhoeffer follows Augustine and Luther in identifying two different objects of love: "in one case, I myself, in the other, God and my neighbor." We must choose between these two loves. "Self-love is misguided love . . . that is basically enmity toward God and one's neighbor because they only disturb the immediate circle of myself."[50] Sin, Matt Jensen concludes, is "a radical self-centeredness in which we assert an insidious gravitational force, seeking to pull all others into our orbit."[51] Instead of respecting other people, we

---

George MacDonald. Against Calvinistic limited atonement, Erskine emphasized the loving side of God's nature. MacDonald also defends a God who is tender rather than severe, a God who welcomes sinners home rather than rejects them in anger. God, he says, saves us from our sins—not from punishment for our sins. Hell is a place of purification to prepare us to enter heaven. For both Erskine and MacDonald, God is relational and personal, not legal and judgmental. See Partridge, "George MacDonald's Theology." Also see Montgomery et al, *Relational Theology*. Thanks to my editor, Robin Parry, for pointing this out to me

46. Hahn, *Rome Sweet Home*, 30.

47. Augustine, *On Christian Doctrine*, 1.27–28. Verhey (*Christian Art of Dying*, 271–72) points out that Augustine's conception of love draws on Plato's notion of *eros*—the desire of the soul for what is truly good, beautiful, and immortal. By the object of our love we are oriented either toward God or away from God. "Every human being loves; every human being is in motion toward something drawn to it by its attractive power. . . . Created by God, we yearn for fulfillment . . . in God, but in our sin we look for fulfillment elsewhere. . . . Sin disorders and disorients our yearning souls." Also see Smith, *Desiring the Kingdom* and *Imagining the Kingdom*.

48. Augustine, *City of God*, 14.13, 572–73.

49. Luther, *Lectures on Romans*, 291 and 313. Original sin "turns the finest gifts of God in upon itself. . . . Thus the prophet Jeremiah (17:9) says: 'the heart is perverse above all things, and desperately corrupt . . . ,' that is, is . . . curved in on itself."

50. Bonhoeffer, "Unbelieving Way of Love," in Kelly and Nelson, *Testament to Freedom*, 245–46.

51. Jenson, *Gravity of Sin*, 2. Murdoch (*Sovereignty of Good*, 52 and 78) says that sin

actively use them for personal gain or passively ignore their needs. We also use God, "loving" God, not for God's own sake but for what God does for us. Sin is choosing to live apart from God and in disregard of others, as the Episcopal Church Prayer of Confession acknowledges, "we have not loved you with our whole heart, we have not loved our neighbors as ourselves."[52] Sin is betrayal in relationships.

Sinful behavior (external actions) comes from a sinful state of being (internal dispositions). While we are born with sinful natures "prior to any act of conscious choice"—Thomas says—sinful habits are "deepened by conscious acts." Repeated behaviors create and maintain attitudes and habits which become second nature to us.[53] But evil goes beyond personal failure to unjust social systems. It involves what St. Paul calls "the cosmic powers of this present darkness" (Eph 6:12; cf. Rom 8:38; Col 1:16), which are not demonic beings but social and cultural forces—economic, organizational, and political institutions (such as the media) that control our thinking, desiring, and acting. These orders of creation, which are meant to serve human well-being, have become twisted and harmful.[54]

---

is deeply-rooted selfishness: "the enemy is the fat relentless ego," the "individual relentlessly looking after itself." Pannenberg (cited in Thiselton, *Life After Death*, 183) agrees: we are "caught fast in the self" as the center of our concern. A number of Christian psychologists and feminist theologians have challenged the idea that self-love is the cardinal sin. Some individuals struggle, not with pride and thinking of themselves too highly, but with feelings of inadequacy, inferiority, and shame; lacking self-acceptance, they feel defective and unlovable. Many women struggle, not with self-elevation, but with self-sacrifice in service to others. Instead of self-centeredness, the basic problem may be failing to be a self—undervaluing oneself as a person created in God's image, losing oneself in others, not living up to one's potential and participating in one's own exploitation. See Cooper, *Sin, Pride and Self-Acceptance*.

52. Episcopal Church, *Book of Common Prayer*, 360. See Pinnock and Brow, *Unbounded Love*, 90.

53. Thomas, *Introduction to Theology*, 102. The direction of causation goes both ways. 1. The kinds of actions we do arise naturally from the kinds of persons we are, from settled dispositions we follow without thinking. We do what we do because we are what we are; sinful actions are the result of sinful natures. 2. The kinds of persons we are result from the kinds of actions we do. Sinful actions reinforce sinful natures. Actions both show who we are and shape who we are.

54. Smith (*Imagining the Kingdom*, 140–41) points out that individualist accounts of sin ignore "the social forces and systemic factors that prime and shape our imaginations, creating dispositions and tendencies within us toward unjust action and sinful behavior.... Through a vast repertoire of secular [influences] we are quietly assimilated to the earthly city of disordered loves." Many people who are committed to social justice are unaware, for example, of how their normal way of life exploits children halfway around the world.

The result of sin, Thomas says, is that "our existence is in contradiction to our essence, . . . our relation to God, neighbor, self, and nature is disrupted."[55] Refusing to live in relationship with God and neighbor reverses what we are meant to be. We stop being *persons* who interact with others, John Hick says, and become *egos*—self-enclosed individuals seeking our own interests and using, rather than respecting, others.[56] Sin creates a problem between us and God (it alienates us from God objectively); in legal terms, we are guilty and stand condemned, deserving of punishment—in personal terms, we are estranged from God. It also causes a problem within us (it makes us self-centered subjectively)—we have corrupt and defiled natures, what Lewis calls the "fierce imprisonment in the self."[57] Sin has, in addition, disrupted human relationships and devastated all of nature, which is now cursed—as the Fackres point out—"with the cancer cell that fells the seven-year-old . . . , an earthquake that slides a city into the ocean or a flood that wipes out a region's food supply."[58] The whole creation is "groaning" in "bondage to decay" (Rom 8:21–22).

The Restoration of God's Purpose Is Relational: Salvation

God, Jacques Ellul says, "has never acquiesced in the break which was brought about in Adam."[59] The Christian Reformed Church confession puts it well: "while justly angry, God did not turn God's back on" the sinful world, but "turned God's face to it in love. With patience and tender care God set out on the long road of redemption, to reclaim the lost as God's people and the world as God's Kingdom. Although Adam and Eve were expelled from the garden . . . God held on to them in love [and] promised to crush the evil forces they unleashed."[60] Salvation is the healing of broken relationships.

The inner life of the triune God is one of persons-in-communion, and we are meant to enjoy that fellowship eternally. Sin cuts us off from

---

55. Thomas, *Introduction to Theology*, 99.
56. Hick, *Death and Eternal Life*, 450.
57. Lewis, *Problem of Pain*, 140.
58. Fackre, *Christian Basics*, 24–25.
59. Ellul, cited in Yancey, *Prayer*, 328.
60. Christian Reformed Church, "Our World Belongs to God," Sections 19–20, 1025.

relationship; it makes participation in the divine life of love impossible. We cannot return to God by our own efforts without assisting grace; we need atonement—action that brings estranged parties together. In Jesus Christ God acted to rescue a world ruined by sin, to set right what has gone wrong. Christ reconciles us to God (2 Cor 5:19); he puts things right between God and us, and welcomes us back into fellowship with God.[61] Each of the three main theories of atonement speaks to a different element of human estrangement from God: Christ's death 1. defeats the powers of evil (the victory theory), 2. offers a substitutionary sacrifice making divine forgiveness possible (the satisfaction theory), and 3. shows us how to love others selflessly (the moral theory).[62] Salvation is

---

61. The cross, Pinnock and Brow (*Love Unbounded*, 102) emphasize, reconciles *us* to God—not *God* to us, as the satisfaction theories of Anselm and Calvin suggest. Jesus died to change our attitude to God, not God's attitude to us. Jesus' death is not a penal offering that persuades an angry God, who must be appeased, to love us. (To be fair, Calvin and his heirs never claimed that the atonement was to make God love us; rather, God sent Jesus because God already loved us.) *Objective justification* means that, because of Christ's perfect life and sacrifice, God is now reconciled to all human beings. God's saving work is already accomplished. All obstacles—like divine anger that must punish sin—have been removed and all persons are forgiven by God. *God is reconciled to us apart from anything we do—but this does not mean that we are reconciled to God. Subjective justification* is our assimilation of what God has done for us. We cannot enjoy this reconciliation until we appropriate Christ's merits by faith. A person in prison may be pardoned, but they are not actually free until they believe they are and act on it by walking out the open door. See Kronen and Reitan, *God's Final Victory*, 119–23.

62. Each theory of atonement, Beilby and Eddy (*Nature of Atonement*, 12) suggest, "sees the central thrust of the work of Christ as designed to address a different fundamental problem that stands in the way of salvation." 1. The patristic *Christus Victor* model is Satanward in focus; it understands the work of Christ as conflict with and triumph over the forces of evil. It emphasizes Christ's resurrection. 2. The medieval and Reformation satisfaction model is Godward in focus; it understands the work of Christ as addressing a demand of God. Anselm argues that sin offends God's infinite honor—and that Christ paid the debt that we could not. Luther and Calvin assert that sin deserves punishment—and that Christ took the penalty we owe. It emphasizes Christ's death. 3. The modern moral exemplar model is humanward in focus; it understands the work of Christ as changing human beings who, motivated by Christ's example of love, repent of sin and learn to serve the neighbor in need. It emphasizes Christ's life and ministry. There are, Borg (*Meeting Jesus Again*, 121–27) says, three biblical "macro-stories," each saying something different but important about what is wrong with our lives and describing a solution to that problem. 1. For the Hebrews enslaved in Egypt, the problem was bondage—and the solution was liberation; Christ defeats the powers of evil. 2. For the exiled Jews in Babylon, the problem was exile—and the solution was homecoming; Christ shows us the how to return to God. 3. For the priests with their Temple rituals, the problem was sin and guilt—and the solution

multifaceted, but its essence is not legal acquittal; it is restored relationship. The mending of our separation from God requires action on both sides: God must offer salvation and assist us to respond (by enlightening our minds and enabling our wills)—and we must repent, turn from sin, and follow a new path of love.

To be saved is to be made healthy (from the Latin word *salus*). Sin, recall, not only damages our relationship with God by creating guilt—it also deforms our characters by creating selfish dispositions and habits. Salvation brings health to both dimensions of human sinfulness: our outward standing of guilt and our inward condition of pollution. Sin alienates us from God *objectively*; justification forgives the guilt of sin and puts us right, restores us to favor, with God. God accepts us back into fellowship and adopts us as children (Rom 8:15; Gal 4:5; Eph 1:5).[63] Forgiveness is being given a new status and happens instantly. Sin also makes us self-centered *subjectively*; sanctification frees us from sin's power and makes us loving as we "grow into salvation" (1 Pet 2:2) and are "transformed into the likeness of Christ" (2 Cor 3:18; cf. Gal 4:19). Holiness is developing a new character and happens gradually.

Being forgiven and becoming holy are two different things. A change in God's attitude to us does not automatically transform us; justification does not affect our moral condition or purify our hearts. Despite being pardoned, we remain self-centered, unable to love with our whole being. "Even after our guilt is forgiven," David Currie points out, "the effect of

---

was forgiveness; Christ offers a substitutionary sacrifice. The Fackres (*Christian Basics*, 45–62) describe Calvin's three-fold office of Christ: the *royal* Jesus who liberates the world from the "powers," the *priestly* Jesus who offers sacrifice for the sins of the world and the *prophetic* Jesus who tells us of the world God intends and calls us to serve the neighbor in need.

63. Buechner (*Wishful Thinking*, 48) notes that "in printers' language to 'justify' means to . . . put the printed lines in the right relationship with the page they're printed on and with each other. The religious sense of the word is very close to this. Being justified means being brought into right relation. St. Paul says simply that being justified means having peace with God (Rom 5:1)." Walls ("Purgatory for Everyone," 10) points out that "the traditional view was that justification involves actually making us righteous. . . . It was a Protestant innovation to separate justification from sanctification." Or as Hahn (*Rome Sweet Home*, 30–31; slightly modified) points out, the Reformation theory of justification as a legal exchange where Christ takes our sin and gives us his righteousness falls short of the full truth of the gospel. "Being justified means sharing in the grace of Christ as God's sons and daughters. . . . God's grace is something much more than divine favor; it is the actual gift of God's life in divine sonship." Salvation is restoration as children in a family room, not a legal decree of acquittal in a courtroom.

sin remains on our wills."⁶⁴ Our characters, M. Robert Mulholland says, are "the deep-seated attitudes and inner orientations out of which our behavior patterns flow" (Mark 7:20–23; Luke 6:45). As sinners we have developed "a whole structure of habits, attitudes, perspectives, dynamics of relationships, ways of reacting and responding to the world around us" which are harmful and unhealthy. This complex network of attitudes and habits "go way down deep into our being"—even after we are forgiven they are still there.⁶⁵ An alcoholic son—for example—does not stop having a drinking problem just because his parents pardon him for wrecking the family car and pay the damages he caused. He still needs moral reform. In the same way, restored relationship with God requires more than forgiveness—we need, Wadell says, to "unlearn the habits and practices of sin" through what Iris Murdoch calls the slow, lifelong "process of unselfing."⁶⁶ As long as we are focused on ourselves, we cannot give ourselves to God in love or participate in God's relational life. Friendship with God requires sanctification holiness (actual transformation of character) not simply justification holiness (declaration of a change in status or attribution of an alien righteousness that belongs to someone else). While not mutually exclusive, and while salvation brings both forgiveness and healing, it is, Hick says, "this reality of persons transformed, or in process of transformation, from self-centeredness to God-centeredness, that constitutes the substance of Christian salvation."⁶⁷

Life Here and Now is Relational: Ethics and Ecclesiology

There is a necessary connection between who God is and who we are called to be. God is love—and so being filled with God is being filled with love. Individually and corporately we are to live out God's love and

---

64. Currie, *Born Fundamentalist*, 123.

65. Mulholland, *Invitation to Journey*, 85 and 125–27.

66. Wadell, *Happiness*, 167–73 and Murdoch, *Metaphysics as Guide to Morals*, 17. Sanctification is not simply a matter of human effort—we are assisted by divine grace. Nor is sanctification a purely individual matter—we are assisted by the community of the church.

67. Hick, *Interpretation of Religion*, 44. Walls (*Heaven*, 50) agrees: "the heart of salvation is to change us so we gladly love and obey God. This is how we are united to God in a relationship of mutual love.... The essence of salvation is real transformation that allows us to love God and enjoy fellowship with God. The element of forgiveness, although crucial, is secondary to this."

pursue God's reign of justice and peace. We serve God through loving others.

Compassion is the primary quality of God and the defining mark of a life full of God. We are to be "imitators of God," St. Paul says (Eph 5:1–2), people who "live in love, as Christ loved us." "If we want to be Christians," Bonhoeffer asserts, "it means that we are to take part in Christ's greatness of heart"—imitating "Christ's freeing and redeeming love." As Jesus is "being for others" so "participation in the being of Jesus" means "a new life in 'being there for others.'"[68] Loving God cannot be separated from loving other people; love of neighbor is part of love of God. In both Hebrew and Christian Scripture love is more than negative—avoiding harm, actions that make others worse off; it is also positive—performing good, actions that make others better off. Jesus made the reign of God real in the world and we participate in the coming of that same kingdom by caring for orphans, widows, and strangers (Lev 9:10; Deut 10:18; 14:29), doing justice and loving kindness (Mic 6:8), healing the sick and feeding the hungry (Matt 25:31–46).[69] The fruit of the Spirit—love, peace, kindness, gentleness (Gal 5:22–23)—are a sign of growth in the way of Jesus.

We live out God's love, Rachel Held Evans says, "in community and for the community."[70] The church is *internally relational*—a community of people in friendship with God and one another. Christians are called into "life together"—as Bonhoeffer puts it; "whoever is baptized [is] incorporated into the Church-community" and becomes a member of the body of Jesus Christ (Rom 12:5).[71] We need each other as companions on the way and must be involved in relationships of mutual encouragement, support, accountability and insight. The church is also *externally relational*—commissioned to take God's self-giving love into the world. Christ's

---

68. Bonhoeffer, *Letters and Papers*, 49; *Ethics* 80 and 83; *Letters and Papers*, 501.

69. In Jesus' warning about judgment (Matt 25:31–46), the sheep are rewarded for what they did do positively ("I was hungry and you gave me food, I was thirsty and you gave me something to drink"), not for the sins they refrained from committing—and the goats are punished for what they did not do ("I was hungry and you gave me no food, I was thirsty and you gave me nothing to drink"), not for the sins they committed.

70. Evans, *Searching for Sunday*, 104.

71. Bonhoeffer, *Life Together* and *Discipleship*, 219. Wright (*After You Believe*, 216) says: "the living God . . . chooses to dwell particularly in one place. And that place is no longer a building in Jerusalem. . . . It is a family, the family of those who belong to the Messiah." Two contemporary hymns express this well—"We are God's People" and "The Servant Song."

life is not over, Bonhoeffer says. He continues to live in his church—and as Christ was incarnate in the world, so Christ-existing-as-church must be incarnate in the world. The church is not to be turned inward on itself but is sent out in love to care for others—"the Church is Church only when it is there for others," not for its own sake.[72] Our baptismal vows commit us to "seek and serve Christ in all persons, loving our neighbors as ourselves" and to "strive for justice and peace among all people."[73] Medical care, education, and work on behalf of the poor are part of the mission of the church to the world. As God's heart beats with reconciliation, so we are called to be Christ's ambassadors of reconciliation in the world (2 Cor 5:18–19).

The Completion of God's Purpose Is Relational: Eschatology

"Eschatological fulfillment," Lane says, is "the culmination and consummation of that which God has already set in motion in and through the gift of creation."[74] The story begins with creation and ends with new creation—the renewal of all things when God's presence fills all the world, when all God's purpose of love is fulfilled. Final consummation is—first—*cosmic*. The prophets declare that peace and prosperity will be established in the kingdom when the wolf lies with the lamb (Isa 11:1–9; 65:25), orchards replace thorn bushes and creation claps its hands in delight (Isa 55:12–13). "In God's ultimate future," the Fackres say, "every wrong is righted, every flaw mended, every brokenness healed."[75] We will be at peace in ourselves, at peace with those around us, at peace with the natural world and at peace with God. While the intermediate hope is a temporary place of restful happiness in the presence of God, the ultimate hope is the renewal of the entire cosmos, including bodily resurrection and the return of Jesus to a world made new. Salvation is not liberation *from* the material world and the physical body, but redemption *of* them.[76]

72. Bonhoeffer, *Letters and Papers*, 501 and 503. Luther, Bonhoeffer points out (*Discipleship*, 46–49), left the monastery to return to the world—and Calvin, Matthew Boulton (cited in Smith, *Imagining the Kingdom*, 156–57) observes, "envisions a reformed way of life robustly engaged in ordinary affairs that is nevertheless unconformed to their prevailing patterns and protocols."

73. Episcopal Church, *Book of Common Prayer*, 304–5.

74. Lane, *Keeping Hope Alive*, 23.

75. Fackre, *Christian Basics*, 150.

76. Wright, *Following Jesus*, 60. Also see *Surprised by Hope*, 5, 19, 26, 29 and *For All Saints*, 20.

Final consummation is—second—*collective*. "The eschatology of the Scriptures," Stephen Cook asserts, "is remarkable for its grand, world-encompassing scope." On the last day the nations make pilgrimage to Jerusalem (Ps 72:8–11) and foreigners join Israel's worship of *Yahweh* (Isa 56:6–7 ; 66:18–21; Zeph 3:9–10; Rev 7:9). Even God's enemies, Egypt and Assyria, come to Zion and are claimed by God as God's own people (Ps 87:4–6; Isa 19:18–25). This eschatological vision is the consummation of God's promise to bless all families of the earth through Abraham (Gen 12:3; 28:14; Isa 51:1–6).[77] Final consummation is—third—*personal*. Heaven, purgatory, and hell are all relational realities.

Relational Heaven

Heaven fulfills the promise that God will dwell with humanity in a redeemed creation. Eastern Orthodox theology describes the Trinity as *sobornost*—a spiritual community—and so is heaven: the spiritual community of God and the blessed. Theocentric views of heaven have no place for human community, only private communion with God alone. Such models emphasize individuality, a self that is independent, detached and separate—enjoying personal salvation. Social views of heaven, by contrast, emphasize relationality, a self that is interdependent, connected, and communal—experiencing corporate salvation.[78] Because we are persons-in-relationship, heaven cannot be individualistic, but is life together with God and others. Heaven is not a private encounter with God, but includes, Thomas Aquinas says, "the pleasant companionship of all the blessed."[79] It involves, Joseph Ratzinger adds, "fellowship with other hu-

---

77. Cook, "Eschatology of the Old Testament," 301–2.

78. See Lane, *Keeping Hope Alive*, chapter 3.

79. Aquinas, *Summa Theologiae*, Vol. 16, 1a2ae q4 a8, 115. Aquinas—who seems to depict heaven as theocentric beatific vision—was well aware that Scripture depicts eternal life in communal terms and that we are social beings for whom good relationships are necessary to flourishing. Perfect happiness in heaven, therefore, cannot consist solely in God but must include human friendship. While nothing besides God is necessary for perfect joy, other things do play a role in it. Aquinas thinks embodiment is necessary for supreme happiness, and so the soul's joy increases after resurrection. In the same way, while an individualistic heaven would be happy, a social heaven is happier. As the pleasure of a visit to the Grand Canyon is enhanced by being shared with other people, so the private enjoyment of God is not as extensive as it would be if shared with friends also enjoying it. Seeing God in solitary fashion is less good than seeing God in the community of saints. See Brown, "Friendship in Heaven."

man beings. [We are] not engaged in a solitary dialogue with God. [We do] not enter an eternity with God which belongs to [us] alone." Heaven is a collective reality: "if heaven depends on being in Christ, then it must involve a co-being with all those who, together, constitute the body of Christ." [80] Scripture pictures this as a feast of joy and peace—what Bruce Cockburn calls the "festival of friends."[81]

Relational Purgatory

Heaven is participation in the exchange of love which is God's very being—and a necessary condition of heaven is an ability to love with all our hearts. Self-preoccupation cuts us off from relationship—and so sharing the life of God requires the reordering of our characters so that we turn outward to others in self-giving love. Few people achieve such holiness in this life; even those in right standing with God remain self-centered at death, unable to love perfectly. Forgiveness, recall, reconciles us to God but does not heal our damaged characters; "our faith does not just cover up our rebellious wills," Currie emphasizes, "so that we can slip into heaven."[82] God cannot unilaterally and instantaneously give us a radically altered nature at the moment of death. Therefore, there is some kind of process in the period after death that completes our moral transformation into the kind of beings who can enter the fellowship of the Trinity eternally. Purgatory has a relational function: only when we can love wholly are we ready for heavenly life together.

Relational Hell

God has only one purpose in creation (that all persons freely choose relationship with God)—not two (that some be saved and some damned). But we can choose life apart rather than life together, and hell is what happens when we do. A good God will condemn evil, and so there is such a thing as judgment and punishment. As Miroslav Volf says, there must be "exclusion" before there can be "embrace"; evil must be dealt with

---

80. Ratzinger, *Eschatology*, 159 and 235.

81. Cockburn, "Festival of Friends." In heaven, the Episcopal Church catechism (*Book of Common Prayer*, 862) says, "we are united with all the people of God, in the joy of fully knowing and loving God and each other."

82. Currie, *Born Fundamentalist*, 123.

before there can be reconciliation.[83] But we must not separate divine justice from divine love, exclusion from embrace. From the plagues of Egypt (Exod 7–12) to the prophetic warnings to Israel and Judah, from Jonah's admonition to the foreign city Nineveh to St. Paul's excommunication of a sexually immoral man (1 Cor 5:1–13), threats and acts of punishment are meant to bring people back to God. Hell is a place of separation, a natural consequence of rejecting God and living a self-centered life. To enter hell is to miss the purpose for which we are created. But while hell is possible—and sadly—actual, it is not permanent. Those in hell can return to God since God will never finally reject some persons by withdrawing grace and giving up trying to save them, and no person will finally reject God, continuing to choose personal misery by refusing God's persuasive love. Hell serves a relational purpose as a means to salvation.

Expressing Relational Concern: Prayer

Finally, since this is a work on prayer, let me say a word about that. Contemplative prayer builds relationship with God while petitionary prayer is an act of love toward other people. In prayer we represent other individuals to God, as Bonhoeffer comments: "offering intercessory prayer means nothing other than . . . bringing one another into the presence of God . . . as poor human beings and sinners in need of grace."[84] Prayer arises "because we are so bound up in love for our fellow [human beings] that we feel their need as acutely as our own. To make intercession for [others] is the most powerful and practical way in which we can express our love for them," John Calvin is claimed to have said.[85] Praying for other people makes us aware of their needs, turns us away from preoccupation with ourselves and—by seeking their good—develops the virtue of compassion.

Prayer for the departed assumes the doctrine of the communion of saints.[86] God's people include all Christians, living and dead, one "family in heaven and on earth" (Eph 3:15; cf. 4:25). The mystical bond and

---

83. Volf, *Exclusion and Embrace*. Also see Wright, *Surprised by Hope*, 179.

84. Bonhoeffer, *Life Together*, 90.

85. This quote is widely attributed, without citation, to Calvin.

86. See Chapman, "Rest and Light Perpetual," 45–46. The Episcopal Church catechism (*Book of Common Prayer*, 862) says that "the communion of saints is the whole family of God, the living and the dead . . . bound together in Christ."

interaction between God's people on earth and God's people in heaven is not broken by death. Jürgen Moltmann explains: "the fellowship of Christ consists of two semi-circles, so to speak. The one is the community of the living, the other the community of the dead." When we die "we simply move to the other half of the circle." In Christ we, the living, are "joined with the dead in love for each other."[87] Because we are "related to others," Ratzinger says, "the possibility of helping . . . does not cease to exist on the death of the Christian. Rather does it stretch out to encompass the entire communion of saints, on both sides of death's portals."[88] We are not independent individuals before God, but members of a community with corporate relationships. In the communion of saints, we have responsibilities for each other's welfare; given this spiritual interdependence, we can be helped by the prayers of the saints and the dead can be helped by the prayers of the church. Timothy Ware states it well:

> it is precisely here, in this awareness of the all-embracing communion and in the sense of mutual love, that there may be found the key to . . . understanding . . . intercession for the departed. . . . If . . . as members of a single family we are united by the bond of mutual prayer, and if within this family there is no division between the living and departed, then it should surely be considered normal and natural that we pray for the departed.[89]

Just as intercessions help the living, so consummation, growth, and purification prayers can help the faithful departed.

Praying for *all* the departed reminds us that all human beings are part of a common humanity loved by God. The unsaved dead, Thomas Howard says, "are still part of the huge fabric of creation, and nothing

---

87. Moltmann, *Coming of God*, 106–7.

88. Ratzinger, *Eschatology*, 232–33. Lee (*Christian Doctrine of Prayer for Departed*, 190–92) says that "death does not . . . destroy that network of mutual interests and sympathies which bind us together." This means that "it is God's will to save [people], not as isolated and unconnected units, but as members of a body and common subjects of a holy Kingdom; and to bring this great truth home to them God makes them necessary to each other." The collective nature of salvation implies that we are our brother's and sister's keepers; "this principle of mutual interdependence runs through the whole of [a person's] . . . moral and spiritual life." The great evil of human nature, Lee continues, is selfishness—the repudiation of our responsibilities to each other. "How does God contrive to cure us of that selfishness? By making us necessary to each other. . . . Hardly one of [God's] good gifts is bestowed on [someone] directly from on high. They all reach him through the ministry of his fellows"—including prayer.

89. Ware, "One Body in Christ," 188–98.

in that fabric is beyond the scope of mercy."[90] St. Paul urges "that supplications, prayers, intercessions . . . be made for everyone" (1 Tim 2:1). Frederick Lee comments: "every person . . . is our neighbor, whom by God's . . . commands we are enjoined to love, and for whom consequently we should continually offer up our prayers. . . . All . . . are to be included in our generals acts of intercession, without . . . exception."[91] The church's petitions are not limited to believers but include—in the words of the Episcopal Prayers of the People—"those who do not yet believe, and . . . those who have lost their faith, that they may receive the light of the gospel."[92] As we pray for non-believers in this life, so we should make salvation prayers that the unsaved in hell seek and find forgiveness.

Concluding Remarks

When theology is encountered as a set of individual doctrines it can be hard to see how they fit together and what the central message is that lies at the heart of Christian faith. But, Thomas notes, theology is an organic whole: "the doctrines of creation, salvation and eschatology are mutually implied in each other. [They are] not independent acts of God but rather moments in God's one great action in relation to the world."[93] Michael Peterson summarizes: God is

> a personal-social being. . . . The divine persons of the Trinity are forever engaged in reciprocal relations of love and joyful self-giving. . . . God's project in creation . . . is to bring human persons to participate in God's own blessed life. The human *telos*, the true end and fulfillment of our being, is for us to be brought into intimate fellowship with God, sharing mutual love relations as intimately as do the persons of the blessed Trinity.[94]

We are loved into existence by God—and God does not create us to abandon us but to draw us into the divine life. We are all called to enter a

---

90. Howard, *Evangelical Is Not Enough*, 124–25. Sophronius Sacharov, a twentieth-century Eastern Orthodox theologian, prayed for the salvation of the whole world. "The being of all humankind, in its source and by its nature, is one being, one human. Hence the 'natural' impulse of our spirit is to pray for all people" (cited in Ramelli, *Christian Doctrine of Apokatastasis*, 510).

91. Lee, *Christian Doctrine of Prayer for Departed*, 184.

92. Episcopal Church, *Book of Common Prayer*, 390.

93. Thomas, *Introduction to Theology*, 121.

94. Peterson, "Eschatology and Theodicy," 528.

friendship with God that grows and deepens in this life and throughout eternity. Prayer for the departed integrates and expresses these central elements of theology.

The most basic prayer for the departed is this: "we commend to your mercy all who have died, that your will for them may be fulfilled." In this chapter I have outlined *what* we pray for—the completion of God's creative and redemptive purpose, that all persons participate in the mutual love of the Trinity. In the next volume I discuss *whom* we pray for—why we commend all, saved and unsaved alike, to God's mercy. But since prayers for the dead are prayers of hope, I end this foundational volume by considering the nature of hope.

chapter 9

HOPE, EXPECTATION, AND PRAYER FOR THE DEAD

ON A SPRING MORNING we stand beside the grave of Gerry, my brother-in-law, as the minister commends him to God and commits his body to the ground "in sure and certain hope of the resurrection to eternal life through Jesus Christ our Lord."[1] It is all wrong, of course, to be burying a fifty-three-year-old man, professionally successful and loved by his family, struck down while bicycling by a careless driver. We know the years ahead hold desperate pain and difficult challenges, dark nights and silent grief. And yet . . . through our tears our aching hearts draw hope from the prayers we say for Gerry—resurrection and reunion when the great trumpet sounds. God haste the day when, like the triumph of Easter Sunday overcoming the tragedy of Good Friday, our mourning is followed by Morning.

Immanuel Kant maintains that the question "what may I hope for?" is one of the fundamental questions in philosophy and human life.[2] Hope is what Thornton Wilder calls "a climate of the mind"—what

---

1. These traditional words, included in many committal services, come from Vander Zee, *In Life and In Death*, 133—the pastoral guide for funerals from Gerry's denomination, the Christian Reformed Church. Also see Episcopal Church, *Book of Common Prayer*, 501.

2. See Beck, *Kant Selections*, 16-20. The other fundamental problems are "what can I know?" and "what should I do?" Kant conceived of both eschatological hope (the attainment of happiness in proportion to virtue in the next life) and historical hope (political progress and a human moral community—"the kingdom of God on earth").

John Day calls a "prospective emotion."[3] It is a way of seeing the future: where despair sees a negative future, hope sees a positive one. Hope, John Macquarrie says, is "an affirmation of the future, a trust in the future, an investment in the future."[4] "Prayers of petition," Josef Pieper points out, are "nothing other than the voicing of hope"—and prayers for the dead are acts of eschatological hope.[5] Consummation prayers express hope that God hasten the coming of Christ and the day of resurrection. Growth prayers for those in heaven express hope that they enter more and more into God's joyful service. Purification prayers for those in purgatory express hope that their characters be sanctified quickly so they enter the fullness of heaven. Salvation prayers for those in hell express hope that they respond to God's continuing offer of grace. Before examining each particular prayer of hope in the second volume, it will help to understand the nature of hope in general and of specifically Christian hope.

Ordinary Hope and Religious Hope

The phrase "sure and certain hope" seems contradictory: if something is sure then it is not hope, and if it is hope then it is not sure. To say "I am not certain but I hope so" makes sense, but to say "I am certain but I hope so" does not. There is an important difference between ordinary hope and religious hope. Ordinary hope has an uncertainty requirement; hoping that Ted brings his rum eggnog to the party entails that it might or might not happen. Christian eschatological hope, however, has a certainty requirement—God *will*, not might, establish the eternal kingdom and fulfill God's purpose of love. In ordinary language, hope and expectation differ—but in religious usage, they are equivalent.[6] As Emil Brunner writes, "in our everyday experience to 'hope for' means the expectation of a wished-for event in the future. There is . . . implied in it the element of . . . uncertainty. But the Christian hope is of another kind. It is no uncertain expectation based on a wish, but the expectation of the

---

3. Wilder, cited in Martin, *How We Hope*, 3 and Day, "Hope," 91.
4. Macquarrie, *Christian Hope*, 4.
5. Pieper, *On Hope*, 70.
6. Christian theology has a stipulated definition of hope. Lexical definitions convey how a term is commonly used (as defined in a dictionary). Stipulated definitions, by contrast, give a specific—and sometimes different—meaning to a term for a particular purpose.

future that has its basis in the known will of God and therefore shares in ... certainty."[7]

Philosophical Analysis of Ordinary Hope

Hope assumes that we are teleological beings moving forward from what is "already" to what is "not yet." We are not static beings who have reached completion of our purpose—union with God in love. Instead, we are dynamic becomings—*homo viators* on pilgrimage from the present to a future that does not yet exist. "To be a *viator* means 'one on the way,'" Pieper notes. "The *status viatoris* is ... 'the condition ... of being on the way.' ... One who has ... arrived is no longer a *viator*." The virtue of hope, he asserts, "is preeminently the virtue of the *status viator*; it is the proper virtue of the 'not yet.'"[8] He draws this from Thomas Aquinas, who says that hope "exists only in those who are still *en route*."[9] It is not only the living who are *viators*; God's will for the dead is not yet entirely fulfilled, and so they too are on their way to God's good future. That is why we hope and pray for them.

The Logical Structure of Hope

Hope has a desire-belief structure. Robin Downie states that "there are two criteria which are independently necessary and jointly sufficient for 'hope that.' The first is that the object of hope must be desired. ... The second ... is that the object of hope [must be believed to] fall within a range of ... possibility, which includes the improbable but excludes the certain and the merely logically possible."[10] Hope has two psychological

---

7. Brunner, cited in Muyskens, *Sufficiency of Hope*, 139. He blurs the concepts of wish and hope (which involve uncertainty) and expectation (which requires certainty).

8. Pieper, *On Hope*, 21 and 11.

9. Aquinas, *Summa Theologiae*, Vol. 33, 2a2ae q18 a3, 37.

10 Downie, "Hope," 248–49. Day ("Hope," 89) says that the phrase "person A hopes that outcome x will happen" means that "A wishes [or desires] that x, and A thinks that x has some degree of probability, however small." Martin (*How We Hope*, 13) agrees: "to hope for an outcome is to desire it while believing it is possible but not certain to obtain." This definition has a long history. Hope, Aquinas (*Summa Theologiae*, Vol. 21, 1a 2ae q45 a2, 7) says, requires four conditions: it is "a movement of appetite aroused by the perception of what is agreeable, future, arduous, and possible of attainment." Thomas Hobbes (*Leviathan*, 123) defines hope as "appetite with an opinion of attaining"; desire, "without such opinion, [is] despair." Rene Descartes

ingredients: a conative element (desire for an outcome) and a cognitive element (belief that it may occur, that its probability is greater than 0 but less than 1). When we are confident a good outcome will happen, we feel joy—and when a bad outcome is certain, we despair. When we are not sure of a good outcome, we hope for it—and when we are unsure that a bad outcome can be avoided, we are afraid.

If I hope for something, I want it to happen and think that it may. Each element comes in degrees, and so hope has two axes of variation: fervency and strength.[11] The conative axis concerns the intensity of desire—a fervent hope is for an outcome considered very important while a mild hope is for one that is unimportant. The cognitive axis concerns belief about how probable the outcome is—high hope means the evidence is thought to favor it while faint hope means the odds are thought to be against it. These two axes are independent of each other: there can be fervent but faint hope or mild but high hope. Hope can also be evaluated along these two dimensions. It can be morally good or bad (depending on the desire involved)—and it can be epistemically reasonable or illusory (depending on whether evidence warrants the degree of hope felt).[12] Fantasy hope, wishful thinking, is based on insufficient reasons; justified hope, by contrast, has an adequate rational basis. Hope has two contrar-

---

(*Passions of Soul*, 137–38 and 189–90) says that evidence "which indicates to us that it is likely [we will obtain what we desire] arouses hope" while "that which indicates that it is unlikely arouses apprehension." When "hope is so strong that it completely drives away apprehension, it . . . is called confidence or assurance"—and "when apprehension is so extreme that it removes all reason for hope, it is converted into despair." Benedict Spinoza (*Ethics* 3.18 Note 2, 278) understands hope as a mental "pleasure, arising from the image of something future . . . of which we do not yet know the issue. Fear . . . is [a] pain . . . arising from the image of something concerning which we are in doubt. If the element of doubt be removed . . . , hope becomes confidence and fear becomes despair." John Locke (*Essay Concerning Understanding*, 440) says "hope is that pleasure of the mind, which everyone finds in himself upon the thought of a probably future enjoyment of a thing which is apt to delight him." David Hume (*Treatise of Human Nature* 2.3.9) agrees: "when good is certain or probable, it produces joy. When evil is in the same situation there arises . . . sorrow. When either good or evil is uncertain, it gives rise to fear or hope, according to the degrees of uncertainty on the one side or the other."

11. This paragraph draws on Day, *Hope*, 19–24 and Smith, "Analysing Hope," 10–11.

12. Justified hope, Day (*Hope*, 39 and 80) says, requires justified desire (the desire is moral) and justified belief (the belief is reasonable, that is, probable). There are, of course, qualifications to be put on this statement. Philosophers such as Martin (*How We Hope*) defend the rationality of desperate hope in particular situations.

ies: fear and despair. Hope and fear differ in terms of *desire*; when I hope I desire an outcome, but when I fear I desire a different outcome from the one I expect. Hope and fear form a continuum, and hope always involves some degree of fear; hope and fear move up and down as our assessment of the probabilities changes.[13] Hope and despair differ in terms of *belief*; when I hope I believe that an outcome is likely, but when I despair I believe it unlikely.

There are important distinctions between wishing, expecting, and hoping. When there is little likelihood that an outcome will occur, my desire is *wish*. "I wish that my wife Jenna would return from her trip tomorrow" means that I feel certain she will not, but want her to. When an outcome is certain it creates *expectation*. "I expect Jenna to return tomorrow" means that I am sure she will.[14] But where wishing and hoping are always for something desired, expecting may not be—I may or may not want Jenna to return. When there is some, perhaps even strong, likelihood that an outcome will happen, my desire is *hope*. "I hope that Jenna returns tomorrow" means that I want her to and think she may (but am not certain). Hope, then, requires both desire and non-confident belief.

The Lived Experience of Hope

Adrienne Martin notes that two people with identical beliefs and desires (cancer patients undergoing chemotherapy, for example) can have different attitudes about an outcome—one hopeful, one not. This means that believing and desiring, while necessary, are not sufficient conditions for hopefulness.[15] In addition, the hopeful person *incorporates* her beliefs and desires into her way of life, making it part of her thoughts, feelings, and actions; the despairing person does not. Hope is a disposition of the whole person—how we think, how we feel, how we will. As

---

13. Day (*Hope*, 31–32) points out that hope is always mixed with fear: when person A hopes for item x, A realizes there is a chance of not-x happening—and A simultaneously hopes that x and fears that not-x.

14. This is why probability has a central role in hope. When person A desires item X and is certain that X will happen, then A no longer hopes—A expects. Conversely, when A desires X and is certain that not-X will happen, A no longer hopes—A despairs. See Day, *Hope*, 12, 19, 23–25, 32–33, and 63.

15. Martin (*How We Hope*, chapter 2, 105) defends what she calls "the incorporation analysis:" hope "involves assigning a probability to an outcome, and seeing that probability as licensing certain feelings and thoughts about that outcome, as well as hedged reliance on that outcome in one's plans."

James Muyskens puts it, "one who hopes for [something] arranges their life and emotions as if [it] were the case."[16] Hope involves thinking—imagining what the hoped-for outcome would be like. Hope involves feeling—positively expecting the best. Hope involves acting, where possible, to bring about the outcome. Nicholas Smith calls hope an "investment of desire" in which we commit ourselves to thinking, feeling, and acting in ways congruent with what we hope for.[17]

Jane Waterworth claims that hope involves anticipation rather than expectation.[18] To *expect* means, etymologically, to "look out for" and "await" the probable occurrence of an event. We expect things that are likely to happen—that the taxi will arrive on time because the service is reliable, for example. Since we are sure it will occur, we simply wait. To *anticipate*, by contrast, means to "seize or take possession beforehand"—to take appropriate action in advance of an event. Anticipating that my friend may drink too much when he visits, I prepare by hiding the whiskey in the garage. Where expectation involves assurance and is passive, anticipation involves uncertainty and is active. The distinction between expectation and anticipation is not absolute. My pregnant niece expects a safe birth since its probability is high—and she just has to wait for the natural process to run its course. But she also anticipates the baby's arrival by actively preparing for it—painting the nursery, for example.

Hope has important existential value. "The soul," Gabriel Marcel says, "exists only through hope.... Hope is perhaps the very stuff of which our soul is made." It exists "only as an active struggle against despair."[19] Life sometimes presents us with trials—situations with no exit (such as a prisoner in captivity)—to which we can respond with despair or hope. *Despair* sees present conditions as permanent, the future as closed. There is no way out and everything will turn out poorly. When we accept a situation as final, we become demoralized and capitulate—we "go to pieces," Marcel says, and "disarm."[20] Feeling trapped before a fate which seems inevitable, we lose heart and give up—collapsing into apathy and "inert

---

16. Muyskens, *Sufficiency of Hope*, 14–15. Pettit ("Hope and Its Place in Mind," 158–59) agrees that hope involves a cognitive resolve to act as if something we desire will or is likely to happen.

17. Smith, "Analysing Hope," 20.

18. Waterworth, *Philosophical Analysis of Hope*. Smith ("Analysing Hope," 16–17) summarizes Waterworth's analysis.

19. Marcel, "Desire and Hope," 283 and Marcel, cited in Schumacher, *Philosophy of Hope*, 122.

20. Marcel, cited in Godfrey, *Philosophy of Human Hope*, 105.

waiting." This abdication becomes self-fulfilling; our passivity lessens the chances of the desired event happening. When we despair, Day agrees, we become apathetic and do nothing to secure that which we desire; if Braden despairs of winning his race then he will not even try.[21] *Hope*, by contrast, sees the present condition as temporary, the future as open. Because it does not accept the situation as final, hope results in motivation, resolve, standing our ground, and not surrendering. Hope, Marcel states, means "active waiting"—"preparation or mobilization of the self in anticipation of" the coming event.[22] We do not just passively wait; instead, we act to bring about what we hope for. Hope, Day notes, is intrinsically linked to action because we try to get what we want to have. When a person hopes, they try to bring the event about; the higher Braden's hope of winning the race, the harder he will try to win it.[23] We "hope and work," Joseph Godfrey says, rather than "hope and wait."[24] By doing so, we make a difference in whether the event happens or not—thus hope, too, is self-fulfilling. "There can strictly speaking be no hope except where the temptation to despair exists," Marcel concludes. Hope occurs in a situation of uncertainty, where the future looks bleak. "Hope is the act by which this temptation is actively . . . overcome."[25] Where despair breeds helplessness, hope—a sense of confidence in the future—restores morale and fortitude, courage and patience, persistence and action. As John Stuart Mill puts it, "a hopeful disposition gives a spur to the faculties and keeps all the active energies in good working order."[26]

Hope is a general attitude of openness to the future. It refuses to believe that all is lost; instead, it affirms that, as Pieper says, "things will turn out well, they will have a good ending—for myself and . . . the world in its totality."[27] As a stance toward the future, Dermot Lane observes,

---

21. Day, *Hope*, 65 and 83.

22. Marcel, "Desire and Hope," 278–82. Existentialism, with its emphasis on a future with open possibilities for the world and individuals, values hope. The future is constituted by possibility, not actuality—reality is not pre-determined but a process of coming-to-be.

23. Day, *Hope*, 56 and 60.

24. Godfrey, *Philosophy of Human Hope*, 235.

25. Marcel, cited in Godfrey, *Philosophy of Human Hope*, 104.

26. Mill, cited in Day, *Hope*, 44.

27. Pieper, cited in Schumacher, *Philosophy of Hope*, 158.

hope "prevents people from falling into despair when historical hopes [both ordinary and ultimate] collapse."[28]

These, then, are the necessary conditions for hoping that an outcome will occur: the person

1. *desires* the outcome—wants it to happen
2. *believes* that the outcome is possible but not certain—thinks that it may happen
3. *incorporates* their desire and belief into their way of being and acting.

As Alice and Robert Evans write, "what persons hope for affects what they value, what they live for, what they desire from day to day, what they say, what they do, and . . . who they are."[29] Hope, Smith adds, is "something we do, . . . an active orientation, a stance we take up and not just a feeling" that passively happens to us. Hope is "not just something we find ourselves with, like eyes of a certain color, but something we are . . . to some degree responsible for."[30] Hope is a virtue we learn; by nurturing hope, we become hopeful people. As Christians we should desire and believe in final consummation, spiritual growth, moral purification, and posthumous—even universal—salvation. One way we incorporate these hopes into our consciousness is through praying for the dead.

Biblical and Theological Definitions of Religious Hope

Where ordinary secular hope is desire plus non-confident belief in fulfillment, Christian eschatological hope is desire plus confident belief. Seung Yang defines hope as "looking forward *with confidence* to a future good"—and Karl Donfried says hope is "the *expectation* of a favorable future under God's direction."[31] John Calvin defines hope as "the *expectation* of those things which . . . have been truly promised by God."[32] While ordinary hope means being unsure whether things will work out, Christian hope is sure and certain conviction that they will, a "settled,

---

28. Lane, *Keeping Hope Alive*, 62.
29. Evans, *Introduction to Christianity*, 119.
30. Smith, "Analysing Hope," 18 and 7.
31. Yang, "Hope," 434, and Donfried, "Hope," 434.
32. Calvin, *Institutes*, Book 3.2.42, 590.

unwavering confidence"—as Tom Wright puts it.[33] The *Catechism of the Catholic Church* defines eschatological hope as "*confident expectation* of . . . the beatific vision of God."[34] Christian hope, David Winter says, "is not the weak, unsubstantiated optimism that we express when we say 'I hope so,' but a *confident belief* that what God has promised, God will do."[35] Hope, Jürgen Moltmann simply states, is "*expectation*-thinking."[36]

Biblical Teaching on Hope

Biblical hope concerns both present and future. We wait for God's historical actions during this present lifetime (e.g., Ps 37:9, 34; 2 Cor 1:10) and for God's eschatological actions at the end of history (e.g., Zeph 3:8; 1 Thess 1:10).

Hope in Hebrew Scripture

Several Hebrew words are translated in English as "hope."[37] *Batah* means to trust or rely on someone, to be full of confidence—and *yahal* means to wait for an expected good. In Isaiah 40:31 the word *qawal* is translated both as "hope" ("those who hope in the Lord will renew their strength"— *NIV*) and as "wait" (*NRSV*). "I will wait for the Lord," the prophet says, "and I will hope in him" (Isa 8:17; cf. 25:9; 64:4). The Hebrew terms, Anthony Thiselton points out, combine desire and expectation. They have a variety of meanings—impatient waiting, eager waiting, desperate waiting (e.g., Ps 130), waiting in quietness and trust (e.g., Ps 131).[38] Yahweh is the individual's hope ("you, O Lord, are my hope"—Ps 71:5), the nation's hope ("hope of Israel"—Jer 14:8), creation's hope ("hope of all the ends of the earth"—Ps 65:5).

The source of hope is a God who makes promises, who "keeps covenant and steadfast love" (Neh 1:5). The Bible's opening chapter is a narrative of hope, as Lane explains: "the point of [the] creation account in

---

33. Wright, *After You Believe*, 203.
34. Roman Catholic Church, *Catechism of Catholic Church*, Section 2090, 507 and Section 1817, 447.
35. Winter, *Living Through Loss*, 71.
36. Moltmann, *Theology of Hope*, 35.
37. This section draws on Donfried, "Hope" and Yang, "Hope."
38. Thiselton, *Life After Death*, 55–56.

Genesis 1 seems to be the restoration of confidence in God ... at a time, namely the Babylonian exile ..., when everything seemed to be lost. The significance of this creation story is that the God who brought order out of chaos at the beginning of time is the same God who will rescue the people of Israel from the chaos of ... captivity."[39] God made promises to the patriarchs: to Noah (Gen 8:22) and Abraham (Gen 15:18–20). When childlessness threatened the promise, the barren matriarchs—Sarah, Rebekah, and Rachel—were given sons (Gen 21:2; 25:21; 30:22). God promised, in the covenant at Sinai, to make Israel God's treasured people (Exod 19:5–8)—and, despite their disobedience, repeatedly delivered them (Judg 2:11–19). God promised an eternal monarchy to King David (2 Sam 5:3, 19; 7:14; Ps 132:11); when this promise seemed canceled, the prophets announced that restoration would follow judgment. They portray God as a faithful husband calling back an unfaithful wife (Hos 2:19), a faithful parent seeking a rebellious child (Hos 1:1–9). Jeremiah, before deportation, purchased land in hope of return (32:9–5)—"I know the plans I have for you, says the Lord, ... to give you a future with hope" (29:11). Zechariah (9:9–12) calls the exiled people "prisoners of hope" awaiting deliverance and renewal. Even the lament psalms (e.g., 6:4; 35:23–25), Yang says, "are hopeful because they are ... an expectation that Yahweh ... will rectify the situation."[40]

"The faithfulness of the Lord endures for ever" (Ps 117:2). God's unwavering *hesed*—steadfast love—shown repeatedly in Israel's history was the foundation for trust that God will fulfill God's future promises. "Our ancestors have told us what deeds you performed in their days," the psalmist prays, so "rise up, come to our help" (Ps 44:1,26). The prophet Isaiah (51:1–6) encourages the exiled Hebrews to have faith in the future deliverance promised by God. He points to Abraham and Sarah as models of hope who believed, against enormous odds, that God would lead them to a land whose name they did not know, that a child would be born in their old age and that God would be faithful even if they obediently sacrificed their son. This is a model for hope, Walter Brueggemann says, "for belief and trust that God can create newness out of defeat, barrenness and even death."[41] The exiles looked back (vv. 1–2), Derek Kidner emphasizes,

---

39. Lane, *Keeping Hope Alive*, 179.

40. Yang, "Hope," 886.

41. Brueggemann, *Threat of Life*, 57–58; slightly modified. He adds (19) that when God says "I am the God of your fathers, the God of Abraham, the God of Isaac, the God of Jacob" (Exod 3:6) God means "I am ... the One who came upon hopeless old

"to look ahead to the promised consummation both in this world (v. 3–5) and in the next (v. 6)."[42] History—promise and fulfillment—grounded Israel's hope in times of anxiety.

Hope in Christian Scripture

The primary Greek words translated as "hope" or "expectation" are *elpis* and *elpizo*. "In hope we were saved" (Rom 8:24), St. Paul says; "may the God of hope fill you with all joy and peace . . . , so that you may abound in hope" (Rom 15:13). Hope is directed toward the eschatological events of *parousia* and resurrection (Acts 23:6; 24:15; 26:6–7)—"hope of sharing the glory of God" (Rom 5:2; cf. Col 1:27), "hope of eternal life" (Titus 3:7). Ours is a "living hope" (1 Pet 1:3)—constant and unfading, vibrant and active. Hope, the author of Hebrews (6:19) says, is a "steadfast anchor of the soul" that holds us firm to the promises of God so we do not lose our moorings. The "hope of salvation" is "a helmet," St. Paul says, that protects against the enemy of despair (1 Thess 5:18).

Hope, Rudolf Bultmann and Karl Rengstorf state, includes "the three elements of expectation of the future, trust, and the patience of waiting." First, hope means "*expectation* with the nuance of counting upon"—looking forward to an event which is certain to occur.[43] We are "waiting for the coming of our Lord Jesus Christ" (1 Cor 1:7), St. Paul says, "expecting a Savior" (Phil 3:20)—"we eagerly wait for the hope of righteousness" (Gal 5:5; cf. Heb 9:28). The Greek word used in these verses is *apekdechomai*—"to expect eagerly" or "to await eagerly." The entire creation "waits with eager longing" for final redemption (Rom 8:19). The word here is *apokaradokia*—"longing and eagerly expecting." It suggests, Terrence Pendergast notes, "an attitude of craning one's neck to observe what is coming about"—standing on tiptoe and stretching forward in anticipation.[44]

---

people and gave them children . . . , the One who came among wandering sojourners and promised them land, the One who came where life was all closed down and promised them a future they could not imagine or invent for themselves."

42. Kidner, "Isaiah," 617.
43. Bultmann and Rengstorf, "Elpis," 531 and 530.
44. Thiselton, *Life After Death*, 56 and Pendergast, "Hope, NT," 284.

Second, Bultmann and Rengstorf say, hope means "certainty of *trust* in a divinely given future."⁴⁵ "You have come to trust in God," St. Peter (1 Pet 1:21) declares, "so that your faith and hope are set on God." St. Paul points to Abraham's trust, despite all evidence, in God's promise. "Hoping against hope" he believed that the God "who gives life to the dead and calls into existence things that do not exist" would give him lineage and land. Abraham "considered him faithful who had promised" (Heb 11:11); "no distrust made him waver . . . , but he [was] fully convinced that God was able to do what he had promised" (Rom 4:17–21). We, too, must have "steadfastness of hope" (1 Thess 1:3; cf. Rom 15:4) and "hold firm the confidence . . . that belongs to hope" (Heb 3:6). Faith brings "assurance of things hoped for" (Heb 11:1; cf. 6:11)—and trust in the promises of "God, who never lies" gives "hope of eternal life" (Titus 1:2).

Third, Bultmann and Rengstorf say, in hope "*patient waiting* . . . is emphasized."⁴⁶ "We wait for the blessed hope" of Christ's return in glory (Titus 2:13; cf. 1 Thess 1:10)—and "we wait for it with patience" (Rom 8:19,25). This waiting is more than anxious endurance; instead, we "rejoice in hope" (Rom 12:12). Nor is this waiting passive, but implies being ready and prepared. Jesus' apocalyptic discourses contain parables of watchfulness (Matt 24:36—25:30) urging us to be "alert" and "at work" when he appears (Luke 12:37, 38, 43). St. Paul also stresses that "it is now the moment for you to wake from sleep. For salvation is nearer to us now than when we became believers" (Rom 13:11–12). Hope is like expectation in being certain, not doubtful—and like anticipation in being actively incorporated, not passively waited.

Theological Reflection on Hope

Christian hope is expectation that is sure and certain. While we have historical hopes, our ultimate hope is eschatological—we await the fulfillment of God's purpose for the entire world and all people. Ultimate hope, if it is not to be pure fantasy and wishfulness, requires a rational foundation; confident belief is necessary for hope. The source of hope—the "hope-maker," in philosophical jargon—is divine promise and faithfulness. In "the hope-giving word of promise," Moltmann says, "we have

---

45. Bultmann and Rengstorf, "Elpis," 531.
46. Ibid., 522.

a key word of [the biblical] religion of expectation."[47] Thiselton agrees: "we may look beyond the present only on the basis of promise. If the future were the product of human imagination..., it would remain sheer speculation."[48] Peter Geach identifies three elements of Christian hope: "expectations regarding the future would fall into chaos but for *trust* in the *promises* of God, who is ... *faithful* to God's own word once given."[49]

1. *Trust.* Bernard Schumacher points out that we only hope for things which we cannot bring about on our own—and so hope requires trust in, counting on, something outside ourselves.[50] *Hoping that* a favorable outcome will occur requires *hoping in*—which is, Godfrey says, "closely bound up with trust."[51] A cancer patient hopes *that* their condition will be cured because they hope *in*—or trust—the doctors treating them. Trust is confident expectation that another person will act for our good. We cannot trust at will; instead, trust requires having reasons to believe in the other's goodness (they are well-disposed to me) and competence (they are able to achieve what I trust them for).[52] Praying for and hoping *that* final consummation, spiritual growth, moral purification, and universal salvation will occur involves trusting *in* a God who wants to and is able to accomplish them.

2. *Promises.* Promises are not simply hypothetical assertions concerning the future; instead, they are speech-acts that create it. John Searle distinguishes two directions of fit between words and the world: "some [utterances]... get the words to match the world, others... get the world to match the words."[53] Statements of fact ("Jim was married on July 1") describe the world while promises ("Jenna, I will love you in sickness and in health") shape it. Promises are what John Austin calls "performatives"—speech-acts by authorized persons "in which to say something is to do something," as when my pastor father says over my daughter "I

---

47. Moltmann, *Theology of Hope*, 120.
48. Thiselton, *Life After Death*, 20. This section draws on Thiselton, chapters 2–4.
49. Geach, *Virtues*, 54.
50. Schumacher, *Philosophy of Hope*, 75.
51. Godfrey, *Philosophy of Human Hope*, 37. Day (*Hope*, 27) points out that sometimes hope involves reliance on other people—person A hopes that person B will do action X. For Christians this means we hope that God will bring consummation (for example).
52. For philosophical analysis of trust see McLeod, "Trust."
53. Searle, cited in Thiselton, *Life After Death*, 26.

baptize you, Becky."[54] Divine promises make things happen—they are divine actions, performed by the saying of words, that define the future. A promise, Searle adds, "commits the speaker to a certain course of action." Promises are obligations that bind—and the God of the covenant, in promising to Noah, Abraham, Moses, and David, becomes duty-bound to specific actions in the future.[55]

3. *Faithfulness.* Biblical hope is *hesed*-based, John Polkinghorne says.[56] Fulfillment is certain because of the steadfastness of God; our "hope is in the Lord . . . who keeps faith forever" (Ps 146:5–6). We "hold fast to the confession of our hope without wavering, for he who has promised is faithful" (Heb 10:23). Where pagan deities are arbitrary—Elijah mocked *Ba'al* for being on a journey or asleep (1 Kgs 18:27)—the God of Israel is "the faithful God who maintains covenant loyalty" (Deut 7:9). Remembrance of God's past faithfulness and expectation of God's future faithfulness cannot be separated, Moltmann says: "hope's *assurance* springs from the . . . faithfulness of the God of promise. Hope's *knowledge* recalls the faithfulness of this God in history. . . . Assurance of hope without such knowledge would be vague adventuring"—wishful thinking. Two great past acts of God—the exodus (the center of Jewish history) and Easter (the center of Christian history)—are the foundation of hope in the future.[57] "The promise-fulfillment schema," Macquarrie concludes, "forms the framework" for hope—for confidence in the coming victory of God and the mending of creation, the pilgrimage of nations to Jerusalem, and the ingathering of all people to God.[58]

---

54. Austin, cited in Thiselton, *Life After Death*, 26.

55. Searle, cited in ibid. In "Grace We Are Owed" and "Earning, Deserving" I argue that God has duties—that in creating human beings God commits Godself to them and becomes duty-bound to pursuing their welfare.

56. Polkinghorne, *God of Hope*, 95.

57. Moltmann, *Theology of Hope*, 119–20; emphasis added. He says (297–98): "it is in order to awake confidence in [God's] faithfulness in the future that the historic experiences of former times are recounted." Fackenheim (*God's Presence in History*) distinguishes root experiences and epoch-making experiences. A root experience (such as the exodus and Easter) is the key historical event of God's action and presence that creates a people's identity and self-understanding. An epoch-making experience (such as the exile or crucifixion), by contrast, is a historical event that challenges those core beliefs. In such times, despair threatens to swallow us and completely define our lives. For people of faith it is root experiences, not immediate traumas, which shape our outlook on the future.

58. Macquarrie, *Christian Hope*, 32.

Put philosophically, eschatological hope is grounded in a God who is both benevolent and powerful. The argument is simple:

1. God has good will (and so wants to complete the promised future).
2. God is competent (and so can complete the promised future).
3. If God wants to and can complete the promised future, then God will.
4. Therefore, God will complete the promised future.

"With the Lord there is steadfast *love*, and with him is great *power*," therefore God "*will* redeem Israel" and all of creation—the psalmist (130:7–8) declares. "The symbol of the anchor," Muyskens observes, "expresses succinctly the function of hope in biblical . . . thought. In the battering storms of life, the wayfarer's hope in God remains an anchor in a stormy sea—a constant source of security, calm and respite. One's hope for the future . . . is fastened to God's promise and faithfulness."[59] George Frideric Handel's oratorio *Messiah* begins with the promise that God's redeeming activity—valleys exalted, the crooked made straight, and rough places a plain (Isa 40:1–5)—will be revealed and all humanity shall see it together. The tenor recitative sings "saith your God" in three forceful notes that rise, and are repeated, as hope rises—and the chorus concludes with confident finality: "for the mouth of the Lord has spoken it."[60]

Living between promise and fulfillment, we are pilgrims—*viators*—on this earth: "here we have no lasting city, but we are looking for the city that is to come" (Heb 13:14; cf. 11:8–16). Sometimes we are tempted to despair: "we walk through dark corridors with no hope," John Crossin acknowledges, "buffeted by the crises and disappointments of life."[61] The sin of despair involves both *acedia* (apathy, lack of caring, weariness, fatigue) and *tristitia* (sadness, melancholy).[62] Peter Brown points out that the Latin term "*disperare* means, literally, *de-sperare*—to 'un-hope' oneself. It means to give up hope, to cease to expect, even . . . to give no thought to."[63] Discouragement creates indifference to spiritual duties and moral

59. Muyskens, *Sufficiency of Hope*, 135–36.
60. See Bullard, *Messiah*, 12–13.
61. Crossin, *Everyday Virtues*, 22–23.
62. Evagrius of Pontus identified two sins, later combined into one—sloth—by Gregory the Great. See DeYoung, *Glittering Vices*, chapter 4; Fairlie, *Seven Deadly Sins*, chapter 5; Schimmel, *Seven Deadly Sins*, chapter 8.
63. Brown, *Ransom of Soul*, 156; slightly modified.

obligations. Resignation saps energy and paralyzes the will: difficulty and injustice are so prevalent in the world that we cannot change them—and so, since action is futile, we do nothing. The virtue of hope cures these ills. It counters, Moltmann's states, "the dejection which leads to inertia, the despondency which infects everything."[64] This is the moral character of hope: it affects intellect, emotion, and will, creating confident belief, trusting mood and positive action.

Hope is a disposition to act as if what we hope for is true and will happen. *Action-hope* enables us to endure, to "not grow weary in doing what is right" (Gal 6:9; 2 Thess 3:13), to "toil and struggle, because we have our hope set on the living God" (1 Tim 4:10). "Waiting," Moltmann says, "does not mean a passive waiting-it-out; it means an active expectation. . . . With every doing of the right, we prepare the way for the 'new earth' on which righteousness will 'dwell.'"[65] "Hope," Augustine of Hippo is claimed to have said, "has two beautiful daughters: anger and courage. Anger at the way things are and courage to see that things do not stay the way they are."[66] The Roman Catholic International Theological Commission states that there is an "intimate bond between the firm hope of future life and the possibility of responding to the demands of Christian life."[67] "Buoyed up by hope," the *Catechism of the Catholic Church* adds, we are "preserved from selfishness and led to . . . charity."[68] Because God will have the victory we are to be "steadfast, immovable, always excelling in the work of the Lord" (1 Cor 15:58). When we hope we are committed to taking action to bring about what we hope for—we do not simply wait for it to arrive. Hope, as Joseph Grady puts it, is the *prolegomena*—the ground and precursor—to ethics. It creates impatience with the present state of affairs and enables actions of effort and sacrifice toward the future.[69] In acting we become agents of hope to a despairing world. As Robert Kennedy says, "each time a person stands up for an ideal, or acts to improve the lot of others or strikes out against injustice, he or she sends forth a tiny ripple of hope."[70] When we hope, Richard Norris emphasizes,

---

64. Moltmann, *In the End*, 93.
65. Moltmann, *Ethics of Hope*, 7–8.
66. This quote is widely attributed, without citation, to Augustine.
67. International Theological Commission, "Current Questions," 209.
68. Roman Catholic Church, *Catechism of Catholic Church* 1820, 448.
69. Grady, "Marcel: Hope and Ethics," 61.
70. Kennedy, cited in Felten and Procter-Murphy, *Living the Questions*, 174.

we reach out to God's future, acting "to make the world in which we presently live look, if only a little bit, like the new creation which God is bringing."[71] Because we hope, we start building the future today.

Hope is also a disposition to think and feel in positive ways. *Attitude-hope* creates a sense of optimism—feelings of serenity and joy: "happy are those . . . whose hope is in the Lord" (Ps 146:5). Hope, Calvin says, "strengthens faith, that it may not waver in God's promises, or . . . doubt concerning their truth. . . . Hope refreshes faith, that it may not become weary. . . . It invigorates faith . . . with perseverance."[72] Martin Luther agrees: "though we are uncertain of the future, yet we hope with certain hope, and hereby we are . . . buoyed up, lest falling into . . . despair, we should break down under the present evil."[73] The *Catechism of the Catholic Church* says that "hope keeps [us] from discouragement" and "affords us joy even under trial."[74] Where despair breeds sadness and passive apathy, hope creates joy and active energy.

Hope, Allen Verhey observes, "sometimes takes the form of lament." Praise belongs to hope—but so does an honest recognition that death and evil still deny God's reign. "Blessed are those who mourn," Jesus says (Matt 5:4). It is because they hope that they are distressed, Verhey points out.

> The mourners are those who have heard the good news of God's good future and weep because it is not yet, and their eyes fill with tears because they see it challenged and contradicted in the present. Their spirits ache for the coming of the Kingdom Jesus announced. . . . Their hope does not keep them from grieving. Indeed, it is precisely their hope for that day that prompts their tears and the cry "How long, O Lord."[75]

We long for the fulfillment of God's promise, we hunger and thirst for the future when peace will flourish—and weep because it is not yet, because the Lord seems slow to keep the promise (2 Pet 3:1–9). It is because we hope that we mourn and ask "my God, where are you?"

Hope is a stable disposition of character infused by divine grace and acquired by human practice. Just as there is the learned helplessness

---

71. Norris, *Understanding the Faith*, 253.
72. Calvin, *Institutes*, Book 3.2.42, p. 590.
73. Luther, in Kerr, *Compend of Luther's Theology*, 240.
74. Roman Catholic Church, *Catechism of Catholic Church* 1818, 447.
75. Verhey, *Christian Art of Dying*, 336–37; cf. 276, 334, and 344.

of despair, so there is learned hopefulness and optimism.[76] Living in a world where "despair lies in wait at every instant," Marcel says, "we have the *duty* of fighting against this temptation."[77] We develop the habit of hope through a long process of formation until it forms a part of our being. The Bible commands us to actively cultivate hope—to seize it (Heb 6:18), hold fast to it (Heb 10:23), set our minds on it (1 Pet 1:13). Hope is nourished, sustained and, when it fails, restored by the passing of time, the support of caring friends, personal and communal prayer—and by what Brueggemann calls "vigorous, active remembering."[78] Prayer for the dead, I claim in the second volume, is one way of cultivating hope in final consummation, spiritual growth, moral purification, and universal salvation.

Concluding Remarks

The Bible is full of crises of hope—from Abraham to the exiles, from the prophet Habakkuk to the church at Thessalonica. Perhaps the most poignant crisis, however, is recorded by St. Luke (24:21). "We had hoped that he was the one to redeem Israel." The two disciples on the road to Emmaus, speaking about the crucifixion of the man who had looked so promising, admit their sad defeat to the traveler who joins them. Barbara Brown Taylor comments: "'We *had* hoped.' Hope in the past tense, one of the saddest sounds a human being can make. We had hoped he was the one. We believed things might really change, but we were wrong. He died. It is over now. No more fairy tales. No more illusions. Back to business as usual." Their hope had shriveled, killed by disappointment. They are not alone, Taylor adds; "everyone has walked [that road] at one time or another." Shaken and hardened by life, we give up hope and settle in cynicism. But Jesus comes to us, people with broken dreams in a broken world—"the disappointed, the doubtful, the disconsolate"—as he came to Cleopas and his companion. "Take heart," he says, "do not despair."[79]

---

76. See Seligman, *Helplessness* and *Learned Optimism*. Some people, having been conditioned to pessimism, are more likely to give up in the face of adversity and to suffer from depression. Optimistic people, by contrast, believe bad events to be temporary rather than permanent; optimism can be learned by training positive ways of interpreting and responding to adversity.

77. Marcel, "Hope and Desire," 278; emphasis added.

78. Brueggemann, *Threat of Life*, 57.

79. Taylor, *Gospel Medicine*, 22–25; emphasis added. The phrase "settle in cynicism"

Human existence is either a tragedy (a sad and painful story ending in ruin and disappointment) or a comedy (a wonderful and glorious story ending with joy and happiness). "No person can live without hope," Dietrich Bonhoeffer writes from prison days after the failure of the assassination attempt on Adolf Hitler—a time when he anticipated further punishment for being part of the resistance circle. "For the Christian ... the only important thing is to have well-founded hope.... How great ... is the power that an absolutely grounded hope has for life." But many people suffer from hope-deprivation, seeing life as tragic.[80] Lack of hope is poignantly expressed in Samuel Beckett's absurdist play *Waiting for Godot*—in which two men wait in vain for the arrival of someone or something named Godot. Both naturalism and traditional Christianity are tragic.

1. A naturalist worldview excludes ultimate hope for anyone. Since life ends absolutely in "a death without hope," Albert Camus reasons, it is the "final defeat" that dooms all plans and meaning to extinction and non-fulfillment.[81] Some, like Bertrand Russell, defiantly embrace despair.

> [Nothing] can preserve an individual life beyond the grave; ... all the labors of the ages, all the devotion, all the inspiration, all the noonday brightness of human genius, are destined to extinction in the vast death of the solar system, and ... the whole temple of man's achievement must inevitably be buried beneath the debris of a universe in ruins.... Only within the scaffolding of these truths, only on the foundation of unyielding despair, can the soul's habitation henceforth be safely built.[82]

2. Traditional Christian doctrine excludes ultimate hope for many people since only a few achieve heaven while most of humanity are eternally condemned. At the gates of Dante's Inferno is posted the sign "Abandon every hope, all you who enter."[83] Given the reality of a hugely-populated hell, Kenneth Kantzer bluntly admits, "the biblical answer [concerning afterlife destiny] ... is a hard and crushing word, devastating

---

comes from Brueggemann, *Threat of Life*, 115.

80. Bonhoeffer, *Letters and Papers*, 488. The phrase "hope-deprivation" comes from Smith, "Concept of Hope," 18.

81. Camus, cited in Schumacher, *Philosophy of Hope*, 156.

82. Russell, cited in Talbott, *Inescapable Love*, 213–14.

83. Dante, *Portable Dante*, 14.

to human hope."⁸⁴ If sinners remain in hell forever then God's purpose in creating them (that they be united with rather than separated from God) is defeated rather than fulfilled. A permanently occupied hell means an ultimate dualism in which evil is not entirely eliminated from reality; instead, a force opposed to God exists eternally alongside God.

Where naturalism and classical Christianity are tragic, the gospel is comedic. It is, Moltmann declares, "wholly and entirely confident hope."⁸⁵ "I'm an optimist," Billy Graham says. "I've read the last page of the Bible and God's going to win."⁸⁶ Jacques Ellul agrees, in words that reverse Russell's despair: "I am not pessimistic because I believe that the history of the human race, no matter how tragic, will ultimately lead to the Kingdom of God. I am convinced that all the works of humankind will be reintegrated in the work of God, and that each one of us, no matter how sinful, will ultimately be saved."⁸⁷ In the comforting words of Julian of Norwich, "all shall be well, and all shall be well, and all manner of things shall be well."⁸⁸ We have hope, the Christian Reformed Church confession says, because "our world belongs to God—not to us or earthly powers, not to demons, fate or chance. . . . The future is secure because . . . our world, broken and scarred, still belongs to God."⁸⁹ Biblical hope is not naïve optimism or vague wish but sure confidence that we will receive what God has promised. It is grounded, Brueggemann reminds us, in a God who "can keep promises against all odds."⁹⁰ Polkinghorne agrees: hope holds fast to promises despite apparent contradiction since "the One who is trustworthy is the ground of hopeful expectation."⁹¹ Because God will keep God's promises we can live with joyful hope. Hope acknowledges the twin realities expressed by Bruce Cockburn: we are "grim

---

84. Kantzer, cited in Talbott, *Inescapable Love*, 37.

85. Moltmann, *In the End*, 87.

86. Graham, "Responding to God's Glory," 145.

87. Ellul, cited in MacDonald, *Evangelical Universalist*, 156.

88. Julian, cited in Hick, *Death and Eternal Life*, 156.

89. Christian Reformed Church, "Our World Belongs to God," Sections 7, 13, and 18, 1021 and 1023–24.

90. Brueggemann, *Threat of Life*, 5. Faith involves a dialogue: "one voice says, 'can you imagine!' The other voice answers 'yes, but.'" Consider Abraham: "can you imagine a new son . . . ? . . . can you imagine land given to a landless people? Not: can you implement it . . .—only: can you entrust possibilities to God that go beyond your own capacity for control?" (6).

91. Polkinghorne, *God of Hope*, 47 and 88.

travelers"—we live and lament in a broken world, but in the midnight of despair history is tinged with the sunrise of hope. We have, he sings elsewhere, heard "rumors of glory."[92]

Hope is like a hurricane lamp—an oil lantern with a glass chimney designed to shelter the flame from the wind so it is not blown out but continues to burn and give out soft light. Hope has an intellectual aspect; it is a way of understanding and seeing the world, a set of beliefs and desires. It has an emotional aspect—a positive mood of trust and expectancy that overcomes despair and fear. It has a volitional aspect; because the future is open, not closed, we can imagine a new state of affairs and act toward it.[93] The hopeful Christian

1. *desires* particular eschatological outcomes: final consummation of all things, continual growth toward God, perfectly holy character and salvation of every person;

2. *believes* confidently that these outcomes will occur, given God's promises and faithfulness, power and love; and

3. *incorporates* these desires and beliefs into their way of being and doing.

Christian hope combines elements of expectation and anticipation. We expect the last things because we are certain they will happen; "we stride confidently toward the promised future," Moltmann says.[94] We anticipate them because, as we await their arrival, we prepare ourselves and our world for them. The promise that those in exile would return to Zion inspired hope: "strengthen the weak hands, and make firm the feeble knees. Say to those who are of a fearful heart, 'Be strong, do not fear'" (Isa 35:3–4). St. Paul exhorts the Thessalonians with hope that gives courage and comfort: since "we will be with the Lord forever . . . , encourage one another with these words" (1 Thess 4:18).[95] Where despair brings hopelessness that makes action meaningless, hope—believing the future is open, not closed—makes a difference in how we think, feel, and live now.

---

92. Cockburn, "Grim Travelers" and "Rumors of Glory."

93. See Maquarrie, *Christian Hope*, chapter 1.

94. Moltmann, *Theology of Hope*, 298.

95. Day (*Hope*, 57 and 91) says that when we convey our hope to others it encourages and supports them. In such a situation person A causes person B to hope that event X will take place.

The *nature* of eschatological hope is confident expectation, its *source* is God's future promises and past faithfulness, and its *content* is fourfold:

1. *consummation hope*—joyful resurrection and life in eternal communion with God and neighbor on a new earth of justice and peace;
2. *growth hope*—ever-deepening awareness of and relationship with God;
3. *sanctification hope*—personal purification from sin and selfishness; and
4. *salvation hope*—inclusion of all persons in the joys of heaven.[96]

Not to desire and believe in these things—and not to pray them for the dead—is to sin against hope. As Pieper says, "one who despairs does not petition because he assumes that his prayer will not be granted." Not to pray for the dead, Robert Ombres asserts, is "to be guilty of a real failure in the exercise of Christian hope."[97]

Hope is a formed disposition of character, a virtue acquired through habitual actions that train our thoughts, emotions, and actions. Prayer is one way hope is nurtured, through which we come to desire, believe in and incorporate hope into our characters. Prayer—Pope Benedict XVI says—is a "school of hope'" by which we "draw the future into the present, so that . . . the present is touched by the future reality."[98] Crossin agrees: "prayer is a key to hope"—through it "we live once again in hope for heaven and for God's grace today."[99] Praying for the dead maintains eschatological expectation and protects from eschatological despair; it cultivates a positive vision for the future.

The second volume of this work examines in detail the hopes expressed in prayers for the departed: consummation hope, growth hope, purification hope, and salvation hope. There is hope for the blessed, hope for the imperfect, hope for the unsaved, hope for all creation. Through

---

96. Some Christians do not hope, but merely wish, for universal salvation (since they think there is little likelihood that it will occur). Others—some Calvinists, for example—do not even wish for universal salvation (since they think God has revealed that some individuals are damned for the glory of God and to desire their salvation is to be more charitable than God).

97. Pieper, *On Hope*, 36 and 70 and Ombres, *Theology of Purgatory*, 59, slightly modified. Ombres is referring specifically to prayer for those in purgatory; I have broadened his meaning to include all the dead.

98. Pope Benedict XVI, *Spe Salvi*, 17.

99. Crossin, *Everyday Virtues*, 22–23.

these prayers of hope—perhaps better, prayers of expectation—we incorporate belief and desire for spiritual growth, moral purification, universal salvation, and final consummation into our characters and practice the promises of God.

Afterword

LOOKING AHEAD: A PREVIEW OF VOLUME TWO—

The Theological Meaning and Spiritual Value of Praying for the Dead

LARRY AND I WERE once more having breakfast. A good friend of his had died several weeks earlier, and we were talking about Henry. "I've never prayed for any dead person before," Larry reported. He paused . . . "But I feel compelled to pray for him." "Why do you think that is?" I wondered. "Well . . . I prayed so long for his healing from cancer that I can't just stop now," Larry replied. "It just seems natural to continue praying for him." Another silence. "What do you pray for him?" I asked. "That anything which separates him from God be healed and removed," Larry said.

This is the essence of every prayer for every departed person. Our prayers entrust all of the dead into God's loving care, asking that God's purpose for them—joyful and eternal union with God—be fulfilled. But questions remain. First, what is the theological meaning of the specific petitions for each particular group of the departed—the blessed, the imperfect, the unsaved? What do we pray for them? Second, what is the spiritual value of praying for all the departed? How does it form our lives as followers of Jesus? The second book of this project answers these questions.

- Chapter 1 briefly restates the philosophical and theological assumptions of volume one.

- Chapters 2 through 5 examine in detail the four types of prayer for the dead. They discuss the substance of prayer for final consummation of all things, growth of the blessed in heaven, purification of the imperfect in purgatory, and salvation of the unsaved in hell—identifying the necessary conception of the afterlife required by each particular prayer. Consummation and growth prayers are fully in line with Scripture and church tradition. Purification and salvation prayers, however, raise controversial questions and are more theologically divisive—they are analyzed in some detail.
- Chapters 6 and 7 reflect on how praying for the dead is spiritually and morally forming for the living—how it enhances faith, builds hope, and sharpens discipleship.
- Chapter 8 provides sample prayers that may be used in both public worship and private devotion.

Prayers for the dead create particular beliefs and desires in us—and they help us incorporate those beliefs and desires into our habits of life. Praying for consummation, growth, purification, and salvation instills confidence in the good future God will bring and makes us ready to live in the light of eternity.

It seems right to end this book on prayer with several prayers.

> A consummation prayer:
>
>> Loving God, in your infinite mercy bring N., together with the whole church, living and departed in the Lord Jesus, to a joyful resurrection and the fulfillment of your eternal purpose. Unite us together again to rejoice in your kingdom and sing your praise forever and ever. Through Jesus Christ our Lord, who has come and is coming again. Amen.
>
> A growth prayer:
>
>> Receive, O Lord our God, our brother/sister N. into your love. Grant to him/her those things which eye has not seen, nor ear heard, nor the human heart imagined. Feed him/her at the table of eternal life where the voice of those who keep high festival never ceases, and where endless is the sweetness of those who behold the beauty of your countenance. May N. grow in deeper reverence and love, for you are the true happiness of those who know you. Amen.

LOOKING AHEAD: A PREVIEW OF VOLUME TWO—

A purification prayer:

Jesus, gentle shepherd—lead N. out of his/her blindness and weakness. Set them on the path of holiness and wholeness. Conform them to your image as you cleanse their hearts and minds. Make your love the reality of their lives—that they may love you fully. Re-creating God, hear our prayer. Amen.

A salvation prayer:

Lord Jesus, you stretched out your arms on the hard wood of the cross that everyone might come within the reach of your saving embrace. Bring N., who did not know you, to love you and rest in your dwelling place. Let the light of your grace shine upon him/her. Christ, Mediator and Redeemer, have mercy. Amen.

APPENDIX

THEORIES OF HUMAN NATURE and personal identity are complicated—problems confront each view and conclusions are far from established. Here is a brief overview of some key elements.

1. Arguments for and against Dualism

Several arguments support dualism. First, the mind is not the brain. The law of identity states that if thing 1 is identical to thing 2 then every property of 1 is a property of 2 (and *vice versa*). If, however, two things have different properties then they are separate and distinct items. Mind and brain *do* possess different properties (and are thus numerically-distinct and ontologically-different types of things). Mind is conscious and brain is not—brain cells do not have experience. Brain processes have a location in space (specific parts of the brain perform specific functions), but mental events do not (my desire for ice cream is not located to the left of my belief that 2+2=4). Brains have mass and volume, but thoughts do not. And, as Rene Descartes points out, I can doubt the existence of my body but not my mind. In addition, my inner experience is private (no one else can know what the color yellow looks like to me) but brain processes are public (scientists can map activity in particular neurological regions when I see yellow). Since mind has psychological properties that brain does not, and since brain has physical properties that thoughts do not, they are two different things.

Second, the soul is the subject of conscious experience. In addition to the various experiences there is the being, the self, who has them. Descartes' *cogito ergo sum* means that I must exist in order for the thinking I am doing right now to take place. We are aware of ourselves as the permanent subject having sequential experiences across time and as the single subject having simultaneous experiences at one time. According to William Hasker organisms with complex brains generate both conscious states (a set of temporary fragmented mental events) *and* subjects having those conscious states (the unified and enduring self where the constant flow of experiences appears).[1] The soul, then, is an independent reality from the thoughts and feelings that it experiences.

Third, scientific evidence clearly shows a causal relationship between brain and mind in this world—but it does not show that brain is necessary for mind in all possible worlds. Saul Kripke imagines zombies—physical duplicates identical to ourselves, that have material bodies just like ours and behave exactly as we do, but without consciousness of any kind. If a zombie is pinched, it says "ouch"—but feels no pain, since on the inside nothing is going on.[2] Since zombies are possible (that is, there is nothing logically contradictory about the idea of beings in which brain activity is not accompanied by conscious feelings), brain and mind, neurological processes and consciousness, are not the same thing. Science also cannot explain why specific mental states (such as pains but not itches) are correlated with specific brain states. Inverted qualia worlds (where different brain states are correlated with other mental states—the mental state of seeing red being caused by the brain state usually associated with seeing blue) suggest that the correlations are not necessary—and thus require explanation.[3]

Dualism also faces serious difficulties. Take just one—mind-brain interaction. "The physical world," David Papineau says, "appears to be causally complete. The causes of physical effects always seem to be other physical causes."[4] The causal completeness of physical systems only allows material causes and leaves no room for mental causes (mind cannot influence matter). Events in the body and brain cause events in consciousness (light rays from the sun hit my eyes, creating a mental state—I see bright colors) and events in consciousness cause events in the brain and body (I decide to wear sunglasses, and this mental state creates a bodily action—I put them on). Dualism cannot explain this two-way causal interaction between physical and non-physical things. Since soul is non-physical, the interaction cannot be physical; a physical process in the brain cannot

---

1. Hasker, "Persons as Emergent Substances," 111, 116, and "On Behalf of Emergent Dualism," 64.
2. Kripke, cited in Papineau, *Consciousness*, 56, 80, and 100.
3. See Moreland, "Argument from Consciousness," 439.
4. Papineau, *Consciousness*, 65.

cause a non-physical experience in the soul. And since the brain is physical, the interaction cannot be non-physical; a non-physical thought in the mind cannot cause a neuron in the physical brain to fire.

2. Arguments for and against Materialism and Constitutionism

Several arguments support materialism and constitutionism. First, neuroscience connects mental states with brain processes. Science shows that mind—conscious states—does not exist apart from body. My mind goes where my body goes, and what happens in my mind is affected by what happens in my brain. My son David is developmentally disabled as the result of a prenatal brain injury that adversely impacts his academic performance, verbal communication, and adaptive functioning. Localization studies have identified specific regions and systems in the brain that perform particular functions: language, emotion, face recognition, memory, decision-making.[5] Science thus contradicts dualism: mind changes depending on what happens to the brain. Since mental states are correlated with and caused by brain states, consciousness requires a properly-functioning brain. Ockham's razor states that we should adopt the simplest explanation of a phenomenon: consciousness is not something extra to—but just is—brain activity (in the same way that temperature is not something extra to but just is mean kinetic energy). Materialists deny that zombies are possible: our physical duplicates must be our conscious duplicates as well—brain processes without consciousness are not possible.[6]

Second, there is evolutionary continuity between human beings and animals. Because we have the same biological origins, what makes human beings distinctive is not having a special part (a non-physical soul created by God) but having special abilities (enabled by a vast network of brain cells). In both animals and human beings, minds depend on brains which are made of the same material; consciousness does not depend on brains for animals and on souls for humans. Materialism explains where and why consciousness, rationality, and volition develop during evolutionary and fetal development: they enter when physical brains reach a certain level of complexity.

---

5. See Jeeves, "Brain, Mind and Behavior."
6. See Papineau, *Consciousness*, 83 and 105.

APPENDIX

Like dualism, materialism and constitutionism face serious difficulties. Take just one—it cannot explain how conscious states emerge from physical states, how minds with subjective experiences emerge out of brains made from non-experiencing matter. Physical states are not subjective, but mental states are. Mental experiences have a qualitative feel; there is something it is like for me when I see the color yellow, hear thunder, or taste coffee. While mental states feel a certain way, physical processes in the brain—neurons firing—do not; they are mindless events without phenomenal character. Because the subjectivity of conscious experience is an extra element above and beyond the objective physical state of the brain, we cannot know what is happening in someone's mind by knowing what is happening in their brain. (This is called the "problem of qualia"—we cannot see the mind but can see the brain, therefore they are not identical things.) How does the physical functioning of the brain give rise to subjective experiences in the mind? Why does a neuron firing feel like anything? Thomas Nagel gives the example of bats which fly accurately in the dark using a unique mental ability—echolocation. Suppose a scientist knows everything that is going on in the bat's brain—she still has no idea what it is like to be a bat, what the bat's subjective experience of echolocation is like (whether they sense objects as bright or dark, textured or colored or shaped—as we do). Or a blind scientist could know all the details of what is happening in the brain of a sighted person—but that will not give him knowledge of what the color yellow looks like.[7] No physical description of the world can define what goes on in the mind; in academic jargon, the mental is not reducible to the physical. The fact that a complete biological account of consciousness fails to capture its first-person, subjective features suggests that while conscious experiences accompany and depend on brain activity, they are not identical to it. There is an "explanatory gap" between physical processes in the brain and conscious events in the mind; they are separate realms. For further criticism of materialism and its inability to account for consciousness, to explain subjective states in entirely physical terms, see Chalmers, *Conscious Mind* and Koons and Bealer, *Waning of Materialism*.

---

7. Nagel, "What Is It Like to Be a Bat?" and Jackson, "What Mary Didn't Know." Also see Baggini, *Pig That Wants to Be Eaten*, 37–39, 217–19 and 277–79.

APPENDIX

3. The Metaphysics of Constitutionism

Constitutionalism raises questions concerning the relationship of 1. human bodies to the material parts that make them up and 2. human persons to human bodies. These involve difficult issues in substance, change, parts, and wholes.[8] Heraclitus of Ephesus was the first to consider the oneness of things that are different, asking whether we can step into the same river twice. The answer depends on what we mean by "same river." If we mean the same collection of water molecules, then no (the water you step into the second time is different)—but if we mean the same continuing entity which is composed of different water molecules at different times, then yes. As Norman Melchert says, "it is the same river, although the water that makes it up is continually changing. A river is not identical with the water that makes it up but is a kind of structure or pattern that makes a unity of ever-changing elements. It is a one that holds together the many." Just like the river, all things are in flux—"ever-changing, yet preserving an identity through the changes."[9] The river co-exists with, but is distinct from, a particular collection of water molecules; it is constituted by, but not identical to, a specific set of water drops. This is because one set of molecules compose the river at one time and a different set compose it at another time. The same is true of the tree in my yard; if it was identical to a particular set of parts, then it would cease to exist when a single leaf falls from it. The river or tree endures as the parts come and go. They continue to exist year after year, surviving the loss and addition of component parts—the same is true of cars and other items. Each is what Sydney Shoemaker calls a "continuant"—a successive entity that persists through time, having different properties and being composed of different sets of molecules at different times.[10] Take another example. Clay composes a statue but is not identical to the statue. Since the clay exists before (and perhaps after) the statue does, the clay and the statue are discernible—and thus not identical. Even when the clay and statue co-exist they are not identical—since something is true of the clay that is not true of the statue.

There are two kinds of change. A *substantial change* involves something beginning or ceasing to exist; if my car was destroyed by an

---

8. This note draws on Carter, *Elements of Metaphysics*, chapters 5, 6, and 7. Also see Conee and Sider, *Riddles of Existence*, chapter 7.

9. Melchert, *Philosophical Conversations*, 19.

10. Shoemaker, cited in Carter, *Elements of Metaphysics*, 77.

explosion it would undergo a substantial change. A *qualitative change* involves something being in one state or condition at one time and in a different state or condition at another time; when my car is painted a new color it undergoes a qualitative change. *Mereological change*—which occurs when something gains or loses parts—is a type of qualitative change. Continuants (such as rivers, trees and cars) have different parts at different times—and so are not identical to the parts that now make them up.

What is true of statues, trees, rivers, and cars is also true of human bodies and persons: both are continuants. The relationship of my body and its material components is similar to the relationship between trees or rivers and their molecular constituents. *My body* co-exists with and is composed by different collections of molecules at different times; it changes qualitatively if I lose all my hair. The relationship of persons and bodies is similar to the relationship between statues and clay. The statue is constituted by but not identical to the clay that composes it—and *I as a person* co-exist with and am constituted by a particular body but am not identical to that body. I can exist without the body I now have, just as a river can exist without the water molecules it is now composed of. Because I can exist when my earthly body has perished, I cannot be identical to that body—because I can exist in circumstances where my body does not exist, I am not the same thing as my body. I am my consciousness—so if my consciousness ends, Rene Descartes says, I end. "I am, I exist; that is certain. For how long? For as long as I am experiencing. . . . If I wholly ceased from experiencing, I should at once wholly cease to be." John Locke adds that while identity requires consciousness, that consciousness can be housed in or constituted by different bodies. "It being the same consciousness that makes a man be himself to himself, personal identity depends on that only, whether it be annexed solely to one individual substance, or can be continued in a succession of several substances."[11] In body-switching the mind is transferred from one body to another. These bodies can be qualitatively different: Jim 1 can be tall and thin and Jim 2 short and fat—but so long as bodies have the same psychological essence, then they constitute the same person.

---

11. Descartes and Locke, cited in Carter, *Elements of Metaphysics*, 93 and 96 respectively.

APPENDIX

4. Responsibility and Identity

Responsibility—as well as punishment and reward—require a substance view of persons rather than a process view. We must be substantial entities (subjects who have experiences) rather than a collection of psychological states or a set of temporal segments. Different parts of our selves exist at different times; Alice's morning self, for example, is happy while Alice's evening self is sad. In order for someone to bear responsibility for past actions these temporal selves must belong to one enduring person. "It is hard to see," William Carter says, "how your evening self could be responsible for the misdeeds of your morning self, if . . . two different selves are at issue. If Evening Alice and Morning Alice are distinct selves, why blame Evening Alice for Morning Alice's kicking of the cat?"[12] David Mellor agrees: "no one can be held responsible for an earlier action unless he or she . . . is identical with whoever . . . did that earlier action." Responsibility requires "the self-same entity to be . . . present both when the deed was done and later when being held accountable for it." The process view of persons gives everyone a "temporal alibi" for any charge of wrongdoing: my present self did not do the act, one of my previous selves did.[13] We cannot justly punish or reward my present self for the actions of my previous selves. Responsibility, then, requires that our present selves be identical with our previous selves.

5. Why Soul without Personality Lacks Identity

John Locke imagines one and the same soul substance being present in you and in Nestor, counselor of the Greeks at Troy—but with no trace of memory connecting you and him. "This would no more make [you] the same person with Nestor, than if some of the particles of matter that were once a part of Nestor were now a part of [you]; the same immaterial substance, without the same consciousness, no more making the same

---

12. Carter, *Elements of Metaphysics*, 117. I had a student whose brother was in a coma following a car crash. After several weeks someone woke up, but it was not her brother, she said, since the new person had complete amnesia and an entirely different personality. Suppose we call the pre-accident person "brother 1" and the post-accident person "brother 2." Now imagine that brother 1 robbed a bank, but was only linked by DNA to the crime when brother 2 existed. Should brother 2 be punished for the crime? No—while the same body was present at the crime, a different person, brother 1, was there.

13. Mellor, cited in Carter, *Elements of Metaphysics*, 119.

person ... than the same particle of matter, without consciousness, ... makes the same person."[14] Widespread and permanent amnesia transforms us into someone else. This is why reincarnation—in which the same soul, erased of all memories and psychological traits, migrates from body to body—means personal extinction rather than personal survival. Emmett Barcalow puts it well: "if I have a taped copy of the movie *Star Wars* and I erase it, the tape still exists but it is no longer a tape of *Star Wars*.... Similarly, if your soul continues to exist but your [psychological essence] has been erased from it..., then that soul is no longer ... you."[15] What lives on is some spiritual "stuff" that has no value to *me* since I lose my individual identity. Thus the soul theory of identity is redundant. If soul is the same as personality, then the soul view just is the personality view (and soul is superfluous). But if soul is different from personality, then the soul view is of no interest—since personality is what matters to identity. Either way, soul is irrelevant. My soul without my memories and personality is not me; survival of the self requires psychological continuity. Identity is determined by personality, not by body or soul.

6. Personality and the Duplication Problem

The personality view faces a serious difficulty—the duplication problem.[16] Amoebas can split into two identical creatures, so imagine that persons can too—resulting in multiple copies of the same personality existing after death. Suppose that two men with my personality appear after my death—Jim 1 in Chicago and Jim 2 in Toronto. There are three possibilities as to which of the new Jims is the original. *First*, perhaps Jim 1 is the real me and Jim 2 is not. But this is completely arbitrary; since the two men are exactly identical, there is no reason to pick one rather than the other as being the real me. *Second*, perhaps both Jim 1 and Jim 2 are the real me. But this is not possible; separate things cannot be one and the same thing. Jim 1 and Jim 2 are qualitatively identical but numerically distinct. (Derek Parfit suggests that, while neither Jims are identical to me, both continue me. Since what matters is the right kind of continuity between me and my future self, there can be survival without identity.[17])

14. Locke, *Essay Concerning Human Understanding*, II, xxvii, 14.
15. Barcalow, *Open Questions*, 130.
16. See Kagan, *Death*, 145–49.
17. See Baggini, *Pig That Wants to Be Eaten*, 136–38.

Third, perhaps neither Jim 1 nor Jim 2 is the real me. But this refutes the personality view; while my personality survives, I do not—and so personality cannot be the essence of identity.

The duplication problem can be answered by adding a uniqueness requirement stipulating that there be no splitting of persons—and thus no equally-qualified candidates for identity. If only one person in the future has my personality—which a provident God can ensure—then I survive. It might be objected that the uniqueness requirement violates a fundamental feature of personal identity—that it depend on intrinsic facts about the person themselves, not on extrinsic facts about other people. But the "no-splitting" rule makes identity rely on contingencies outside the person—whether there is any competitor person. In reply, Stephen Davis distinguishes two types of personal properties. Some, like being fifty-eight years old, are non-relational and intrinsic; they are independent of the properties that other people possess. Other properties, however, like being the oldest child in a family, are relational and extrinsic; they do depend on the properties of others. Identity across time is a relational property—and so the uniqueness requirement is not problematic.[18]

7. Models of Resurrection

How materialists (and dualists too) understand resurrection provides a background for theories of an embodied intermediate state. Some theologians conceive of resurrection as reassembly of the very same material body. Gregory of Nyssa says that our risen bodies will be reassembled from the elements of our earthly bodies and reunited with our souls.[19] The Council of Toledo states that "not in . . . any other widely different flesh . . . will we rise again, but . . . in this self-same flesh in which we live"—and the *Westminster Confession* agrees that "all the dead shall be raised up, with the self-same bodies, and none other."[20] God locates the original matter that composed the earthly body and reassembles those particles into a resurrection body.

---

18. Davis, *Risen Indeed*, chapter 7 and "Physicalism and Resurrection," 240–44.

19. See Ramelli, *Christian Doctrine of Apokatastasis*, 421.

20. Council of Toledo, cited in Ratzinger, *Eschatology*, 135 and *Westminster Confession*, chapter 32, 82.

Reassembly raises a number of questions. The first cluster of issues concern the matter God can—or must—use. If God uses the very same particles then the resurrection body is numerically identical to the original earthly body rather than a qualitatively identical but numerically distinct duplicate of it. This "same matter" requirement has several difficulties. First, the *distribution problem*. Suppose my body is eaten by a cannibal, and the particles that made up my body now make up hers. Which resurrection body—mine or hers—gets the shared atoms? The church fathers offered various solutions—from "the body cannot digest human flesh" to "first owner gets the atoms." Second, the *destruction problem*. If I am killed in a nuclear explosion or undergo cremation that annihilates my atoms, then even God could not reassemble the very same matter into a resurrection body. Perhaps, though, basic particles like quarks are always preserved and available for reassembly. Third, the *arbitrariness problem*. In making my resurrection body, which atoms will God use—those that composed my body as a five-year-old boy or as a fifty-eight-year-old man? God has no principled way to choose.

One solution to arbitrariness insists on numerical identity between earthly and afterlife bodies and stipulates a "last state requirement": a person can exist again only if they return as they last existed.[21] A baseball game stopped for a rain delay in the sixth inning must resume play in the sixth, not the second inning—and so the resurrection body must be reassembled in the same condition it was in at death. My father cannot die as a frail eighty-year-old and be reassembled as a vigorous thirty-year-old; in order to maintain continuity the afterlife body must begin existence exactly like the earthly body at death. To prevent the person, reassembled in a damaged body, from simply dying again, God must heal them either immediately or—more likely—gradually (by running the aging or injuring process in reverse). William Hasker agrees: while the biblical portrayal of resurrection is of radically transformed bodies, perhaps "re-created bodies are initially very similar to the bodies that died, but . . . once re-creation has occurred, a process of transformation is begun that preserves personal identity yet results in a glorified resurrection body." Other philosophers such as Trenton Merricks argue that, given our nature as successive entities, the last state requirement is mistaken.[22]

---

21. See Hershenov, "Metaphysical Problem."
22. Hasker, *Emergent Self*, 214. See Merricks, "Resurrection of Body," both articles.

Other thinkers allow reassembly with different matter. Human beings are not, Dean Zimmerman says, static entities but successive entities (or continuants)—things that gain or lose parts over time.[23] Our bodies are constituted by living matter, not building blocks; matter flows through the body like water through a river, and so God does not need to use the same matter. Among the church fathers who discussed the reassembly model only Origen of Alexandria realized that the human body is a pattern of change, not a static entity—that the body changes its elements and constituent parts over time. He distinguished between two principles within the body, Joseph Ratzinger says. "On the one hand, there is matter, in continuous flux and failing to retain its full identity from one day to the next. On the other hand, there is the persisting form in which the individual gives himself permanent expression."[24] None of the matter that made up my boyhood body remains today in my middle-age body, and yet I survived this complete replacement of atoms without ceasing to exist. "Personal identity," Stephen Davis says, "does not . . . require the resurrection of the same matter of which the old body consisted." God can use different particles, as long as the afterlife body is configured as the earthly body.[25] Some scholars believe that while God *need not* use all original matter, God *cannot* use all replacement matter; while my car survives partial replacement of parts, if it has all new parts it does not remain the same car. This is the ancient "ship of Theseus" riddle: if a ship's wooden planks are replaced one by one until eventually all are new—is it still the same, numerically identical ship or is the original ship gone?

A second set of questions with reassembly concern whether one and the same item can cross a time gap of non-existence. Reassembly assumes intermittent bodily existence—that the body is disassembled, and thus non-existent, in the intermediate state. Kevin Corcoran and David Hershenov (who are materialists) and Zimmerman (a dualist who believes that materialism is compatible with afterlife survival) contend that persistence of identity across time gaps is possible and so resurrection *via* reassembly can preserve identity across temporal gaps. There are many gap-inclusive items that *come into* existence only once but can *resume* existence after a period of non-existence. A watch can be disassembled for repair and reassembled as the very same watch, not a different one,

---

23. Zimmerman, "Christians Should Affirm Mind-Body Dualism," 321.
24. Ratzinger, *Eschatology*, 176–77. Also see Nichols, *Death and Afterlife*, 62.
25. Davis, *Risen Indeed*, 99 and 107.

weeks later; reassembly preserves one and the same watch across a time gap. Intermittent existence does seem possible.

Peter van Inwagen rejects survival by body reassembly; a time gap when the earthly body disintegrates makes the new body a replica, not a continuation of the original.[26] After death we hope to be the same person, not just someone very similar. The replica problem arises if the afterlife body is qualitatively but not numerically identical to the earthly body. Take an analogy. A manuscript written in Augustine of Hippo's own hand is destroyed by fire in the year 457 CE. But a scholar today claims to have the very manuscript that was destroyed, miraculously recreated by God in 458 CE. The existing manuscript, however, is a perfect duplicate—a replica—rather than the original work. Again: if dad rebuilds a Lego house that daughter originally made, but which fell over and broke apart, it is not the same house because different causal processes—dad's action rather than daughter's action—are responsible for the earlier and later houses. In the same way, a body at one time is identical to a body at a later time only if the proper material and causal continuity connects them. But in reassembly an act of God, not the earthly body's own processes, is responsible for the afterlife body's existence—and so it lacks proper causal connection with the earthly body. Reassembly does not avoid the replica problem.

Even if van Inwagen is wrong and the very same body could exist again after a period of non-existence, reassembly is irrelevant to the metaphysics of an intermediate state body that is continuously connected to the earthly body. The reassembly view of the resurrection body fits with a future embodied state after a period of bodily disassembly; it does not fit with a materialist view of an embodied intermediate state.

8. An Argument for Afterlife Existence via Body Switching

John Hick offers three linked scenarios which suggest that survival involves personality switching bodies.[27]

1. A person *disappears* in London and the very next instant an identical person—with complete identity of personality—appears in Chicago. As long as there is psychological continuity, the person survives location-switching. Perhaps the Chicago person has the

26. Van Iwagen, "Possibility of Resurrection," 242–43.
27. Hick, *Death and Eternal Life*, chapter 15.

very same body as the London person (the same bits of matter compose both bodies) or perhaps the Chicago person has a different body made of distinct bits of matter (the London body has been destroyed and a new Chicago body created). Either way, as long as personality continues across two different locations, the London person survives—whatever happens to the body. And whether the Chicago person appears immediately or in three months—is also irrelevant.

2. A person *dies* in London and the very next instant a psychologically-identical person appears alive in Chicago. The person has experienced a this-life recreation since their personality continues uninterrupted.

3. A person dies in London and the very next instant a psychologically-identical person appears in the intermediate state. The person has been recreated in the afterlife since the two individuals are psychologically continuous.

The logic connecting the cases is this: if case 1 is possible, then so is case 2—and if case 2 is possible, then so is case 3. Case 1 is clearly possible—there is nothing logically incoherent about location-switching; but then post-mortem survival *via* body-switching is also possible.

9. Prayer for the Dead and Temporary Non-Existence

There is nothing incoherent about intermittent existence since identity can cross time gaps, periods of non-existence. An extinction-recreation view of the afterlife is possible. But since non-existence during the intermediate state conflicts with Scripture, it is not a feasible afterlife scenario. Extinction-recreation also appears to rule out prayer for the dead (which disallows non-existence, a gap in time between death and resurrection). It may, however, be possible for those who believe in extinction-resurrection to pray for the dead. Jerry Walls suggests that temporary non-existence is not logically incompatible with purgatory—and, by extension, prayer for the dead. Trenton Merricks attempts to square the practice of prayer *to* the saints (and, by implication, prayer *for* the dead) with denial of a conscious intermediate state.[28] It is possible that God stores up our prayers for the dead and answers them after the resurrection.

28. Walls, *Purgatory*, 191 and Merricks, "Resurrection of Body," in *OHPT*, 485–86.

APPENDIX

In the extinction-recreation scenario we pray for individuals who, by definition, do not exist now. *Consummation prayers* can be effective in bringing resurrection to pass more quickly for those now non-existent persons. *Growth, purification,* and *salvation prayers* take effect after the dead return to consciousness at the last day (such prayers are actually for post-resurrection not pre-resurrection persons). It is logically possible that prayers for the dead which I make now will not reap results until after final consummation. I may make salvation prayers now for a dead friend who—because he is non-existent now—will not repent until after final consummation has taken place. The same may be true of sanctification prayers. This assumes, of course, that salvation and sanctification can occur after final judgment.

At the very minimum, prayer for the dead requires that the individuals prayed for be conscious *at some point* after death, not that they be conscious *immediately* at death. As long as they eventually become conscious, prayers for them can make sense since they will exist again to enjoy the fruits of our prayers. Although prayer for the dead is compatible with non-existence between death and resurrection, it fits more nicely with a conscious intermediate state.

Furthermore, my prayers may be effective after final consummation *even if* the dead are conscious now. Suppose that I pray for a loved one who died yesterday but final consummation happens today—before sufficient time has elapsed for them to become perfectly holy or repent from sin. Their purification or salvation will occur after final consummation, with my prayers offered *now* being effective *then*.[29]

---

29. Thanks to my colleague Timothy Linehan and editor Robin Parry for pressing me on this point.

ABBREVIATIONS

AFCF — *Ancient Faith for the Church's Future.* Edited by Mark Husbands and Jeffrey Greenman. Downers Grove, IL: IVP, 2008.

ANF — *Ante-Nicene Fathers.* Edited by Alexander Roberts and James Donaldson. 10 Vols. Peabody, MA: Hendrickson, 2004.

CD — *Contemporary Debates in Philosophy of Religion.* Edited by Michael Peterson and Raymond VanArragon. Oxford: Blackwell, 2004.

EP — *The Encyclopedia of Philosophy.* Edited by Donald Borchert. 2nd ed. Farmington Hills, MI: Macmillan / Thomson Gale, 2006.

IEP — *Internet Encyclopedia of Philosophy.* Edited by James Feiser and Bradley Dowden. Online: iep.utm.edu.

LW — *Luther's Works.* Edited by Oswald Hilton, Helmut Lehman, and Jaroslav Pelikan. 55 Vols. Philadelphia: Fortress, 1999.

NIDB — *New Interpreters Dictionary of the Bible.* Edited by Katharine Doob Sakenfeld. 5 Vols. Nashville: Abingdon, 2009.

NPNF — *Nicene and Post-Nicene Fathers.* First Series. 14 Vols. Edited by Philip Schaff. Peabody, MA: Hendrickson, 2004.

NPNF — *Nicene and Post-Nicene Fathers.* Second Series. 14 Vols. Edited by Philip Schaff and Henry Wace. Peabody, MA: Hendrickson, 2004.

OHE — *The Oxford Handbook of Eschatology.* Edited by Jerry Walls. Oxford: Oxford University Press, 2008.

ABBREVIATIONS

OHPT	*The Oxford Handbook of Philosophical Theology*. Edited by Thomas Flint and Michael Rea. Oxford: Oxford University Press, 2009.
RCPR	*The Routledge Companion to Philosophy of Religion*. Edited by Chad Meister and Paul Copan. 2nd ed. London: Routledge, 2013.
REP	*Routledge Encyclopedia of Philosophy*. Edited by Edward Craig. 10 Vols. London: Routledge, 1998. Online: routledge.com.
SBS	*Soul, Body and Survival: Essays on the Metaphysics of Human Persons*. Edited by Kevin Corcoran. Ithaca, NY: Cornell University Press, 2001.
SEP	*Stanford Encyclopedia of Philosophy*. Edited by Edward Zalta. Online: plato.stanford.edu.
TDNT	*Theological Dictionary of the New Testament*. Edited by Gerhard Kittel and Gerhard Friedrich. 10 Vols. Grand Rapids: Eerdmans, 1984.
TDOT	*Theological Dictionary of the Old Testament*. Edited by Johannes Botterweck, Helmer Ringgren, and Heinz-Josef Fabry. 15 Vols. Grand Rapids: Eerdmans, 2003.
WHS	*Whatever Happened to the Soul? Scientific and Theological Portraits of Human Nature*. Edited by Warren Brown et al. Minneapolis: Fortress, 1998.

BIBLIOGRAPHY

A Monk of St. Tikhon Monastery. *These Truths We Hold—The Holy Orthodox Church: Her Life and Teachings.* South Canaan, PA: St. Tikhon Seminary Press, 1986. Online: stots.edu.

Aben, Tersur. *African Christian Theology.* Bukuru, Nigeria: African Christian Textbooks, 1988.

Alcorn, Randy. *Heaven.* Carol Stream, IL: Tyndale House, 2004.

Alfeyev, Hilarion. "Eschatology." In *The Cambridge Companion to Orthodox Christian Theology*, edited by Mary Cunningham and Elizabeth Theokritoff, 107–20. Cambridge: Cambridge University Press, 2008.

Allen, Richard. "On Not Understanding Prayer." *Sophia* 10 (1971) 1–7.

Ambrose of Milan. "On the Death of Valentinian." In *Funeral Orations by Saint Gregory Nanianzen and Saint Ambrose*, edited by Leo McCauley et al., 265–99. New York: Fathers of the Church, 1953.

Anderson, Ray. "On Being Human: The Spiritual Saga of a Creaturely Soul." In *WHS*, 175–94.

———. *Theology, Death and Dying.* Oxford: Blackwell, 1986.

Anglican Church in New Zealand. *New Zealand Prayer Book.* San Francisco: Harper, 1997.

Anglican-Orthodox Dialogue. *The Dublin Agreed Statement 1984.* Online: anglicancommunion.org.

Aquinas, Thomas. *Summa Theologiae.* Blackfriars ed. New York: McGraw-Hill, 1964.

———. *Summa Theologica.* 2nd rev. ed. Vol. 3. New York: Benzinger Brothers, 1948.

Archbishops' Commission on Christian Doctrine. *Doctrine in the Church of England.* London: SPCK, 1938.

———. *Prayer and the Departed.* London: SPCK, 1971.

Arnobius of Sicca. "Against the Heathen." In *ANF*: 6: 413–539.

Atwell, Robert. "From Augustine to Gregory the Great: An Evaluation of the Emergence of the Doctrine of Purgatory." In *Journal of Ecclesiastical History* 38 (1987) 173–86.

Augsburg Confession. Online: bookofconcord.org.

Augustine of Hippo. *City of God.* Harmondsworth, UK: Penguin, 1972.

———. *Confessions.* Oxford: Oxford University Press, 1991.

———. *Enchiridion.* In *NPNF*, First Series 3: 237–81.

———. *On Christian Doctrine.* In *NPNF*, First Series 2: 519–97.

———. *Sermons.* New Rochelle, NY: New City, 1992.

Badham, Paul, and Linda Badham. *Immortality or Extinction?* Totowa, NJ: Barnes and Noble, 1982.

Baggini, Julian. *The Pig That Wants to be Eaten*. New York: Plume, 2005.
Baker, Lynne Rudder. "Christians Should Reject Mind-Body Dualism." In *CD*: 327–38, 341–42.
———. *Persons and Bodies: A Constitution View*. Cambridge: Cambridge University Press, 2000.
———. "Material Persons and the Doctrine of Resurrection." *Faith and Philosophy* 18 (2001) 151–67.
———. "Persons and the Metaphysics of Resurrection." *Religious Studies* 43 (2007) 333–48.
Baker, Sharon. *Razing Hell*. Louisville: Westminster John Knox, 2010.
Bakken, Kenneth. *Journey into God*. Minneapolis: Augsburg-Fortress, 2000.
Balthasar, Hans Urs von. *Dare We Hope That All Men Be Saved?* San Francisco: Ignatius, 1988.
Barcalow, Emmett. *Open Questions: An Introduction to Philosophy*. 3rd ed. Belmont, CA: Wadsworth, 2001.
Barr, James. *Biblical Words for Time*. 2nd ed. Naperville, IL: Allenson, 1969.
Barry, Vincent. *Philosophical Thinking about Death and Dying*. Belmont, CA: Wadsworth, 2007.
Basinger, David. *The Case for Free Will Theism*. Downers Grove, IL: IVP Academic, 1996.
———. "God Does Not Necessarily Respond to Prayer." In *CD*: 255–64, 266–67.
———. "Why Petition an Omnipotent, Omniscient, Wholly Good God?" *Religious Studies* 19 (1983) 25–41.
Bauckham, Richard, and Trevor Hart. "The Shape of Time." In *The Future as God's Gift: Explorations in Christian Eschatology*, edited by David Fergusson and Marcel Sarot, 41–72. Edinburgh: T. & T. Clark, 2000.
Beck, Lewis White, ed. *Kant Selections*. New York: Macmillan, 1988.
Beilby, James, and Paul Eddy, eds. *The Nature of the Atonement: Four Views*. Downers Grove, IL: IVP Academic, 2006.
Bell, George. *Randall Davidson: Archbishop of Canterbury*. London: Oxford University Press, 1935.
Bell, Rob. *Velvet Elvis: Repainting the Christian Faith*. Grand Rapids: Zondervan, 2005.
———. *Love Wins: A Book about Heaven, Hell and the Fate of Every Person Who Ever Lived*. New York: Harper Collins, 2011.
Belshaw, Christopher. *10 Good Questions about Life and Death*. Oxford: Blackwell, 2005.
Bennett, Arthur. "Prayer for the Departed." *Churchman* 81 (1967) 252–64.
Bierma, Nathan. *Bringing Heaven Down to Earth*. Phillipsburg, NJ: P. & R., 2005.
Bilateral Working Group of The German National Bishop's Conference and the Church Leadership of the United Evangelical Lutheran Church of Germany. *Communio Sanctorum: The Church as the Communion of Saints*. Collegeville, MN: Liturgical, 2004.
Bloesch, Donald. *Essentials of Evangelical Theology*. Vol. 2. New York: Harper and Row, 1978.
———. *The Last Things: Resurrection, Judgment, Glory*. Downers Grove, IL: IVP, 2004.
Boggis, R. J. Edmund. *Praying for the Dead: An Historical Record of the Practice*. London: Longmans, Green and Co., 1913.
Bonhoeffer, Dietrich. *Creation and Fall*. Minneapolis: Fortress, 1997.
———. *Discipleship*. Minneapolis: Fortress, 2003.

———. *Ethics*. Minneapolis: Fortress, 2009.
———. *Letters and Papers from Prison*. Minneapolis: Fortress, 2010.
———. *Life Together*. Minneapolis: Fortress, 1996.
Borg, Marcus. *The Heart of Christianity*. San Francisco: Harper San Francisco, 2003.
———. *Meeting Jesus Again for the First Time*. San Francisco: Harper San Francisco, 1994.
Borg, Marcus, and N. T. Wright. *The Meaning of Jesus: Two Visions*. New York: Harper One, 1999.
Brenner, Andrew. "Aquinas on Eternity, Tense and Temporal Becoming." *Florida Philosophical Review* 10 (2010) 16–24.
Brown, Christopher. "Friendship in Heaven: Aquinas on Supremely Perfect Happiness and the Communion of Saints." In *Metaphysics and God: Essays in Honor of Eleonore Stump*, edited by Kevin Timpe, 225–48. New York: Routledge, 2009.
Brown, Peter. *The Ransom of the Soul: Afterlife and Wealth in Early Western Christianity*. Cambridge: Harvard University Press, 2015.
Brueggemann, Walter. *The Collected Sermons of Walter Brueggemann*. Louisville: Westminster John Knox, 2011.
———. *The Psalms and the Life of Faith*. Minneapolis: Fortress, 1995.
———. *The Threat of Life*. Minneapolis: Fortress, 1996.
Brummer, Vincent. *What Are We Doing When We Pray?* Farnham, UK: Ashgate, 2008.
Buechner, Frederick. *The Eyes of the Heart: A Memoir of the Lost and Found*. New York: Harper One, 1999.
———. *Wishful Thinking: A Theological ABC*. New York: Harper and Row, 1973.
Bullard, Roger. *Messiah: The Gospel according to Handel's Oratorio*. Grand Rapids: Eerdmans, 1993.
Bultmann, Rudolf. "Is Exegesis Without Interpretation Possible." In *Existence and Faith: Shorter Writings of Rudolf Bultmann*, edited by Schubert Ogden, 289–96. New York: Meridian, 1960.
Bultmann, Rudolf, and Karl Rengstorf. "Elpis, Elpizo." In *TDNT* 2: 517–34.
Buttrick, George. *Prayer*. New York: Abingdon, 1942.
Byassee, Jason. "Emerging from What, Going Where?" In *AFCF*: 249–63.
Bynum, Caroline. *The Resurrection of the Body in Western Christianity, 200–1336*. New York: Columbia University Press, 1995.
Calvin, John. *Institutes of the Christian Religion*. Philadelphia: Westminster, 1960.
Carter, William. *The Elements of Metaphysics*. New York: McGraw-Hill, 1990.
Casey, John. *Afterlives: A Guide to Heaven, Hell and Purgatory*. Oxford: Oxford University Press, 2009.
Cavarnos, Constantine. *The Future Life According to Orthodox Teaching*. Etna, CA: Center for Traditionalist Orthodox Studies, 1985.
Chalmers, David. *The Conscious Mind*. Oxford: Oxford University Press, 1997.
Chapman, David. "Rest and Light Perpetual: Prayer for the Departed in the Communion of Saints." *One in Christ* 34 (1998) 39–49.
Christian Reformed Church. "Our World Belongs to God." In *Psalter Hymnal*, 1019–38. Grand Rapids: CRC, 1988.
Chrysostom, John. *The Homily of St. John Chrysostom on the First Epistle of Paul the Apostle to the Corinthians*. Oxford: Parker, 1939.
———. "On the Priesthood." In *NPNF*, First Series 9: 33–86.
Church of England. *Common Worship*. Online: churchofengland.org.

BIBLIOGRAPHY

———. *Homily on Prayer*. Online: anglicanlibrary.org.
———. *Report of the Royal Commission on Ecclesiastical Discipline*, 1906. Online: anglicanhistory.org.
Church of Jesus Christ of Latter Day Saints. "Baptism for the Dead." Online: lds.org.
Church of the Brethren. *For All Who Minister*. Elgin, IL: Brethren, 1993.
Cockburn, Bruce. "Festival of Friends." *In the Falling Dark*. True North Productions, 1976.
———. "Grim Travelers." *Humans*. True North Productions, 1980.
———. "Rumors of Glory." *Humans*. True North Productions, 1980.
Cocksworth, Christopher. *Prayer and the Departed*. Cambridge: Grove, 1997.
Cohoe, Caleb. "God, Causality and Petitionary Prayer." *Faith and Philosophy* 31 (2014) 24–45.
Conee, Earl, and Theodore Sider. *Riddles of Existence: A Guided Tour of Metaphysics*. 2nd ed. Oxford: Oxford University Press, 2014.
Congregation for Divine Worship and the Discipline of the Sacraments. *Directory on Popular Piety and the Liturgy: Principles and Guidelines*. Vatican City: 2001. Online: vatican.va.
Connelly, Douglas. *The Promise of Heaven*. Downers Grove, IL: IVP, 2000. *Constitutions of the Holy Apostles*. In *ANF* 7: 385–508.
Cook, Stephen. "Eschatology of the Old Testament." In *NIDB* 2: 299–308.
Cooper, John. "Biblical Anthropology and the Body-Soul Problem." In *SBS*: 218–28.
———. *Body, Soul and Life Everlasting: Biblical Anthropology and the Monism-Dualism Debate*. Grand Rapids: Eerdmans, 1989.
Cooper, Terry. *Sin, Pride and Self-Acceptance: The Problem of Identity in Theology and Psychology*. Downers Grove, IL: IVP, 2003.
Copi, Irving, and Carl Cohen. *Introduction to Logic*. 11th ed. Upper Saddle River, NJ: Prentice Hall, 2002.
Corcoran, Kevin. "The Constitution View of Persons." In *In Search of the Soul: Four Views of the Mind-Body Problem*, edited by Joel Green and Stuart Palmer, 153–76. Downers Grove, IL: IVP Academic, 2005.
———. "Persons and Bodies." *Faith and Philosophy* 15 (1998) 324–40.
———. "Physical Persons and Postmortem Survival without Temporal Gaps." In *SBS*: 201–17.
Craig, William Lane. *No Easy Answers*. Chicago: Moody, 1990.
———. *God, Time and Eternity*. Dordrecht: Kluwer Academic, 2001.
———. "Time, Eternity and Eschatology." In *OHE*: 596–613.
———. "Divine Eternity." In *OHPT*: 145–66.
Crisp, Oliver. "John Calvin and Petitioning God." In *Engaging with Calvin*, edited by Mark Thompson, 136–57. Nottingham, UK: IVP, 2009.
Crossin, John. *Everyday Virtues*. Mahwah, NJ: Paulist, 2002.
Crump, David. *Knocking on Heaven's Door*. Grand Rapids: Baker, 2006.
Cullmann, Oscar. *Immortality of the Soul or Resurrection of the Dead?* London: Epworth, 1958.
———. *Christ and Time: The Primitive Christian Conception of Time and History*. Rev. ed. Philadelphia: Westminster, 1964.
Currie, David. *Born Fundamentalist—Born Again Catholic*. San Francisco: Ignatius, 1996.
Cyprian of Carthage. "Epistle 36." In *ANF* 5: 314–15.

Cyril of Jerusalem. "Catechetical Lecture 23, 'On the Mysteries: On the Sacred Liturgy and Communion.'" Book 5.9–10. In *NPNF*, Second Series 7: 153–57.
Daley, Brian. *The Hope of the Early Church*. Cambridge: Cambridge University Press, 1991.
———. "Old Books and Contemporary Faith." In *AFCF*: 53–68.
Damer, T. Edward. *Attacking Faulty Reasoning*. Belmont, CA: Wadsworth, 1980.
Dante Alighieri. *The Divine Comedy*. In *The Portable Dante*, edited by Mark Musa. New York: Penguin, 1995.
Davis, Stephen. *After We Die: Theology, Philosophy and the Question of Life after Death*. Waco, TX: Baylor University Press, 2015.
———. *Logic and the Nature of God*. Grand Rapids: Eerdmans, 1983.
———. *Risen Indeed: Making Sense of the Resurrection*. Grand Rapids: Eerdmans, 1993.
———. "Physicalism and Resurrection." In *SBS*: 229–46.
Davison, Scott. "Petitionary Prayer." In *OHPT*: 286–305.
———. "Petitionary Prayer." In *SEP*.
Day, J. P. "Hope." *American Philosophical Quarterly* 6 (1969) 89–102.
———. *Hope: A Philosophical Inquiry*. Helsinki: Philosophy Society of Finland, 1991.
DeMaris, Richard. "Corinthian Religion and Baptism for the Dead (1 Corinthians 15:29): Insights from Archaeology and Anthropology." *Journal of Biblical Literature* 114 (1995) 661–82.
DeSilva, David. *Sacramental Life: Spiritual Formation through the Book of Common Prayer*. Downers Grove, IL: IVP, 2008.
DeYoung, Rebecca Konyndyk. *Glittering Vices: A New Look at the Seven Deadly Sins and Their Remedies*. Grand Rapids: Brazos, 2009.
Defense of Augsburg Confession. Online: bookofconcord.org.
Descartes, Rene. *The Passions of the Soul*. In *Essential Works of Descartes*, edited by Lowell Bair, 108–210. New York: Bantam, 1961.
Divine Liturgy of St. John Chrysostom. London: Faith, 1922.
Divine Liturgy of St. James. In *ANF* 7: 537–50.
Divine Liturgy of St. Mark. In *ANF* 7: 551–60.
Divine Liturgy of the Blessed Apostles. In *ANF* 7: 561–68.
Donfried, Karl. "Hope." In *Harper Collins Bible Dictionary*, edited by Paul Achtemeier, 434–35. San Francisco: Harper San Francisco, 1996.
Double, Richard. *Beginning Philosophy*. Oxford: Oxford University Press, 1999.
Dowden, Bradley. "Time." In *IEP*.
Downie, R. S. "Hope." *Philosophy and Phenomenological Research* 24 (1963) 248–51.
Duck, Ruth, and Patricia Wilson-Kastner. *Praising God: The Trinity in Christian Worship*. Louisville: Westminster John Knox, 1999.
Duffy, Stephen. *The Graced Horizon: Nature and Grace in Modern Catholic Thought*. Collegeville, MN: Liturgical, 1992.
Dyke, Heather. "Time, Metaphysics of." In *REP*.
Eberl, Jason. "Do Human Persons Persist between Death and Resurrection?" In *Metaphysics and God: Essays in Honor of Eleonore Stump*, edited by Kevin Timpe, 188–205. New York: Routledge, 2009.
Edwards, Paul, ed. *Immortality*. Amherst, NY: Prometheus, 1997.
Elliott, Peter. *Ceremonies of the Liturgical Year according to the Modern Roman Rite*. San Francisco: Ignatius, 2002.

English Roman Catholic–Methodist Committee. "Justification—A Consensus Statement." *One in Christ* 28 (1992) 87–91.
Eno, Robert. "The Fathers and the Cleansing Fire." *Irish Theological Quarterly* 53 (1987) 184–202.
Ephiphanius of Salamis. *The Panarion of Epiphanius of Salamis*. 2d rev. ed. Vols. 2–3. Leiden: Brill, 2013.
Episcopal Church. *Book of Common Prayer*. New York: Seabury, 1979.
———. "The Episcopal Faith." Online: episcopalchicago.org.
Episcopal Church of Scotland. *Scottish Liturgy*. Online: scotland.anglican.org.
Evangelical Covenant Church. *The Covenant Book of Worship*. Chicago: Covenant, 2003.
Evangelical Lutheran Church in America. *Evangelical Lutheran Worship*. Minneapolis: Augsburg Fortress, 2006.
Evans, Alice and Robert Evans. *Introduction to Christianity: A Case Method Approach*. Atlanta: John Knox, 1980.
Evans, Rachel Held. *Searching for Sunday*. Nashville: Thomas Nelson, 2015.
Fabry, Heinz-Josef. "Ruach." In *TDOT* 13: 365–402.
Fackre, Dorothy, and Gabriel Fackre. *Christian Basics: A Primer for Pilgrims*. Grand Rapids: Eerdmans, 1991.
Fairlie, Henry. *The Seven Deadly Sins Today*. Notre Dame, IN: University of Notre Dame Press, 1979.
Fackenheim, Emil. *God's Presence in History*. New York: Harper and Row, 1970.
Fairbairn, Donald. *Life in the Trinity*. Downers Grove, IL: IVP, 2009.
Fedwick, Paul. "Death and Dying in Byzantine Liturgical Traditions." *Eastern Churches Review* 8 (1976) 152–61.
Feinberg, Joel. *Harm to Others*. Oxford: Oxford University Press, 1984.
Felten, David, and Jeff Procter-Murphy. *Living the Questions*. New York: Harper One, 2012.
Florovsky, George. *Creation and Redemption*. Vol. 3. Belmont, CA: Nordland, 1976.
Ford, David. "Prayer and the Departed Saints." Online: protomartyr.org.
———. *Theology: A Very Short Introduction*. Oxford: Oxford University Press, 1999.
Ganssle, Gregory. "God and Time." In *IEP*.
Geach, Peter. *Providence and Evil*. Cambridge: Cambridge University Press, 1977.
———. *The Virtues*. Cambridge: Cambridge University Press, 1977.
Godfrey, Joseph. *A Philosophy of Human Hope*. Dordrecht: Nijhoff, 1987.
Goldingay, John. "The Logic of Intercession." *Theology* 99 (1998) 262–70.
Gordon, Robert. "Exodus." In *The International Bible Commentary*, edited by F. F. Bruce, 149–88. Grand Rapids: Zondervan, 1979.
Gould, James B. "Bonhoeffer and the False Dilemma of German Atheism." *Toronto Journal of Theology* 14 (1998) 61–81.
———. "Bonhoeffer and Open Theism." *Philosophy and Theology* 15 (2003) 57–91.
———. "Broad Inclusive Salvation: The Logic of 'Anonymous Christianity.'" *Philosophy and Theology* 20 (2008) 175–98.
———. "The Grace We Are Owed: Human Rights and Divine Duties." *Faith and Philosophy* 25 (2008) 261–75.
———. "Earning, Deserving and the Catechism's Understanding of Grace." *Anglican Theological Review* 91 (2009) 373–94.
Grady, J. E. "Marcel: Hope and Ethics." In *Journal of Value Inquiry* 4 (1970) 56–64.

Graham, Billy. "Responding to God's Glory." In *Declare His Glory Among the Nations*, edited by David Howard, 141–54. Downers Grove, IL: IVP, 1977.
Green, Joel. "'Bodies—That Is, Human Lives': A Re-examination of Human Nature in the Bible." In *WHS*, 149–74.
———. *Body, Soul and Human Life*. Milton Keynes, UK: Paternoster, 2008.
———. "Eschatology and the Nature of Humans: A Reconsideration of Pertinent Biblical Evidence." *Science and Christian Belief* 14 (2002) 33–50.
———, ed. *What about the Soul? Neuroscience and Christian Anthropology*. Nashville: Abingdon, 2004.
Green, Joel, and Stewart Palmer, eds. *In Search of the Soul: Four Views of the Mind-Body Problem*. Downers Grove, IL: IVP, 2005.
Gregory the Great. *Dialogues*. New York: Fathers of the Church, 1959.
Griffiths, Paul. "Purgatory." In *OHE*: 427–45.
Gulley, Philip, and James Mulholland. *If Grace Is True: Why God Will Save Every Person*. San Francisco: Harper, 2003.
Hahn, Scott, and Kimberly Hahn. *Rome Sweet Home: Our to Catholicism*. San Francisco: Ignatius, 1993.
Hall, Christopher. "Tradition, Authority, Magisterium." In *AFCF*: 27–52.
Hall, Douglas John. *When You Pray*. Valley Forge, PA: Judson, 1987.
Hallote, Rachel. *Death, Burial and Afterlife in the Biblical World*. Chicago: Dee, 2001.
Hardy, Edward. "The Blessed Dead in Anglican Piety." *Sobornost* 3 (1981) 160–78.
Harris, Murray. *Raised Immortal: Resurrection and Immortality in the New Testament*. Grand Rapids: Eerdmans, 1983.
Hasker, William. "Afterlife." In *SEP*.
———. *The Emergent Self*. Ithaca, NY: Cornell University Press, 1999.
———. "Persons as Emergent Substances." In *SBS*: 107–19.
———. "On Behalf of Emergent Dualism." In *In Search of the Soul: Four Views of the Mind-Body Problem*, edited by Joel Green and Stuart Palmer, 75–100. Downers Grove, IL: IVP, 2005.
Hatchett, Marion. *Seven Pre-Reformation Eucharistic Liturgies*. Sewanee, TN: University of the South Press, 1973.
Hebblethwaite, Brian. *The Christian Hope*. Rev. ed. Oxford: Oxford University Press, 2010.
Heidelberg Catechism. Online: crcna.org.
Helm, Paul. "Eternity." In *SEP*.
Hershenov, David. "The Metaphysical Problem of Intermittent Existence and the Possibility of Resurrection." *Faith and Philosophy* 20 (2003) 24–36.
Hick, John. *Death and Eternal Life*. Louisville: Westminster John Knox, 1994.
———. *An Interpretation of Religion*. 2nd ed. New Haven: Yale, 2005.
Hobbes, Thomas. *Leviathan*. Harmondsworth, UK: Penguin, 1985.
Hoekema, Anthony. *The Bible and the Future*. Grand Rapids: Eerdmans, 1979.
Holden, Harrington. *Wesley in Company with High Churchmen*. London: Church, 1870.
Howard, Thomas. *Evangelical is Not Enough*. Nashville: Thomas Nelson, 1984.
Howard-Synder, Daniel, and Frances Howard-Snyder. "The Puzzle of Petitionary Prayer." *European Journal for Philosophy of Religion* 2 (2010) 43–68.
Hume, David. *A Treatise of Human Nature*. Oxford: Clarendon, 1975.
Husbands, Mark. "Introduction." In *AFCF*: 9–23.

BIBLIOGRAPHY

Inbody, Tyron. "The Power of Prayer and the Mystery of Evil." *Anglican Theological Review* 81 (1999) 61–81.
International Theological Commission. "Some Current Questions in Eschatology." *Irish Theological Quarterly* 58 (1992) 209–43.
Jackson, Frank. "What Mary Didn't Know." *Journal of Philosophy* 83 (1986) 291–95.
Jackson, Timothy. *The Priority of Love.* Princeton: Princeton University Press, 2003.
Jeeves, Malcolm. "Brain, Mind and Behavior." In *WHS*: 73–98.
Jenni, Ernst. "Time." In *Interpreter's Dictionary of the Bible*, Vol. 4, edited by George Buttrick, 642–49. Nashville: Abingdon, 1962.
Jenson, Matt. *The Gravity of Sin: Augustine, Luther and Barth on 'homo incurvatus in se.'* London: T. & T. Clark, 2006.
Jeremias, Joachim. "Abyss." In *TDNT* 1: 9–10.
———. "Hades." In *TDNT* 1: 146–49.
Joint Theological Faculties of the Lutheran Church–Missouri Synod. "Study on Intercessory Prayers for the Benefit of the Souls of the Dead." *Concordia Theological Monthly* 34 (1963) 359–61.
Kagan, Shelly. *Death.* New Haven: Yale University Press, 2012.
Kelly, Geffrey, and Burton Nelson, eds. *A Testament to Freedom: The Essential Writings of Dietrich Bonhoeffer.* San Francisco: Harper, 1990.
Kelly, John. *A Commentary on the Pastoral Epistles: I Timothy, II Timothy, Titus.* London: Addison-Wesley, 1987.
Kerr, Hugh, ed. *A Compend of Luther's Theology.* Philadelphia: Westminster, 1966.
Kettner, Edward. "Time, Eternity and the Intermediate State." *Concordia Journal* (1986) 90–100.
Kidner, Derek. "Isaiah." In *New Bible Commentary*, Rev. ed, edited by Donald Guthrie, 588–625. Grand Rapids: Eerdmans, 1970.
Kneale, William. "Eternity." In *EP* 3: 356–59.
Koons, Robert, and George Bealer, eds. *The Waning of Materialism.* Oxford: Oxford University Press, 2010.
Kreider, Alan. *English Chantries: The Road to Dissolution.* Cambridge: Harvard University Press, 1979.
Kronen, John, and Eric Reitan. *God's Final Victory: A Comparative Philosophical Case for Universalism.* New York: Continuum, 2011.
La Due, William. *The Trinity Guide to Eschatology.* New York: Continuum, 2004.
Lamott, Anne. *Help, Thanks, Wow: The Three Essential Prayers.* New York: Riverhead, 2012.
Lane, Dermot. *Keeping Hope Alive.* Mahwah, NJ: Paulist, 1996.
Larchet, Jean-Claude. *Life After Death According to the Orthodox Tradition.* Rollinsford, NH: Orthodox Research Institute, 2012.
Law, Stephen. *The Philosophy Gym.* New York: St. Martin's, 2003.
Le Goff, Jacques. *The Birth of Purgatory.* Chicago: University of Chicago Press, 1984.
Le Poidevin, Robin. "Experience of Time." In *SEP*.
Lee, Frederick. *The Christian Doctrine of Prayer for the Departed.* London: Daldy, Isbister and Co., 1875.
Leftow, Brian. "Eternity." In *A Companion to the Philosophy of Religion*, edited by Philip Quinn and Charles Taliaferro, 257–63. Oxford: Blackwell, 1999.
———. "Eternity (Addendum)." In *EP* 3: 359–60.

Lewis, C. S. *God in the Dock: Essays in Theology and Ethics*. Grand Rapids: Eerdmans, 1970.
———. *The Last Battle*. New York: Scholastic, 1956.
———. *Letters to Malcolm*. San Diego: Harcourt, 1963.
———. *Mere Christianity*. New York: Macmillan, 1952.
———. *Poems*. San Diego: Harcourt, 1964.
———. *Prince Caspian*. New York: Scholastic, 1951.
———. *The Problem of Pain*. London: Fontana, 1940.
Liturgy of St. Gregory. Online: liturgies.net.
Liwak, Rudiger. "Rephaim." In *TDOT* 13: 602–14.
Locke, John. *An Essay Concerning Human Understanding*. 2nd ed. Oxford: Oxford University Press, 1978.
Louth, Andrew. "Eastern Orthodox Eschatology." In *OHE*: 233–47.
———. *Introducing Eastern Orthodox Theology*. Downers Grove, IL: IVP Academic, 2013.
Ludlow, Morwenna. *Universal Salvation: Eschatology in the Thought of Gregory of Nyssa and Karl Rahner*. Oxford: Oxford University Press, 2000.
Luther, Martin. *Lectures on Genesis: Chapters 21–25*. In *LW* 4.
———. *Lectures on Genesis: Chapters 31–37*. In *LW* 6.
———. *Lectures on Romans*. In *LW* 25.
———. *Liturgy and Hymns*. In *LW* 53.
———. *Table Talk*. In *LW* 54.
———. *Word and Sacrament II*. In *LW* 36.
———. *Word and Sacrament III*. In *LW* 37.
———. *Smalcald Articles*. Online: bookofconcord.org.
———. *Small Catechism*. Online: bookofconcord.org.
Lutheran Church-Missouri Synod. *Lutheran Service Book*. St. Louis: Concordia, 2006.
MacDonald, Gregory. *The Evangelical Universalist*. 1st ed. Eugene, OR: Cascade, 2006.
Macquarrie, John. *Christian Hope*. New York: Seabury, 1978.
Marcel, Gabriel. "Desire and Hope." In *Readings in Existential Phenomenology*, edited by Nathaniel Lawrence and Daniel O'Connor, 277–85. Englewood Cliffs, NJ: Prentice Hall, 1967.
Markosian, Ned. "Time." In *SEP*.
Marshall, Peter. *Belief and the Dead in Reformation England*. Oxford: Oxford University Press, 2002.
Martin, Adrienne. *How We Hope: A Moral Psychology*. Princeton: Princeton University Press, 2014.
Masek, Lawrence. "Petitionary Prayer to an Omnipotent and Omnibenevolent God." *American Catholic Philosophical Association Proceedings* 74 (2001) 273–83.
Marx, Karl. *Early Writings*. New York: McGraw-Hill, 1964.
Mavrodes, George. "Prayer." In *REP*.
McGinn, Colin. *Eternal Questions, Timeless Approaches: How to Think Like a Philosopher*. New York: Barnes and Noble Audio, 2004.
———. *The Problem of Consciousness*. Oxford: Blackwell, 1991.
McLaren, Brian. *Finding Our Way Again: The Return of the Ancient Practices*. Nashville: Thomas Nelson, 2008.
———. *A Generous Orthodoxy*. Grand Rapids: Zondervan, 2004.
———. *The Last Word and the Word after That*. San Francisco: Jossey-Bass, 2005.

———. "One, Holy, Catholic and Fresh?" In *Ancient Faith, Future Mission: Fresh Expressions in the Sacramental Traditions*, edited by Steven Croft, et al., 9–19. New York: Seabury, 2010.

McLaughlin, Megan. *Consorting with Saints: Prayer for the Dead in Early Medieval France*. Ithaca, NY: Cornell University Press, 1994.

McLeod, Carolyn. "Trust." In *SEP*.

McTaggart, J. M. E. "The Unreality of Time." In *The Philosophy of Time*, edited by Robin LePoidevin and Murray McBeath, 23–34. Oxford: Oxford University Press, 1993.

Meister, Chad. "Death and the Afterlife." In *RCPR*: 294–306.

Melchert, Norman. *Philosophical Conversations: A Concise Historical Introduction*. Oxford: Oxford University Press, 2008.

Merricks, Trenton. "The Resurrection of the Body and the Life Everlasting." In *Reason for the Hope Within*, edited by Michael Murray, 261–86. Grand Rapids: Eerdmans, 1999.

———. "How to Live Forever without Saving Your Soul." In *SBS*: 183–200.

———. "The Resurrection of the Body." In *OHPT*: 476–90.

Meyendorff, John. *Byzantine Theology: Historical Trends and Doctrinal Themes*. New York: Fordham University Press, 1974.

Miller, Lisa. *Heaven*. New York: Harper Collins, 2010.

Moll, Rob. *The Art of Dying*. Downers Grove, IL: IVP, 2010.

Moltmann, Jürgen. *The Coming of God: Christian Eschatology*. Minneapolis: Fortress, 1996.

———. *Ethics of Hope*. Minneapolis: Fortress, 2012.

———. *The Future of Creation*. Minneapolis: Fortress, 2007.

———. *In the End—In the Beginning*. London: SCM, 2004.

———. *Sun of Righteousness Arise! God's Future for Humanity and the Earth*. London: SCM, 2010.

———. *Theology of Hope*. New York: Harper & Row, 1967.

Montgomery, Brint, et. al. *Relational Theology: A Contemporary Introduction*. Eugene, OR: Wipf and Stock, 2012.

Moore, Brooke Noel. *Philosophical Possibilities Beyond Death*. Springfield, IL: Thomas, 1981.

Moreland, J. P. "The Argument from Consciousness." In *RCPR*: 433–44.

Morris, Leon. "First John." In *New Bible Commentary: Revised*, edited by Donald Guthrie, 1259–69. Grand Rapids: Eerdmans, 1970.

Morris, Thomas. *Our Idea of God*. Downers Grove, IL: IVP Academic, 1991.

Mulholland, M. Robert. *Invitation to a Journey: A Roadmap for Spiritual Formation*. Downers Grove, IL: IVP, 1993.

Murdoch, Iris. *Metaphysics as a Guide to Morals*. London: Penguin, 1992.

———. *The Sovereignty of Good*. New York: Schocken, 1971.

Murphy, Nancey. *Bodies and Souls, or Spirited Bodies?* Cambridge: Cambridge University Press, 2006.

———. "Nonreductive Physicalism: Philosophical Issues." In *WHS*, 127–48.

Murray, Michael. "God Responds to Prayer." In *CD*: 242–55, 264–66.

Murray, Michael, and Kurt Meyers. "Ask and It Will Be Given To You." *Religious Studies* 30 (1994) 311–30.

Muyskens, James. *The Sufficiency of Hope*. Philadelphia: Temple University Press, 1979.

Nagel, Thomas. "What Is It Like to Be a Bat?" *The Philosophical Review* 83 (1974) 435–50.
Newcott, Bill. "The Paradox of Prayer." *AARP Magazine*, February-March 2015.
Nichols, Terence. *Death and Afterlife: A Theological Introduction*. Grand Rapids: Brazos, 2010.
Norris, Richard. *Understanding the Faith of the Church*. New York: Seabury, 1979.
Nozick, Robert. *Philosophical Explanations*. Cambridge: Belknap Press of Harvard University Press, 1981.
O'Callaghan, Paul. *Christ Our Hope: An Introduction to Eschatology*. Washington, DC: Catholic University of America Press, 2011.
Oden, Thomas. *After Modernity . . . What? Agenda for Theology*. Grand Rapids: Zondervan, 1990.
———. *Life in the Spirit*. Vol. 3, *Systematic Theology*. San Francisco: Harper San Francisco, 1992.
Ombres, Robert. *Theology of Purgatory*. Dublin: Mercier, 1978.
Orthodox Church. *The Lenten Triodion*. London: Faber & Faber, 1978.
———. *The Lenten Triodion: Supplementary Texts*. Bussy-en-Othe, France: Monastery of the Veil of the Mother of God, 1979.
———. *Service Book of the Holy Orthodox-Catholic Apostolic Church*. New York: Association Press, 1922.
Padgett, Alan. "Eternity." In *RCPR*: 335–43.
Papineau, David. *Consciousness: A Graphic Guide*. London: Icon, 2010.
Parfit, Derek. *Reasons and Persons*. Oxford: Oxford University Press, 1984.
Partridge, Mike. "George MacDonald's Theology." Online: george-macdonald.com.
Paul, Richard. *Critical Thinking*. Rohnert Park, CA: Sonoma State University Press, 1990.
Payne, David. "2 Peter." In *The International Bible Commentary*, edited by F. F. Bruce, 1564–70. Grand Rapids: Zondervan, 1979.
Pendergast, Terrence. "Hope, NT." In *Anchor Bible Dictionary*, edited by David Freedman, 3: 282–85. New York: Doubleday, 1992.
Penelhum, Terence, ed. *Immortality*. Belmont, CA: Wadsworth, 1973.
Perrett, Roy. *Death and Immortality*. Dordrecht: Nijhoff, 1987.
Peterson, Michael. "Eschatology and Theodicy." In *OHE*: 518–33.
Peterson, Michael, et al. *Reason and Religious Belief: An Introduction to the Philosophy of Religion*. Oxford: Oxford University Press, 1991.
Pettit, Philip. "Hope and Its Place in Mind." *Annals of the American Academy of Political and Social Science* 1 (2004) 152–65.
Pieper, Josef. *On Hope*. San Francisco: Ignatius, 1986.
Piguet, Leo, ed. *100 Prayers for Celebrating the Liturgical Seasons*. Notre Dame, IN: Ave Maria, 1982.
Pinnock, Clark. "Response to Zachary Hayes." In *Four Views of Hell*, edited by William Crockett, 127–31. Grand Rapids: Zondervan, 1992.
Pinnock, Clark, and Robert Brow. *Unbounded Love*. Downers Grove, IL: IVP, 1994.
Plato. *Phaedo*. In *The Dialogues of Plato*, edited by Benjamin Jowett. Vol. 1. Oxford: Clarendon, 1964.
———. *The Last Days of Socrates*. London: Penguin, 1969.
———. *Timaeus*. In *The Dialogues of Plato*, edited by Benjamin Jowett. Vol. 3. Oxford: Clarendon, 1964.

Plumptre, E. H. *The Spirits in Prison and Other Studies on Life After Death*. London: Isbister, 1884.

Polkinghorne, John. *The Faith of a Physicist*. Princeton: Princeton University Press, 1994.

———. *The God of Hope and the End of the World*. New Haven: Yale, 2002.

Pope Benedict XVI. Encyclical Letter *Spe Salvi*. 2007. Online: vatican.va.

Pope Francis. "Homily at the Beatification Mass of Paul VI." Online: zenit.org.

Pope Shenouda III. *The Divine Liturgy of Saint Gregory the Theologian*. Sydney: Coptic Orthodox Theological College, 1999. Online: copticchurch.net.

"Prayer for the Dead." Catholic Online. Online:catholic.org.

"Prayers for the Deceased." Our Catholic Prayers. Online: ourcatholicprayers.com.

"Prayers for the Faithful Departed." About Catholicism. Online: catholicism.about.com.

Presbyterian Church USA. *Book of Common Worship*. Louisville: Westminster John Knox, 1993.

Price, H. H. "Survival and the Idea of 'Another World.'" In *Language, Metaphysics and Death*, edited by John Donnelly, 176–95. New York: Fordham University Press, 1978.

Pruss, Alexander and Joshua Rasmussen. "Time without Creation." *Faith and Philosophy* 31 (2014) 401–11.

Quinn, J. M. "Eternity." In *New Catholic Encyclopedia*, 2nd ed., edited by Berard Marthaler, Vol. 5, 380–83. Washington, DC: Catholic University of America Press, 2003.

Rachels, James, and Stuart Rachels. *Problems from Philosophy*. 2nd ed. New York: McGraw-Hill, 2009.

Rahner, Karl. *Theological Investigations*. Vol. 6. London: Darton, Longman and Todd, 1966.

———. *Theological Investigations*. Vol. 17. London: Darton, Longman and Todd, 1981.

———. *Theological Investigations*. Vol. 19. London: Darton, Longman and Todd, 1983.

Ramelli, Ilaria. *The Christian Doctrine of Apokatastasis*. Leiden: Brill, 2013.

Ratzinger, Joseph. *Eschatology: Death and Eternal Life*. Washington, DC: Catholic University of America Press, 1988.

Rauhut, Nils. *Ultimate Questions: Thinking about Philosophy*. 3rd ed. Upper Saddle River, NJ: Prentice Hall, 2011.

Reaume, John. "Another Look at 1 Corinthians 15:29, 'Baptized for the Dead.'" *Bibliotheca Sacra* 152 (1995) 457–75.

Reichenbach, Bruce. *Is Man the Phoenix? A Study of Immortality*. Washington, DC: University Press of America, 1978.

Rietz, Henry. "Time." In *NIDB* 5: 595–600.

Roberts, Arthur. *Exploring Heaven*. San Francisco: Harper, 2003.

Roberts, Robert C., and Jay Wood. *Intellectual Virtues*. Oxford: Oxford University Press, 2007.

Robinson, John. *In the End God*. 2nd ed. New York: Harper and Row, 1968.

Roman Catholic Church. *Catechism of the Catholic Church*. Ligouri, MO: Ligouri, 1994.

———. Council of Trent. Online: americancatholictruthsociety.com.

Rowell, Geoffrey. *The Liturgy of Christian Burial: An Introductory Survey of the Historical Development of Christian Burial Rites*. London: SPCK, 1977.

Russell, H. Lloyd. "The Intermediate State and Prayer for the Departed." Online: anglicanhistory.org.

Russell, Jeffrey Burton. *A History of Heaven: The Singing Silence*. Princeton: Princeton University Press, 1997.

———. *Paradise Mislaid: How We Lost Heaven and How We Can Regain It*. Oxford: Oxford University Press, 2006.

Russian Orthodox Convent of Our Lady of Vladimir. "The Church's Prayer for the Dead." Online: orthodoxinfo.com.

Saarinen, Risto. *The Pastoral Epistles with Philemon and Jude*. Grand Rapids: Brazos, 2008.

Sacred Congregation for the Doctrine of the Faith. "Letter on Certain Questions Concerning Eschatology." *Origins* 9 (1979) 131–33.

Sanders, John. *No Other Name: An Investigation into the Destiny of the Unevangelized*. Grand Rapids: Eerdmans, 1992.

———. *The God Who Risks*. Downers Grove, IL: IVP Academic, 1998.

Saul, Nigel. "The Living and the Dead: Tomb Monument Commemoration in Hereford Cathedral." Online: herefordcathedral.org.

Schimmel, Solomon. *The Seven Deadly Sins*. Oxford: Oxford University Press, 1997.

Schleitheim Confession. Online: anabaptists.org.

Schmemann, Alexander. *The Eucharist: Sacrament of the Kingdom*. Crestwood, NY: St. Vladimir's Seminary Press, 1988.

Schmutzer, Andrew. "A Theology of Sexual Abuse." *Journal of the Evangelical Theological Society* 51 (2008) 785–812.

Schumacher, Bernard. *A Philosophy of Hope*. New York: Fordham University Press, 2003.

Schweizer, Eduard. "Pneuma." In *TDNT* 6: 332–455.

———. "Psyche." In *TDNT* 9: 608–60.

Second Helvetic Confession. Online: ccel.org.

Second Vatican Council. *Lumen Gentium*. Online: cin.org.

Seebass, Horst. "Nephesh." In *TDOT* 9: 497–579.

Seligman, Martin. *Helplessness: On Depression, Development, and Death*. San Francisco: Freeman, 1975.

———. *Learned Optimism: How to Change Your Mind and Your Life*. New York: Free, 1998.

Sklar, Lawrence. "Time." In *REP*.

Smart, J. J. C. "Time." In *EP* 9: 461–75.

Smith, James K. A. *Desiring the Kingdom: Worship, Worldview and Cultural Formation*. Grand Rapids: Baker Academic, 2009.

———. *Imagining the Kingdom: How Worship Works*. Grand Rapids: Baker Academic, 2013.

Smith, Nicholas D. "Philosophical Reflection on Petitionary Prayer." *Philosophy Compass* (2012) 1–9.

Smith, Nicholas D., and Andrew Yip. "Partnership with God: A Partial Solution to the Problem of Petitionary Prayer." *Religious Studies* 46 (2010) 395–410.

Smith, Nicholas H. "Analysing Hope." *Critical Horizons: A Journal of Philosophy and Social Theory* 9 (1998) 5–23.

———. "From the Concept of Hope to the Principle of Hope." Online: academia.edu.

Smith, Quentin. "Time, Being and Becoming." In *EP* 9: 475–82.

Spinoza, Benedict. *Ethics*. In *The Rationalists*. New York: Anchor, 1974.
Stump, Eleonore. "Petitionary Prayer." *American Philosophical Quarterly* 16 (1979) 81–91.
———. "Eternity." In *REP*.
Stump Eleonore, and Norman Kretzman. "Eternity." *Journal of Philosophy* 78 (1981) 429–58.
Suk, John. *Not Sure: A Pastor's Journey from Faith to Doubt*. Grand Rapids: Eerdmans, 2011.
Swete, H. B. "Prayer for the Departed in the First Four Centuries." *The Journal of Theological Studies* 18 (1907) 500–514.
Swinburne, Richard. *The Christian God*. Oxford: Clarendon, 1994.
———. *The Coherence of Theism*. Oxford: Clarendon, 1977.
———. *The Evolution of the Soul*. Oxford: Clarendon, 1986.
———. "God and Time." In *Reasoned Faith*, edited by Eleonore Stump, 204–22. Ithaca, NY: Cornell University Press, 1993.
———. *Is There a God?* Oxford: Oxford University Press, 1996.
———. *Was Jesus God?* Oxford: Oxford University Press, 2010.
Talbott, Thomas. *The Inescapable Love of God*. 1st ed. Boca Raton, FL: Universal, 1999. (2nd ed. Eugene, OR: Cascade, 2014.)
Taliaferro, Charles. "Human Nature, Personal Identity and Eschatology." In *OHE*: 534–47.
———. "Prayer." In *RCPR*: 677–85.
Taylor, Barbara Brown. *Gospel Medicine*. Lanham, MD: Cowley / Rowman & Littlefield, 1995.
Tertullian of Carthage. "The Chaplet." In *Disciplinary, Moral and Ascetical Works*, edited by Rudolph Arbesmann, 225–31. New York: Fathers of the Church, 1959.
———. "On Monogamy." In *ANF* 4: 59–73.
Thiselton, Anthony. *Life After Death*. Grand Rapids: Eerdmans, 2012.
Thomas, Owen. *Introduction to Theology*. Cambridge: Greeno, Hadden and Co., 1973.
Tickle, Phyllis. "Liturgy and Cultural Engagement." In *Ancient Faith, Future Mission: Fresh Expressions in the Sacramental Traditions*, edited by Steven Croft, et al., 99–109. New York: Seabury, 2010.
Tiessen, Terrance. *Providence and Prayer: How Does God Work in the World?* Downers Grove, IL: IVP Academic, 2000.
Timmons, Mark, and David Shoemaker. *Knowledge, Nature and Norms*. Belmont, CA: Wadsworth, 2009.
Tollinton, Richard. "Prayer for the Departed." *The Modern Churchman* 12 (1915) 252–64.
Toner, Patrick. "Prayers for the Dead." In *The Catholic Encyclopedia*. Vol. 4. New York: Appleton, 1908. Online: newadvent.org.
Tucker, Karen. *American Methodist Worship*. Oxford: Oxford University Press, 2001.
U.S. Lutheran-Catholic Dialogue. *The Hope of Eternal Life*. Edited by Lowell Almen and Richard Sklba. Minneapolis: Lutheran University Press, 2011.
United Methodist Church. *A Service of Death and Resurrection: The Ministry of the Church at Death*. Supplemental Worship Resources 7. Nashville: Abingdon, 1979.
———. *The United Methodist Hymnal*. Nashville: United Methodist Publishing House, 1989.

———. *The United Methodist Book of Worship*. Nashville: United Methodist Publishing House, 1992.
United States Conference of Catholic Bishops. *The Roman Missal*. 3rd ed. International Commission on English in the Liturgy Corporation, 2010. Totowa, NJ: Catholic Book, 2011.
———. *General Instruction of the Roman Missal*. Online: usccb.org.
van Inwagen, Peter. "Dualism and Materialism: Athens and Jerusalem?" *Faith and Philosophy* 12 (1995) 475–88.
———. "I Look for the Resurrection of the Body and the Life of the World to Come." Online: andrewmbailey.com.
———. "The Possibility of Resurrection." *International Journal for Philosophy of Religion* 9 (1978) 114–21.
Vander Zee, Leonard. *In Life and In Death: A Pastoral Guide for Funerals*. Grand Rapids: CRC, 1992.
Vassiliadis, Nikolaos. *The Mystery of Death*. Athens: Orthodox Brotherhood of Theologians, 1997.
Verhey, Allen. *The Christian Art of Dying*. Grand Rapids: Eerdmans. 2011.
Volf, Miroslav. *Exclusion and Embrace*. Nashville: Abingdon, 1996.
Wachter, L. "Sheol." In *TDOT* 14: 239–48.
Wadell, Paul. *Happiness and the Christian Moral Life*. Lanham, MD: Rowman and Littlefield, 2012.
Wainwright, Geoffrey. "The Saints and the Departed: Confessional Controversy and Ecumenical Convergence." *Studia Liturgia* 34 (2004) 65–91.
Walls, Jerry. *Heaven: The Logic of Eternal Joy*. Oxford: Oxford University Press, 2002.
———. "Purgatory for Everyone." *First Things* (April 2002). Online: firstthings.com.
———. "Heaven." In *OHE*: 399–412.
———. *Purgatory: The Logic of Total Transformation*. Oxford: Oxford University Press, 2012.
———. *Heaven, Hell and Purgatory*. Grand Rapids: Brazos, 2015.
Ware, Timothy. *The Orthodox Church*. London: Penguin, 1963.
———. "'One Body in Christ': Death and the Communion of Saints." *Sobornost* 3 (1981) 179–91.
Waterworth, Jane. *A Philosophical Analysis of Hope*. New York: Palgrave MacMillan, 2004.
Webber, Robert. *Ancient-Future Faith: Rethinking Evangelicalism for a Postmodern World*. Grand Rapids: Baker, 1999.
———. *Ancient-Future Evangelism: Making Your Church a Faith-Forming Community*. Grand Rapids: Baker, 2003.
Welsby, Paul. "Prayers for the Dead." *Theology* 69 (1920) 244–51.
Westminster Confession of Faith. Atlanta: Presbyterian Church in America, 1986.
Westphal, Merold. "Faith Seeking Understanding." In *God and the Philosophers*, edited by Thomas Morris, 215–26. Oxford: Oxford University Press, 1994.
White, Joel. "'Baptized on Account of the Dead': The Meaning of 1 Corinthians 15:29 in Its Context." In *Journal of Biblical Literature* 116 (1997) 487–99.
———. "Recent Challenges to the *communis opinio* on 1 Corinthians 15:29." *Currents in Biblical Research* 10 (2012) 379–95.
Williams, Daniel. "*Similis et Dissimilis*: Gauging Our Expectations of the Early Fathers." In *AFCF*: 68–89.

Williams, Rowan. *The Lion's World: A Journey into the Heart of Narnia.* Oxford: Oxford University Press, 2012.
Willimon, William. *Who Will Be Saved?* Nashville: Abingdon, 2008.
Wills, Gary. *What Jesus Meant.* New York: Viking Penguin, 2006.
Winter, David. *Hereafter: What Happens After Death?* Wheaton, IL: Shaw, 1972.
———. *Living through Loss: God's Help in Bereavement.* Wheaton, IL: Shaw, 1986.
Witvliet, John. "Embracing the Wisdom of Ancient Liturgical Practices." In *AFCF*: 189–215.
Wolterstorff, Nicholas. "God Everlasting." In *Contemporary Philosophy of Religion*, edited by Steven Cahn and David Shatz, 77–98. Oxford: Oxford University Press, 1992.
Wright, Charles. "Prayers for the Dead." Church Association Tract 214. Online: churchsociety.org.
Wright, N. T. *After You Believe: Why Christian Character Matters.* New York: Harper One, 2010.
———. *Following Jesus.* Grand Rapids: Eerdmans, 1995.
———. *For All the Saints: Remembering the Christian Departed.* New York: Morehouse, 2003.
———. *The Last Word.* New York: HarperCollins, 2005.
———. *The Resurrection of the Son of God.* London: SPCK, 2003.
———. *Surprised by Hope: Rethinking Heaven, the Resurrection and the Mission of the Church.* New York: Harper Collins, 2008.
Yancey, Philip. *Prayer: Does It Make Any Difference?* Grand Rapids: Zondervan, 2006.
Yang, Seung. "Hope." In *NIDB* 2: 885–89.
Zimmerman, Dean. "Christians Should Affirm Mind-Body Dualism." In *CD*: 315–27, 338–41.
———. "The Compatibility of Materialism and Survival: The 'Falling Elevator' Model." *Faith and Philosophy* 16 (1999) 194–212.
Zwingli, Ulrich. *Articles.* Online: christianhistoryinstitute.org.

NAME INDEX

A Monk of St. Tikhon Monastery, 46n28
Aben, Tersur, 66n20
Acts of Paul and Thecla, 24
Aerius of Pontus, 24
Alcorn, Randy, 114n49, 123, 124n75
Alfeyev, Hilarion, 47
Allen,, Richard, 94n42
Ambrose of Milan, 26, 91
Anderson, Ray, 100n6, 105n19, 113n45
Andrewes, Lancelot, 37
Anselm of Canterbury, 133, 164n61, 164n62
Apocalypse of Elijah, 26
Apocalypse of Paul, 26
Apocalypse of Peter, 25
Apostolic Constitutions, 28
Aquinas, Thomas, 31, 91, 107–8, 118, 132n17, 133, 141–42, 144, 169, 177
Archbishop's Commission, 13n6, 20n28, 31n41, 37n68, 37n71, 53, 39, 62n6, 63n10, 74–75, 86–87, 95, 141n49, 145n65
Aristotle, 107, 111n39, 113n46
Arius of Alexandria, 18
Arnobius of Sicca, 24
Atwell, Robert, 27n24
Augsburg Confession, 36
Augustine of Hippo, 26–27, 133, 158–59, 161, 190
Austin, John, 187

Badham, Paul, 7n21

Baggini, Julian, 19, 109n34, 153n10, 206n7, 210n17
Baker, Lynne Rudder, 109
Baker, Sharon, 16, 68–69, 156
Balthasar, Hans Urs von, 76
Barcalow, Emmet, 106n24, 114n51, 116, 118n59, 210
Barr, James, 145n67
Barry, Vincent, 106n24, 115n51
Barth, Karl, 95, 101n8, 127–28, 137, 156
Basinger, David, 86n10
Bauckham, Richard, 131
Bealer, George, 206
Beckett, Samuel, 193,
Beilby, James, 164n62
Bell, Rob, 3n6, 17n20, 70
Belshaw, Christopher, 106n24
Bennett, Arthur, 37n71
Berdyaev, Nicholai, 77
Bierma, Nathan, 157–58
Bloesch, Donald, 49–50, 76, 100n6, 123, 146
Boethius of Rome, 133
Boggis, Robert, 23n5, 37n68, 56, 71–72
Bonhoeffer, Dietrich, 4, 95, 155, 160–61, 167–68, 171, 193
Book of Common Prayer, 30n35, 36–37, 40n1, 49, 52–54, 62n7, 63n9, 64, 67, 78, 125, 129, 143–44, 152, 162, 168n73, 170n81, 171n86, 173, 175n1

NAME INDEX

Borg, Marcus, 152n4, 154–55, 164n62
Boros, Ladislaus, 127–28
Boultbee, Thomas, 13
Boulton, Matthew, 168n72
Bowker, John, 16
Bramhall, John, 141
Brow, Robert, 152n7, 153, 160n44, 162n52, 164n61
Brown, Christopher, 169n79
Brown, Peter, 22n2, 23n4, 29n31, 32n43, 47n31, 62n8, 63n9, 103n13, 123n72, 141n52, 189
Brown, Warren, 106n24
Brueggemann, Walter, 70, 85, 184, 192, 194
Brummer, Vincent, 86n10, 87n13, 91
Brunner, Emil, 176–77
Buechner, Frederick, 7, 124, 165n63
Bullard, Roger, 189n60
Bultmann, Rudolph, 17, 98n3, 127, 185–86
Buttrick, George, 93–94
Byassee, Jason, 18n23, 69
Bynum, Caroline, 114n50

Calvin, John, 2n4, 34–36, 48, 91n25, 103n13, 164n61, 164n62, 168n72, 171, 182, 191
Camus, Albert, 193
Carter, William, 64n15, 207n8, 209
Casey, John, 100n6, 143
Catechism of Catholic Church, 41, 42n5, 183, 190–91
Cavarnos, Constantine, 47n33
Chalmers, David, 206
Chapman, David, 14, 73, 89, 171n86
Christian Reformed Church, 48, 78, 163, 175n1, 194
Chrysostom, John, 24–25
Church of England, 54
Church of Jesus Christ of Latter Day Saints, 55–56
Church of the Brethren, 49
Clement of Alexandria, 149n75
Cockburn, Bruce, 170, 194–95

Cocksworth, Christopher, 37n71, 95–96, 122n70
Cohen, Carl, 87n13
Cohoe, Caleb, 86n10, 89, 93
Communio Sanctorum, 57, 75
Conee, Earl, 130n13, 207n8
Connelly, Douglas, 120
Cook, Stephen, 169
Cooper, John, 100n6, 102n11, 103n14, 104n18, 105n20, 105n21, 111n39, 112, 120n65, 137–39
Cooper, Terry, 161n51
Copi, Irving, 87n13
Corcoran, Kevin, 109n34, 120–21, 213
Cosin, John, 37
Council of Toledo, 211
Craig, William Lane, 94n44, 130n13, 132n18, 133n19, 135–36, 139n40, 140
Cranmer, Thomas, 36
Crisp, Oliver, 90, 92n31
Crossin, John, 189, 196
Crump, David, 11, 14, 88, 91n27, 155
Cullmann, Oscar, 111n39, 134n24, 137, 140–41, 145n67, 147
Currie, David, 18n21, 22n3, 37n70, 62n8, 66, 69n28, 165–66, 170
Cyprian of Carthage, 24
Cyril of Jerusalem, 1, 24–25

Daley, Brian, 16, 18–19, 47n31, 72, 75n51
Damer, T. Edward, 67–68
Dante Alighieri, 193
Davidson, Randall, 38–39, 72
Davis, Stephen, 7n21, 106n24, 114n49, 120n65, 132n18, 211, 213
Davison, Scott, 86n10, 88, 94–95
Day, John, 176, 177n10, 178n11, 178n12, 179n13, 179n14, 181, 187n51, 195n95
Defense of Augsburg Confession, 34
DeMaris, Richard, 13n4

236

NAME INDEX

DeSilva, David, 55n58
DeYoung, Rebecca, 189n62
Descartes, Rene, 107, 177n10, 203–4, 208
Directory on Popular Piety and the Liturgy, 41–42, 77n63
Donfried, Karl, 182, 183n37
Double, Richard, 107n25
Dowden, Bradley, 130n13
Downie, Robin, 177
Dublin Agreed Statement, 57, 78n64
Duck, Ruth, 154
Duffy, Stephen, 159n37
Dunn, James, 113
Dyke, Heather, 130n13, 132n17

Eberl, Jason, 108n28
Eddy, Paul, 164n62
Edwards, Paul, 7n21
Elliot, Peter, 43n9, 43n10
Ellul, Jacques, 163, 194
English Methodist Church, 51
Eno, Robert, 5, 32
Epiphanius of Salamis, 24
Episcopal Church, 6, 53–55, 78
Epistula Apostolorum, 26
Erskine, Thomas, 160n45
Evagrius of Pontus, 189n62
Evangelical Covenant Church, 152
Evangelical Lutheran Church in America, 51
Evans, Alice and Robert, 182
Evans, Rachel Held, 167
Evodius of Milan, 123n72

Fabry, Heinz-Josef, 112n40
Fackenheim, Emil, 188n57
Fackre, Dorothy and Gabriel, 147, 154, 158, 163, 164n62, 168
Fairbairn, Donald, 158n32
Fairlie, Henry, 189n62
Fedwick, Paul, 44
Feinberg, Joel, 99n4
Florovsky, George, 137
Forbes, William, 14, 74
Ford, David, 62n8, 64

Gadamer, Hans, 65

Ganssle, Gregory, 132n18
Geach, Peter, 92, 187
Godfrey, Joseph, 119n63, 181, 187
Goldingay, John, 93–94
Gordon, Robert, 156
Grady, Joseph, 190
Graham, Billy, 194
Green, Joel, 100n6, 101n8, 104n16, 104n17, 106n24, 120n65
Gregory of Nyssa, 158, 211
Gregory the Great, 27, 189n62
Griffiths, Paul, 33n45
Gulley, Philip, 151

Hadewijch of Antwerp, 76
Hahn, Scott, 160–61, 165n63
Hall, Christopher, 18, 69
Hall, Douglas John, 17
Hallote, Rachel, 103n14
Handel, George Frideric, 189
Hardy, Edward, 36n63, 37n68
Harris, Murray, 101n8
Hart, David, 153
Hart, Trevor, 131
Hartshorne, Charles, 98n3
Hasker, William, 7, 108, 204, 212
Hatchett, Marion, 29n30
Hebblethwaite, Brian, 101n8
Heidelberg Catechism, 36
Helm, Paul, 132n18
Heraclitus of Ephesus, 207
Hershenov, David, 212–13
Hick, John, 113n45, 119, 126, 136, 140–41, 163, 166, 214–15
Hildegard of Bingen, 77
Hobbes, Thomas, 177n10
Hodge, A. A., 2n4
Hoekema, Anthony, 124n75
Homily on Prayer, 36
Hope of Eternal Life, 42n7, 43n12, 57–58, 50n40, 57–58
Howard, Thomas, 75–76, 172–73
Howard-Snyder, Daniel and Frances, 87, 89n18
Hume, David, 177n10
Husbands, Mark, 6n18

Inbody, Tyron, 84

237

NAME INDEX

International Theological Commission, 100n7, 108n28, 141n48, 190
Inwagen, Peter van, 108, 120, 214

Jackson, Frank, 206n7
Jackson, Timothy, 155
Jeeves, Malcolm, 205n5
Jenni, Ernst, 145n67
Jensen, Matt, 161
Jeremias, Joachim, 104n17
Julian of Norwich, 194,

Kagan, Shelly, 106n24, 115n51, 116n53, 116n54, 210n16
Kant, Immanuel, 175
Kantzer, Kenneth, 193
Kelly, John, 12
Kerr, Hugh, 103n13
Kettner, Edward, 145
Kennedy, Robert, 190
Kidner, Derek, 184–85
Kneale,, William, 132n18
Koons, Robert, 206
Kreider, Alan, 36n65
Kretzman, Norman, 136n29
Kripke, Saul, 204
Kronen, John, 6n17, 70–71, 164n61

LaDue, William, 105, 124n75, 127n6
Lamott, Anne, 61
Lane, Dermot, 153, 154n16, 168, 169n78, 181–84
Larchet, Jean-Claude, 47
Law, Stephen, 117n58
LeGoff, Jacques, 33n47
LePoidevin, Robin, 130n13
Lee, Frederick, 23n5, 172n88, 173
Leftow, Brian, 136n28, 140n45
Lewis, C. S., vii, 1, 4–5, 9, 75n50, 89, 92–93, 133, 140, 143–44, 154, 159–60, 163
Liturgy of the Blessed Apostles, 28
Liturgy of John Chrysostom, 28, 44
Liturgy of St. Gregory of Nanzianzus, 28
Liturgy of St. James, 27

Liturgy of St. Mark, 28
Liwak, Rudigar, 103n14
Locke, John, 116n54, 117n58, 177n10, 208–10
Louth, Andrew, 44n16, 47n31
Luther, Martin, 34–36, 50, 65, 103n13, 161, 164n62, 168n72, 191
Lutheran Church–Missouri Synod, 50

MacDonald, George, 160n45
MacDonald, Gregory, 14n9, 122n71
Mackintosh, Hugh, 2
Macquarrie, John, 123n72, 176, 188, 195n93
Marcel, Gabriel, 180–81, 192
Markosian, Ned, 130n13
Marshall, Peter, 29, 30–31, 33
Martin, Adrienne, 177n10, 178n12, 179
Marx, Karl, 4
Masek, Lawrence, 94
Mavrodes, George, 86n10, 94
McGinn, Colin, 100n5, 111n38
McLaren, Brian, 61, 72, 78–79, 151
McLaughlin, Megan, 23n5, 23n6, 30–32
McLeod, Carolyn, 187n52
McTaggart, John, 130
Meister, Chad, 121
Melchert, Norman, 207
Mellor, David, 209
Mennonite Church, 49
Merricks, Trenton, 103n13, 212, 215
Meyendorff, John, 143
Meyers, Kurt, 86n10
Mill, John Stuart, 181
Miller, Lisa, 56
Moll, Rob, 21
Moltmann, Jurgen, 5, 71n35, 131n14, 134n24, 142, 148, 156n25, 157n26, 157n27, 172, 183, 186–88, 190, 194–95
Montgomery, Brint, 160n45
Moore, Brooke, 7n21
Moreland, J. P., 204n3

238

NAME INDEX

Morris, Leon, 156
Morris, Tom, 132n18, 133n22
Mulholland, James, 151,
Mulholland, M. Robert, 166
Murdoch, Iris, 161n51, 166
Murphy, Nancey, 100n6, 107n26, 107n27, 110n37, 111n39, 119
Murray, Michael, 86n10
Muyskens, James, 180, 189

Nagel, Thomas, 206
Newcott, Bill, 94
Newman, John Henry, 38
Nichols, Terence, 100n6, 102n11, 112n40, 148n73, 213n24
Norris, Richard, 190–91
Nozick, Robert, 80–82

O'Callaghan, Paul, 158
Oden, Thomas, 71, 114
Ombres, Robert, 74n46, 196
Origen of Alexandria, 20n27, 66n19, 139, 213

Packer, James, 2n4
Padgett, Alan, 132n18
Palmer, Stuart, 106n24
Pannenberg, Wolfhart, 142n53, 161n51
Papineau, David, 110, 204, 205n6
Parfit, Derek, 115n51, 210
Partridge, Mike, 160n45
Passion of Perpetua and Felicitas, 24
Paul, Richard, 16n13, 61, 69
Payne, David, 95
Pendergast, Terrence, 185
Penelhum, Terence, 7n21
Perrett, Roy, 7n21
Peterson, Michael, 133n19, 173
Pettit, Phillip, 180n16
Pieper, Josef, 176–77, 181, 196
Piguet, Leo, 56
Pinnock, Clark, 74, 152n7, 153, 160n44, 162n52, 164n61
Piper, John, 2n4
Plato, 107, 111n39, 113n46, 133, 161n47

Plumptre, E.H., 23n5, 37n71, 77n61
Polkinghorne, John, 5n15, 121n68, 142, 143n59, 188, 194
Pope Benedict XII, 138n37
Pope Benedict XVI, 196
Pope Francis, 68
Pope Shenouda III, 46n24
Presbyterian Church USA, 48–49
Price, Henry, 118–19
Prudentius of Tarraconensis, 26
Pruss, Alexander, 135n25
Pseudo-Dionysus, 76

Quinn, J. M., 133n19

Rachels, James, 106n24, 115n51
Rahner, Karl, 3n7, 74n46, 76, 120n65, 130, 142n53, 159
Ramelli, Ilaria, 25n15, 25n17, 153n10, 211n19
Rasmussen, Joshua, 135n25
Ratzinger, Joseph, 30, 74, 101n8, 128n7, 137n34, 138, 141–43, 169–70, 172, 213
Rauhut, Nils, 107n25, 115n51
Reaume, John, 12
Reformed Church in America, 48
Reichenbach, Bruce, 103n13, 105n22
Reitan, Eric, 6n17, 70–71, 164n61
Rengstorf, Karl, 185–86
Report of Royal Commission, 38n74
Richard of St. Victor, 154n14
Ricoeur, Paul, 71n36
Rietz, Henry, 145n67
Reno, Russell Ronald, 18
Roberts, Arthur, 119n63
Roberts, Robert, 65, 69, 80
Robinson, John, 7n20, 71n35, 141, 145n67, 146n68
Roman Missal, 42, 43n8, 77
Rowell, Geoffrey, 30, 37n66, 37n67
Rublev, Andrei, 153, 156
Russell, Bertrand, 193
Russell, Charles Taze, 18
Russell, H. Lloyd, 38n74
Russell, Jeffrey Burton, 123n72, 142n56, 152

NAME INDEX

Saarinen, Risto, 12
Sacharov, Sophronius, 77, 173n90
Sacramentary of Gellone, 76
Sanders, John, 3n7, 91–92
Saul, Nigel, 22
Schimmel, Solomon, 189
Schleitheim Confession, 37
Schliermacher, Frederick, 124n75
Schmemann, Alexander, 45
Schmutzer, Andrew, 159–60
Schumacher, Bernard, 187
Schweizer, Eduard, 112, 113n43
Searle, John, 187–88
Second Helvetic Confession, 35
Second Vatican Council, 3n7, 5, 41, 66n19, 77n63
Seebass, Horst, 112 n40
Seligman, Martin, 192n76
Service Book of Orthodox Church, 45–47
Shamblin, Gwen, 18
Shoemaker, David, 107n25, 115n51
Shoemaker, Sydney, 207
Sider, Theodore, 130n13, 207n8
Sklar, Lawrence, 130n13
Smart, J.J.C., 130n13
Smith, James, 161n47, 162n54
Smith, Nicholas D., 86n10, 94
Smith, Nicholas H., 178n11, 180, 182, 193n80
Smith, Quentin, 130n13
Socrates, 15, 149
Spinoza, Benedict, 177n10
Sproul, R.C., 2n4
Spurgeon, Charles, 2n4
Stump, Eleonore, 86n10, 88, 93, 132n18, 136n28, 136n29
Suk, John, 16, 60
Swete, Henry, 23n5, 24, 97–98
Swinburne, Richard, 6n16, 107, 119, 132n18, 134–35, 154n14
Sibylline Oracles, 26

Talbott, Thomas, 19–20
Taliaferro, Charles, 84, 86n10, 106n24
Taylor, Barbara Brown, 192
Temple, William, 150n77

Tertullian of Carthage, 24
Thirty-Nine Articles on Religion, 36, 67
Thiselton, Anthony, 103n13, 136n31, 183, 185n44, 187
Thomas, Owen, 65–68, 152n6, 160, 162–63, 173
Tickle, Phyllis, 72
Tiessen, Terrance, 20, 79, 86n10, 90n23
Tillich, Paul, 98n3, 127
Timmons, Mark, 107n25, 115n51
Tollinton, Richard, 30
Toner, Patrick, 23n5
Tucker, Karen, 51n42

United Methodist Church, 51–53, 78

Vander Zee, Leonard, 175n1
Vassiliadis, Nikolaos, 44–47, 75
Verhey, Allen, 102n12, 104n16, 105, 119n64, 135n27, 156n22, 161n47, 191
Vincent of Lerins, 67
Volf, Miroslav, 170

Wachter, L., 101n9
Wadell, Paul, 159, 166
Wainwright, Geoffrey, 56
Walls, Jerry, 14, 31n41, 106n24, 119n62, 123–24, 126n2, 147, 165n63, 166n67, 215
Ware, Timothy, 43–44, 73–74, 78n64, 172
Warfield, Benjamin, 2n4
Waterworth, Jane, 180
Webber, Robert, 56–57, 72–73, 79
Welsby, Paul, 37n71
Wesley, John, 38, 51
Westminster Confession, 37, 159, 211
Westphal, Merold, 60–61
White, Joel, 13n5
Wilder, Thornton, 175
Williams, Daniel, 72n41, 73n43
Williams, Rowan, 4
Willimon, William, 76
Wills, Gary, 155

NAME INDEX

Winter, David, 121–22, 124n76, 183
Wren, Brian, 154
Wolterstorff, Nick, 131n15, 132n18, 134–35, 136n29
Wood, Jay, 65, 69, 80
Wright, Charles, 83
Wright, N. T., 15–17, 55, 62n8, 100, 112–13, 114n50, 121n68, 138–39, 141, 152, 155, 157, 167n71, 168n76, 171n83, 182–83

Yancey, Philip, 91n29
Yang, Seung, 182, 183n37, 184
Yip, Andrew, 86n10

Zimmerman, Dean, 120–21, 213
Zwingli, Ulrich, 35

SCRIPTURE INDEX

HEBREW SCRIPTURE

Genesis

1	183–84
1:28	4
2:7	112
3:8	156
8:22	184
12:2–3	70, 169
15:18–20	184
18:16–33	85
21:2	184
25:21	184
28:14	169
30:22	184

Exodus

2:23–24	85
3:6	184n41
3:8	156
7–12	171
19:5–8	184
25:8	157
29:45	157
32:12-14	85
33:11	157
34:6–7	155–56

Leviticus

9:10	167
19:31	11, 103
20:6	11, 103
26:11–12	157

Numbers

14:17–20	85

Deuteronomy

4:7	85
7:9	188
10:18	167
14:29	167
30:19	160

Joshua

24:15	160

Judges

2:11–19	184
6:36–40	85

1 Samuel

1	135
28	103

2 Samuel

5:3, 19	184
7:5	157
7:14	184
11–12	135
14:14	101

SCRIPTURE INDEX

1 Kings

6:13	157
17:20–22	85, 134
18:27	188

2 Chronicles

20:7	156

Nehemiah

1:5	183

Job

10:21	101
14:11–12	101
19:25–27	101n10

Psalms

6:4	184
16	102n11
16:10	101
16:11	146
25:20	112
34:4, 6, 17	85
35:23–25	184
37:9, 34	183
44:1, 26	184
49	102n11
49:15	101
50:15	84–85
55:17	112
65:5	183
68:18	157
71:5	183
72:8–11	169
73	102n11
87:4–6	169
88:1	112
88:4–12	101
90:1–4	132, 136
102:25–27	132
115:3	19
115:17	101
117:2	184
130–131	183, 189
132:11	184
139:1–2	134
139:7–8	102n11
146:5–6	188, 191

Ecclesiastes

3:18–21	101
9:7–10	101

Isaiah

8:17	183
11:1–9	168
12:1–6	157
14:9, 16	103
14:10	101
19:18–25	169
25:7–9	139, 183
30:18	156
35:3–4	195
37:12–20	85
38:18–19	101
40:1–5	189
41:7	91
41:8	156
42:9	135, 148
43:18–19	135, 148
44:18	91
46:10–11	19
49:6	70
51:1–6	169, 184–85
54:5–8	157
55:12–13	168
56:6–7	169
60:11	76
64:4	183
65:25	168
66:18–21	169

Jeremiah

10:5	91
14:8	183
17:9	161n49
18:7–10	135n28
29:11	184
32:9–5	184
32:38	157
33:3	84
51:6	146

243

SCRIPTURE INDEX

Ezekiel

32:21	103
37:27	157

Daniel

12:2	101, 113

Hosea

1–3	157, 184
2:19	184

Micah

6:8	167

Habakkuk

2:3	146

Zephaniah

3:8–10	169, 183
3:15	157

Zechariah

2:10–11	157
8:3	157
9:9–12	184

APOCRYPHA

Wisdom of Solomom

3:1–9	40, 102n11

2 Maccabees

7	102
12:39–45	12

CHRISTIAN SCRIPTURE

Matthew

1:23	157
2:20	112
5:3–12	102, 191
5:13–16	4
6:10	102
7:7, 11	85
8:3	155
8:11	102
8:23–27	86
9:18–29	86
10:28	112
10:39	112
13:24–33	102
14:30–31	86
16:19	70
17:1–13	104, 114
18:10–14	76
18:18	70
21:31	155
22:1–10	157
22:23–33	102n12
22:37	112
23:2–3	66
24–25	102
24:1–30, 45–51	102
24:36—25:30	186
25:31–51	19, 102, 114, 167
26:39–42	85
28:20	157

Mark

1:15	146
5:35	vii
7:8	66
7:20–23	166
9:28–29	92
13	102
13:7	139

SCRIPTURE INDEX

Luke

6:45	166
7:36–50	155
8:43–48	155
11:5–8	86
12:4–5	112
12:37–43	186
14:15–24	157
15:11–32	155
16:19-31	104, 114
18:1–8	86
20:34–35	102
20:38	104
21	102
21:8	146
22:32	85
23:43	104
24:21	192
24:39	114

John

1:14	157
3:16	75
4:28–29	102
11:24	102
14:9	154
14:16, 23	157
15:15	157
17:21	56, 157

Acts

1:7	146
4:23–31	86
9: 36–41	86, 134
10	70
12:5–19	86
17:32	114
23:6–8	104, 185
24:15	185
26:6–7	185
28:8	86

Romans

1:9	86
4:17–21	186
5:1	165n63
5:2	185
8:15	165
8:18–25	102, 163, 185–86
8:38	162
12:5	167
12:12	186
13:11–12	186
15:4	186
15:13	185

1 Corinthians

1:7	185
3:1–3	63n10
3:9	93
5:1–13	171
11:1–2	73
11:27–28	151
12:12–27	139n42
13:12	15
15:20	105n21
15:23–24, 52	102, 140
15:29	12
15:37–44	114
15:35–56	99
15:51	103
15:58	190

2 Corinthians

1:10	183
3:18	147, 165
5:1–8	104–5
5:18–19	164, 168
6:16	157
12:7	94

Galatians

4:4	135
4:5, 19	165
5:5	147, 185
5:17	113
5:22–23	167
6:9	190

SCRIPTURE INDEX

Ephesians
1:5	165
3:15	171
4:25	171
4:39	149n75
5:1–2	167
5:22–33	157
6:12	162

Philippians
1:6, 10	102
1:19	86
1:23	105
3:20–21	102, 114, 185
4:6	86

Colossians
1:16, 20	3, 162
1:27	185
2:8	66

1 Thessalonians
1:3	186
1:10	183, 186
4:13–18	13–14, 102, 105, 114, 141n48, 195
5:18	185
5:23	113

2 Thessalonians
1:9	19
2:15	66
3:6	73
3:13	190

1 Timothy
2:1	173
2:4	2, 19, 75
4:10	190
6:14–15	135, 146

2 Timothy
1:16–18	12
2:2	66
2:15	18

Titus
1:2	186
2:13	186
3:7	185

Hebrews
1:1–2	135
1:3	154
3:6	186
6:11	186
6:18	192
6:19	185
9:27	99, 147
9:28	185
10:12–13	140
10:23	192
11:1–16	186, 189
11:39	139n42
12:23	112
13:14	189

James
2:23	156
4:2	86, 88, 92
5:16–18	86–87

1 Peter
1:3	185
1:13	192
1:21	186
2:2	165
3:18–20	104
5:7	86

2 Peter
1:3–4	158
1:20	18
3:1–9	191
3:8	136
3:9	2, 19
3:12	95

1 John

3:21–22	86
4:8, 16	153, 156–57

Revelation

1:3	146
6:9–11	105, 112, 139, 141n48, 147–48
7:9	169
10:6	142n54
14:13	98
19:6–9	157
20:4	112
21:1–5	135, 139, 156–57
21:22	122n71
21:25	76
22:7	157
22:10	146
22:13	132

www.ingramcontent.com/pod-product-compliance
Lightning Source LLC
Chambersburg PA
CBHW031728230426
43669CB00007B/288